Combatting Totalitarianism

Combatting Totalitarianism

The Legacies of St. Paul and Dietrich Bonhoeffer
in the Collapse of the "Murderous Utopias" of
Communism and National Socialism

JOHN A. MOSES

Forewords by Graham Maddox and Brian Douglas

WIPF & STOCK · Eugene, Oregon

Contents

Acknowledgments

OVER A LONG ACADEMIC life, one incurs numerous debts for the help one has experienced along the way. I have many people to acknowledge. Apart from having had kind and tolerant parents, there were priests of the Brotherhood of St Barnabas, who pioneered Anglican ministry in the bush of far North Queensland. These celibate men, mostly Oxbridge-trained Englishmen or Welsh and Irish trained, were all graduates of the ancient universities of the United Kingdom and so they contributed much to our education and culture derived from the values of the Oxford Movement within the Church of England. To that extent they constituted a major element in the evolution of the Australian character that differed from the rival influence of the Irish Roman Catholics, who were also thick on the ground everywhere in the vast island continent of Australia. Despite our cultural and political differences, Anglicans and Roman Catholics eventually learned to tolerate each other and there were even many instances of intermarriage between the two denominations. And that was precisely the case with my parents because my father's parents had become Roman Catholics. Prior to that they were of Antiochian Orthodox obedience, having migrated from what was then Syria to Australia in 1888. My father was born in 1900 and met my mother, from a Scottish immigrant family who had migrated to Australia in 1920. She had been brought up in an Episcopalian household and was very capable of resisting all the RC pressure exerted at that time to convert. Consequently, I was educated in the Church of England, as were all my siblings.

I was sent to the Anglican boarding school of All Souls' in Charters Towers, a former gold rush city in the nineteenth century, but which after the gold petered out developed into a cattle town that also had at least six denominational boarding schools, of which All Souls' was the flagbearer of Anglo-Catholicism. There I learned more about the faith and especially of the essential ecumenical nature of the Church of England. Its agenda at that time was distinctly based on being open to "all sorts and conditions of men," as I shall explain in greater detail below. Having a Cambridge-educated priest-headmaster named Canon Cedric Hurt made us acutely aware of our derivation. I was later in my old age privileged to organize and edit the history of that school together with that of the sister school for girls, named St Gabriel's and founded by the Anglican Sisters of the Sacred Advent.[1]

Later at the age of twenty I landed in Brisbane, where I continued my apprenticeship as a radio mechanic, and there my Anglican commitment was strengthened by attending All Saints' Church, Wickham Terrace, then under the gentle and wise rector Father Richard Pearson. It was he who impressed upon me that I had a priestly vocation and that I should finish my secondary school education and apply for entry into the Anglican theological college of St Francis' in Brisbane. This I did and my performance soon impressed the principal, Father Ivor Church, sufficiently to urge me to go to the University of Queensland and study for a BA degree before returning to finish theological training. This turned out to be a long drawn-out procedure, however, not without its rewards. I duly attended university and did the degree, which included three years of German. Then, with the encouragement of the head of the Department of History, Professor Dr. Gordon Greenwood, I applied for postgraduate scholarships to various British, American, and finally German universities. After one year waiting, spent as a teacher in the Sydney Church of England Grammar School, I was finally offered a grant from the German Student Exchange Service.

The chance to study in then West Germany was a direction-changing move because of my enrolment at the University of Munich for two years, studying chiefly und the notable liberal German Roman Catholic professor Franz Schnabel (1887–1966), and then for a further three years at the University of Erlangen with three equally liberal-minded professors, namely Waldemar Besson (1929–1971), Walter-Peter Fuchs (1905–1997) and Karl-Heinz Ruffmann (1922–1996). The association with these scholars was of crucial pedagogic-cultural significance. I became through their training dedicated to my subject, namely modern

---

1. See *A Remarkable Tribe*.

German history, which meant in the German historiographical peri-
odization the period from the Reformation until the beginning of the
twentieth century. Thereafter it has been called *Zeitgeschichte*, meaning
contemporary history that studies events that have taken place within the
lifetime of living persons. Subsequent important German interlocutors
have been Professor Dr. Klaus Bade and Dr. Bernd Schulte, both of whom
have been staunch supporters. In Australia my former students Professor
Dr. Peter Hempenstall, Dr. Gregory Muno, Dr. Peter Overlack, and Dr.
Bruce Gaunson have become internationally distinguished scholars in
their respective fields. Further, I have had long and productive association with colleagues at the University of Queensland, including Professor
Paul Crook, Dr. George Shaw, Dr. Joseph Siracusa during my tenure, and
later with Professor Dr. Andrew Bonnell. I wish also to express here my
profound gratitude to old friends David and Alison Sloper, especially for
Alison's professionalism in preparing indexes. Finally, in the preparation
of this and other manuscripts I am deeply indebted to the expertise of the
Reverend Graham Lindsay.

On return to Australia at the end of 1965 I quickly gained an appointment as lecturer in my old department thanks to my mentor Professor Gordon Greenwood. I had, of course, not forgotten my priestly
training and after the completion of several essential biblical courses,
the archbishop of Brisbane, Dr. Felix Arnott (1911–1988), ordained
me priest in 1975 to be an honorary assistant curate in my home parish of Kenmore in Brisbane, where I served for seventeen years. Since
then I have assisted in various other dioceses, chiefly in Armidale and
finally in Canberra-Goulburn, always in an honorary capacity. Over
many years, then, I have busied myself researching and publishing in
various fields, including church-related themes. In Canberra I am currently associated with St Mark's National Theological Centre and am an
honorary assistant curate at St Paul's Church, South Canberra. Among
my clerical interlocutors I am proud to name Canon Dr. Scott Cowdell,
Canon Dr. Brian Douglas, and German Swiss-trained Baptist colleague
Professor Dr. Thorwald Lorenzen. All these, who are internationally
outstanding scholars, have been valuable sounding boards for my ideas
and have considerably influenced the precision of some otherwise
loosely formulated ideas.

Finally, I am not forgetting my high-achieving German-born wife,
Professor Dr. Ingrid Moses (neé Heise), who has been my life companion
for over sixty years, and our two alpha-male sons, Professor Dirk Moses

of City College New York and Rolf Moses, who is CEO of the Queensland Law Society. To my family I owe an inestimable debt of gratitude for their unstinting support in all my academic enterprises over many years.

Canberra, September 2023

Abbreviations

BEK	*Bund der Evangelischen Kirchen* (association of Protestant churches in the German Democratic Republic)
DBWE	*Dietrich Bonhoeffer Works*, English edition
DDR	*Deutsche Demokratische Republik* (German Democratic Republic)
EKD	*Evangelische Kirchen Deutschlands* (association of Protestant churches in Germany)
GDR	German Democratic Republic
HRE	Holy Roman Empire
KJV	King James Version of the Holy Bible
KPD	*Kommunistische Partei Deutschlands* (the Communist Party of Germany, formed after the First World War during the founding years of the Weimar Republic)
RES	real existing socialism
RSV	Revised Standard Version of the Holy Bible
SA	*Sturmabteilung* (original paramilitary wing of the Nazi Party)
SED	*Sozialistische Einheitspartei* (Socialist Unity Party, formed after 1945 in East Germany when the KPD absorbed remnants of the Social Democratic Party to follow an essentially Stalinist line)

SPD   *Sozialdemokratische Partei Deutschlands* (Social Democratic
             Party of Germany)

SS   *Schutzstaffel* (a paramilitary wing of the Nazi Party that
             began as a body guard unit for Adolf Hitler)

Stasi   *Staatssicherheit* (secret state police in Communist East
             Germany administered by the Ministry for State Security)

Foreword
by Professor Graham Maddox (Political Scientist)

TOTALITARIANISM HAS LONG BEEN of fascination to literature and to political speculation. Its methods and consequences have been the inspiration for a swathe of dystopian novels, many of them transformed into films that have exercised the popular consciousness. It has been of fascination to political science. At the London School of Economics Professor Leonard Schapiro produced a schema aimed at defining the concept. Schapiro had long been a student of the Stalinist regime in Russia, which was a fruitful ground of authoritarian propaganda. But then to complicate matters, it was Stalin who was largely instrumental in conquering Hitler. Yet it was down to American scholars to produce the outlines of a type of regime that was the antithesis of the free government of America. The stars of this enterprise were such as Zbigniew Brzezinski, special counsel to Presidents Lyndon Johnson and Jimmy Carter, and prominent political scientists Carl J. Friedrich, Michael Curtis, and Benjamin Barber.

Alas for the American undertaking, in 2006 along came the revered scholar of political thought Sheldon S. Wolin, who announced that the United States itself was a totalitarian regime (*Democracy Incorporated: Managed Democracy and the Specter of Inverted Totalitarianism*). He correctly predicted that his work would "invite outrage tempered by disbelief." He said that capitalism was a system of organized aggression, and that the pervasive market ideology of America suppressed all attempts to criticize it, including Wolin's own. His work was met with aggressive insouciance. If anyone had cared to notice, they would have realized that Wolin had overturned the common formulation of totalitarianism. Incidentally, Benjamin Barber was separately moved to call the United States "totalitarian."

And now comes John Moses with another subversive understanding of this vexatious concept. Eschewing the formulation of totalitarianism familiar to political science as a "syndrome" of peculiar characteristics and "contours," he couches his study in the language and conceptual framework of religion. He is uniquely equipped for the task. A student of labor history, a scholar of German history and in particular its intellectual formation, an expert in German war aims, an observer of Dietrich Bonhoeffer, and an Anglican theologian in the Lutheran tradition, it would be difficult to find anyone with more insight into the problem at hand than John Moses. Paradoxically, he finds the ultimate roots of political authoritarianism in St. Paul's Letter to the Romans, a letter that he also describes as a Christian manifesto standing at the root of a Christianity that is the foundation of civilization and the source of "common decency." Romans 13 insists that all the powers that be are ordained of God, and therefore are to be revered as God's agents. Even Paul's own tormentor, Emperor Nero, is to be obeyed.

The force of Romans 13 is deeply ingrained in German tradition, harking back to Martin Luther and Jean Calvin. Luther's two kingdoms doctrine asserts that God presides over two separate realms: the religious order, which is strictly spiritual and has nothing to do with coercion of any kind, and the worldly order, where the safety and welfare of the people are entrusted to the secular regime, which is equipped with coercive powers to contain the sins to which all people are to some degree inclined. While the secular order is answerable to God, it is not subject to control by the religious authorities, who are nevertheless open to teaching restraint and compassion. Calvin too made a strong case for obedience to the powers that be, but his *Institutes* allows that "where the honour of God is involved, we must put God first."[2]

Taking up Luther's position with a passion, the philosopher G. W. F. Hegel taught generations of Germans that the state was the supreme expression of comely organization. In fact, it was the very presence of God's Holy Spirit on Earth. Clothed in this sacred mantle, its rules and instructions were unanswerable. Such teaching was congenial to the Prussian state, which was based on militarism in which orders had to be obeyed. Along with the authors he approves, Moses is convinced of an unbroken connection between Hegel and Bismarck's Prussia, and between the *Kaiserreich* of Wilhem II and the Third Reich of Adolf Hitler.

2. Calvin, trans. Battles, *Institutes*, 4.20, 31.

As a parallel to the paradox of the Letter to the Romans being a support for both authoritarianism and the freedom and liberating truth of Christianity, Hegel's work also underlies contradictory tendencies in interpretation. While most acceptable to Prussian militarism (he even approved of war as a mark of progress), Hegel also inspired a group of young thinkers, including Feuerbach and Karl Marx, who adopted his theory of the dialectic in history, but stood it on its head as "dialectical materialism." Abandoning Hegel's theistic assumptions, Marx encouraged the toiling masses to take their place in history and through dialectical processes overthrow the bourgeois state. That this process should be distorted into creating another brand of totalitarian state marks the paradox.

The Hegelian tradition in German history produces odd results. Here Hitler is caught presiding over a religion—one that replaces humanity and common decency with racial supremacy. Nevertheless, the embedded Christian sensibility in 95 percent of German citizens, who were baptized into the two great Christian churches, persisted. While Hitler clearly cared nothing for Christianity itself, he had his soldiers (bypassing Matt 5) swear an oath "by God": "I swear by God this sacred oath: I will render unconditional obedience to the *Führer* of the German Reich and People, Adolf Hitler . . ." He was happy to have his ideologues hail him as *Heiland* and *Erlöser,* "Savior" and "Redeemer." He was to save the German people from their despair after the humiliating defeat in the First War and the impositions of Versailles, from the socialists and Jews who betrayed the people (stabbed them in the back) in the Weimar government, and restore them to a glorious new providence.

A surprising turn in the story is the thesis of Stefan Heep, who argues that the persecution of the Jews was *incidental.* Hitler wanted to establish the supremacy of the Teutonic race and found a *Deutschtum* (Germandom) to which *Judentum* (Jewishness) was the antithesis. It was a form of social Darwinism that would dovetail with Hegel's dialectic. Heep argues that Hitler got from the Jewish Bible that the Ten Commandments were racist and sexist because the ancient Jew was expected to love their neighbour and hate their enemy; women were regarded as chattels. Such a characterization is truncated because it ignores the humane teachings of the Jewish prophets, and especially the Second Isaiah, who declared Israel's God as the ruler of the whole world (indeed whole creation) and extended his redemptive love to all people (Isa 45). If hate was ever the teaching of the ancient Jews, it was overturned by Jesus: "Love your enemies" (Matt 5:44). But for the *Führer* the Germans were the new chosen people. In some respects, Hitler's ranting speeches resembled the posture of the televangelist browbeating a mammoth audience. His furious eructation was the *mysterium tremendum* of the inspired visionary.

In all of this, John Moses promotes the authority of Christianity as the virtuous opponent of totalitarian regimes. While he is well apprised of the socialism of Stalinist Russia, his focus arises from his immersion in German intellectual history. In the story of the German Democratic Republic, Marxism is fused with Hegelian ideology. He acknowledges the mentorship of Dietrich Bonhoeffer, the young theologian hanged by the Nazis in 1944 for his opposition to Hitler. That opposition was relentless and uncompromising. It put him at odds with the majority of the "German Christians," who supported, or at least tolerated, the Nazi regime. In the GDR the church was severely oppressed by the regime, while *Stasi* operatives made the lives of pastors near impossible. Yet the legacy of Bonhoeffer's heroism, and his theology of service to one master alone, was irrepressible among the teachers of Christianity in East Germany. And while the regime sought to instrumentalize Bonhoeffer's legacy so as to legitimize its own activities, at bottom there was to be no submission to its claim to absolute authority.

In effect, the churches became the surrogate of a public space in the GDR. Theologians welcomed dissidents of all kinds into their cloisters, and the church became the byword for an alternative authority to that of the regime. By the time the Soviet Union was dismantled, the GDR regime was bereft of outside support and its internal power was collapsing. Observing the situation, the bishop of Ely declared that "The love of God provides space to think otherwise about humanity than one is instructed to think." In a poignant recollection of Luther, in June 1988 the pastor from *Lutherstadt* Wittenberg, Friedrich Schorlemmer, presented "twenty theses" for reform in a call for democracy. In October 1989 it was a crowd from the *Nikolaikirche* in Leipzig that soon mingled with hundreds of demonstrators in a peaceful throng that swelled to thousands, while huge crowds in Berlin soon saw the end of the German Communist nightmare.

Although it is acknowledged that Romans 13 provided a thin justification for authoritarian regimes, throughout his account John Moses affirms the resilience of the Christian message. It survived savage persecutions from ancient times, as under the Roman Empire, where its appeal became so strong that Emperor Constantine felt compelled to adopt it as his own creed and required his subjects to follow suit. Although that

compulsion traversed the freedom of the love of God, the story emphasizes the resilience of the Christian message. For Moses the gospel is "the
"yardstick of human dignity," and skeptics need to wonder at the vigor
of its survival against many attempts at its "marginalization and even
extermination" at the hands of authoritarian regimes throughout history.

Whether one affirms his claim or not, John Moses has produced
a fascinating alternative to the political science analysis of totalitarianism, bypassing "objective" formulae and delving into an intellectual history that unanswerably serves to unmask the extraordinary excesses of
authority.

Foreword

by Reverend Professor Dr. Brian Douglas (Theologian)

WHEN JOHN MOSES SUGGESTED to me to consider writing a foreword, he asked me to be sure to signal that he is very much aware of the dominant secularism in the civilized world today. On the other hand, not even secular scholars can deny the cultural-political influence of Christianity in shaping the world we live in. And people of faith still are driven to play a vital role in the affairs of humanity. As he observes by quoting Dietrich Bonhoeffer, the world has come of age; ever fewer people feel obliged to submit their autonomy to any kind of invisible deity in deciding how they live. Nevertheless, the cultural-political traditions of Christendom have had an undeniable impact on at least the "Western" world, not always, of course, for the good. So in a real sense the once impressive fortress of the church has become with passage of time the "little flock" that St. Luke refers to in his Gospel, chapter 12, verse 32. Therein is an admonition to the Christian converts in the imperial city of Rome on how to behave in a situation where they were a distinct minority. Things have come full circle it seems.

In this book John Moses addresses two important questions for the Christian: Is there a creator God? Is Jesus of Nazareth his Son as proclaimed in the Christian creeds? These issues are ones of great importance in human history and religion, and they are set alongside the claims of what Moses calls the "murderous utopias" of Communism and fascism. Herein lies Moses' methodology: to examine the spread of Christianity in contrast to the rise and fall of these two murderous utopias. This method leads him to the question of whether it can be claimed that Christianity is an authentic and ideal way to live. Is faith in the creator God and Jesus

Christ possible? Is faith in God and Christ a reality or merely the figment of human imagination?

In addressing these questions Moses looks at what he calls St. Paul's "manifesto": the Epistle to the Romans and Paul's claim that he is a slave of Jesus (Rom 1:1–7). For Moses this is a crucial claim for Paul in that as a slave he explores the reality and power of Christian faith and the associated paradigm change that Paul proclaims: from law to grace and from law to love. Herein is the way of Christianity: living as a slave in the service of our fellow human beings as we worship the creator God and Jesus Christ.

Moses' work is assisted by his powerful reflection on German scholarship, much of which will be virtually unknown in the English-speaking world. The link to Bonhoeffer is important and known to scholars writing in English, but others such as Franz Schnabel (under whom Moses studied in Germany) are less well known. Moses is adept at bringing their insights to our attention. The way that Schnabel answered Hegel is insightful and useful for English-speaking scholars to hear. All this is surrounded by Moses' powerful historical reflection on Christianity, Communism, and fascism. His valuable contribution here is the bringing of the voices of German scholarship into international focus alongside his up-to-date understanding of and reflection on the sweep of modern German history and its sociopolitical and religious legacy to the twenty-first century.

Moses also applies his historical lens to the analysis of Communism and fascism, coming from lifelong interaction and reflection on the history of these traditions. The ideas and the personalities who featured in these traditions are depicted concisely and perceptively, bringing them alive for the contemporary reader. The role of German Protestantism in the formation of evolution of German political culture is also explored in a way that many Anglophone scholars will find freshly enlightening. This book performs a valuable function and will reward close study.

Prologue

Jesus' Paradigm Change and Paul's Christian Manifesto to the World

THE POINT OF DEPARTURE for this book is the manifest longevity of St. Paul's worldview, which he gained from being born both as a Jew and a Roman citizen by virtue of his birthplace, Tarsus near Antioch. This fact has turned out to be of one of far-reaching consequence in his biography as shall be seen. The organization and bureaucracy of the Roman Empire came to be understood by Paul as orderly government and as such was an essential part of God's design for life on planet Earth. In a word, for there to be human progress, there must be political stability ensured by a strong and just government. That was not regarded as a merely convenient rational arrangement for the economic and cultural growth of human society; Paul stressed in Romans 13:1 that "the powers that be are ordained of God" (KJV). There had to be law and order, otherwise there would be permanent chaos, confusion, and disorder. Paul was indebted to the order imposed by the Roman Empire even though the Emperor and his administration were not Christian and were responsible for his own execution. Jesus himself endorsed obedience to Caesar and the obligation to pay taxes to the administration (Matt 22:21 KJV: "Render therefore unto Caesar the things which are Caesar's"). Secular authority ensured law and order should be obeyed. When, however, that authority relegated to itself the right to be worshipped as a god, Christians experienced persecution for their stance. It took until the reign of Emperor Constantine in the year 312 AD to decree that Christianity should become the official religion of the Empire, thus ushering in what is called the Constantinian Era or Christendom. This meant that the secular government would henceforth protect the Christian church and together both state and church would collaborate in their respective spheres of competence to forge civilized human society. This consisted in two spheres, namely the spiritual, over which the church ruled, beside the secular sphere, under the authority of the prince or king, who was responsible for law, order, and defense. That meant the king was both chief state bureaucrat and war-lord, responsible for day-to-day government and national security.

While that arrangement may have appeared clear-cut, it resulted in centuries of rivalry between church and state over which locus of authority held precedence. Nevertheless, the fiction was maintained that the church was responsible for the spiritual well-being of all subjects while the state was responsible for the domestic and international political sphere. But regardless of the inevitable friction between the two sources of authority, it was assumed that the existence of the church was always sacrosanct. Kings and Emperors always considered themselves as defenders of the faith. Only with the advent of the totalitarian ideologies of Marxism-Leninism and National Socialism did a challenge to the existence of traditional Christianity bring the Constantinian Era to an abrupt end, as will be seen in the following excursus.

Paul's worldview in the first century AD had been the established yardstick for church-state relations for centuries and his image of the world (*Weltbild*) remained the same as that which he acquired as an educated Jew and a Roman citizen. As far as his Judaism was concerned, he obviously did not question the Genesis account that the universe was made by God in six days and that humanity's "first parents" were Adam and Eve. In that sense Paul was an old-fashioned fundamentalist, a child of his times, but his concerns focused more on his image of humanity (*Menschenbild*). Male and female were conceived in sin and so the entire human population was hopelessly alienated from God. The Jewish tribes, however, had come to the awareness, finally under the leadership of the former Egyptian slave Moses, that they had been chosen by God to inherit the Earth and worship only him and follow his law.

As Paul, however, had come to appreciate, this scheme was to prove unworkable essentially because of Jewish tribal exclusiveness and the notion that only they as a race had been saved. The Mosaic law handed down at Sinai in Paul's mind had become derailed and so God sent his Son, Jesus of Nazareth, to preach a new gospel (good news) that replaced the old law. Jesus, via his revolutionary preaching, had changed the original paradigm of humanity's relationship to God entirely. Paul, known first as Saul of Tarsus and as a single-minded Jewish official, had at first rigorously opposed the Jesus paradigm, but after his Damascus road experience he underwent a radical conversion and embraced the Jesus' paradigm with an unmatched crusading zeal. So, the Mosaic or Sinai paradigm was replaced by the one established by Jesus of Nazareth on Calvary. In human history the "green hill" on the outskirts of Jerusalem metaphorically towers above the distant outcrop of Sinai.[1]

As educated Jews, however, Jesus and Paul after him had taken issue with the notion of an angry God who consigns most of his creation to damnation and rescues only a chosen few. That had to be wrong. Consequently, a new enterprise was undertaken to project an image of God as a *loving* and above all else a *forgiving* father of all humanity regardless of race. Jewish exclusivity was at last overturned. There was a new "kingdom of God," "not of this world" (John 18:36) into which humanity is invited to enroll. Therein fraternal relationships among formerly hostile individuals and peoples would be established. Personal and tribal enmities would be replaced with the law of love. In short, a new dispensation had been granted, proclaimed by Jesus and propagated in the world by St. Paul.

The foregoing outline of Christianity is discernible in all the epistles attributed to Paul, but most concisely in Romans. The Christian church, despite its disunity, still lives proclaiming its validity for the world. Further, despite the scandalous behaviour of many Christian leaders throughout the centuries and the efforts of hostile regimes to eradicate the worldview projected in the Bible and replace it with a different code of conduct, the Jesus movement still survives.

If there is a lesson to be drawn from history, then, it is that the Christian assessment of human nature and the code of behavior derived from it remain as valid as they ever were. It is still the *yardstick of human decency.* After the coming of Jesus Christ and Paul's proclamation the world would never be the same again, and atheists and agnostics—indeed, all people who have difficulty with the authenticity or key relevance of the Jesus myth and even call it silly—must answer the question of why it has endured so long and, more particularly, why it has successfully resisted marginalization and even extermination by totalitarian regimes.[2] Indeed, the Christian message has survived the

---

1. This allusion is to the well-known Anglican hymn, "There is a green hill far away outside a city wall where our dear Lord was crucified who died to save us all," composed by Cecil Frances Alexander (1818–1895). See Wallace, *Mrs Alexander.*

2. Among the most vocal denigrators of the Jesus paradigm are the atheists

two most aggressive ideologies in human history, namely Nazism and Marxism-Leninism. It may not yet have conquered the Earth but at least it is still the church, eternally militant here on Earth. For these reasons, then, one is obliged to recall the Christian worldview and explain why in the twentieth century the two most destructive political systems ever to arise and devastate the world came about and how their attempts to exterminate Christianity ultimately failed. In the following pages this process is traced by an Australian Anglican priest who gained his credentials as a historian via lengthy study in Germany beginning in 1961, reinforced by frequent research visits ever since.

Richard Dawkins (see his *The God Delusion*) and Christopher Hitchens(see his *God Is Not Great*). Both these writers evince a remarkable naivety about genuine theological scholarship. Their arguments recall the level of a 6th-form debating competition. They do make a valid point, however: the violations of Christian principles by clergy of all denominations over the centuries are contrary to what Christians claim to believe themselves. Neither Dawkins nor Hitchens, however, seem to grasp that all human beings are flawed, and regardless of whether they are popes, archbishops, or merely parish clergy or religious (monks and nuns). All can all give way to anger, temptation, and commit crimes against people both young and old entrusted to their care. In short, all human beings are sinners, and some are criminals, even the baptized and those affiliated in some branch of formal Christian ministry.

Preface
The Long Road to Now

No DOUBT SOME READERS will for various reasons find this book quirkish. What is St. Paul doing in it? Is it about Christian theology or the struggle by democrats to resist the rise of totalitarian regimes? Can the two themes be reasonably linked? Maybe; it is two books roughly stitched and woven together to form one dissertation. Those with the perseverance to finish it may judge for themselves. That said, it seems to me that given the impact of religions and ideologies on human behavior, the historian must take them very seriously. For example, religious sectarianism has played a toxically divisive role in the political evolution of my country, the white man's modern Australia. Add to that how racism, in various forms such as toward the original inhabitants ("first nations" Australians) on the one hand and the Anglo-Celtic sectarianism on the other, have besmirched the political landscape of the former British colonies in the Antipodes. Further, one may not forget the decades of the White Australia Policy, which discriminated against the immigration of peoples of Asian background. All of that has been and still is a bitter learning experience.

It is noted that every writer has a different past that molds his/her perceptions of the world, so I am not apologizing for my research. Nevertheless, I am very much aware of the essential subjectivity that informs every piece of historical composition because the underlying intent of all historiographies is didactic; the writer wishes to project his or her comprehension of the past and explain why it should be edifying for all contemporaries.

A glance into my past may prove instructive as I certainly have "lived through interesting times." When I was enrolled in primary school in 1936, the entire world had become aware that the "age of dictators" had well and truly arrived. Already in those early years I became enchanted by the media of the day, radio and newsreels. It seems to be a rule that the more distant one is from the cauldron of world politics, the more interested in them one can become. This became especially apparent in the 1930s, when both the airwaves and cinema screens were drenched with news about the *murderous utopias* of Benito Mussolini's fascist Italy and Adolf Hitler's Nazi Germany as well as Emperor Hirohito's militarized Japan. The jury was out on Stalin's Russia. Some citizens on the political left had a rose-tinted view of the accomplishments of the Soviet Union without appreciating the ruthless and inhumane policies and practices of the regime.

While the term "murderous utopias" may not have been in circulation at that time, it certainly entered the vocabulary after the horrors of the Nazi death camps had been made public. The bone-chilling images on the cinema screen of the liberation of Bergen-Belsen, Majdanek, and Auschwitz-Birkenau brought home even to the citizens of the remote Australian bush what the real world of 1939–1945 had become. Indeed, most of the people of North Queensland despite their isolation were consciously citizens of the British Empire. As such they paid close attention to what was going on the "other side," via shortwave radio and, of course, newsreels. People assiduously tuned in to news broadcasts and listened also to the knowledgeable commentators who regularly presented "Notes on the News." In addition, newspapers and magazines featured series of articles on world events by qualified journalists.

Overwhelmingly, Australians identified with the Empire even if they were not of British stock. My father's Lebanese family certainly did so by taking close notice of events so far away. Part of the reason in the first place was because there were many men in our small town of Atherton and in the wider district who were soldiers returned from the Great War of 1914–1918. These veterans always assembled every Anzac Day on April 25 for the parade and memorial service held around the Digger's Cenotaph, located in those days on an intersection in the middle of the main street.[1] We knew by the very presence of these veterans, of whom not a few had served both in the Gallipoli campaign and afterwards in some of the greatest land battles in human history, such as at the Somme

---

1. The term "Diggers" was used for Australian and New Zealand troops in the Great War because during the Gallipoli campaign in 1915 they had to dig trenches and tunnels between their defensive positions. The term continued to be used for theaters of war subsequently where they were engaged.

in France, that our remoteness from the flash points of international conflict was no guarantee that our young dominion was safely located out of harm's way. That became even more apparent during the war in the Pacific in 1940–1945, when the fear of Japanese invasion gripped the entire Australian population.

The second reason why events in Europe of the mid-1930s were of such great interest was the fact that the farming population of Italian origin in North Queensland was very prominent. There were also clusters of Germans. It was inevitable, therefore, that rumors circulated to the effect that some of these families were pro-fascist and/or pro-Nazi. These rumors reached a peak in 1938 during the remarkable visit of a German war hero from the Great War, an ex-naval officer named Count Felix von Luckner (1881–1966). He was touring the Pacific on behalf of the German propaganda ministry for the "New Germany" and his task had been to drum up support among scattered expatriates in the region, including Italian settlers, not a few of whom cultivated fascist sympathies. Not surprisingly, von Luckner's tour of North Queensland had certainly aroused the interest of the Commonwealth's security agency, the Special Branch, whose officers closely monitored von Luckner's progress throughout eastern and southern Australia.[2]

Events such as that of the flamboyant German naval officer's tour heightened our awareness of the world situation. As well, the news media and the speeches held every Anzac Day kept the population well informed about world events and the Empire's stand on all these questions. Having in mind that the young Commonwealth had already fought for "God, King and Empire," the Anglo-Celtic Australian population knew very well where we stood in the event of another German bid for world power. Further, the rise of imperial Japan had always been a concern, and as I was later to learn, the so-called Anti-Comintern Pact of November 1936 between Germany and Japan signaled an ominous turn of events, although that was directed against international Communism controlled by the Soviet Union. It was, however, to get worse. By May 1939 Germany was allied to Italy in the Pact of Steel, which was augmented by the Tripartite Pact the following September to include Japan.

As schoolchildren of enlightened parents in far North Queensland, we took notice of these events via the radio and the newsreels, obviously without understanding how and why they were happening, except we

2. Moses, "Count von Luckner's Tour of Queensland."

sensed they did not augur well for our young democracy. There could be a rerun of 1914–1918. The role of the Soviet Union during the lead up to hostilities in September 1939 was certainly very obscure. Later, of course, after the Japanese attack on Pearl Harbor (December 7, 1941) the British Empire and the United States became firmly determined to resist fascist aggression. We were reminded that just prior to that fateful event, on August 14, 1941, after the meeting held on the mid-Atlantic Ocean between US President Roosevelt and British Prime Minister Churchill onboard the battleship HMS *Prince of Wales*, the Atlantic Charter had already been signed. According to that the kindred nations pledged to join forces to resist the spread of totalitarianism. These were momentous events that would eventually affect us all in remote Australia.

The Japanese attack on Pearl Harbor was followed the very next day by the British surrender to Japan in Singapore, the darkest day in the history of the British Empire. The feeling in Australia about these disasters was understandably one of great anxiety. One puzzled over the question why the Germans, Italians, and Japanese were being so aggressive. Much later I would learn the phrase "place in the sun." This was usually applied to the Kaiser's Germany, a nation that was understood to be driven by the desire to have a great overseas empire such as the British and French already had. Not surprisingly all imperial powers were pursing their imagined place in the sun. I learned, too, that each nation was driven by its so-called *self-perception*, its own sense of mission that was presumed to be of divine origin. Thinkers within each great power, that is, historians, philosophers, statesmen, theologians, novelists, and journalists, had formulated and published what they each perceived was unique about their nation's culture that should be bestowed on the underdeveloped states and peoples in Africa and Asia but also in Europe.

All imperial powers perceived themselves as dispensing a superior civilization or, as in the German case, a higher *Kultur*. There is a subtle and enigmatic distinction between mere *civilization* and what the Germans understood by *Kultur*. This subject is to be more deeply explored later in these pages. Remarkably, each power concerned asserted that it was acting in accordance with the will of God or an Emperor who was regarded as being the agent of God on Earth. In the decades prior to 1914 Christian empires such as those of Britain, Germany, France, Russia, and the United States of America were all rivals for a place in the sun. One assumes, though, their leaders, especially their religious hierarchies, were aware of the absurdity that they were often at enmity with each other while each one claimed they were acting in accordance with the will of their common, benevolent Creator.

This subject has attracted numerous historians.[3] What is obvious is that each of the great powers, but also even smaller ones with a long and tortuous history such as Poland, developed a sense of mission (*Sendungsbewusstsein*) that inspired their subjects to undertake great imperial projects. These goals were rationalized by arguing that almighty God sanctified the force of arms because their aims were intended for the long-term benefit of the world at large. But each great power had a subtly different concept of their calling. Here it is important to be aware of the typically English example of national self-perception under a benevolent deity.

A FORGOTTEN FACTOR DEFINING ANGLICAN POLITICAL CULTURE[4]

In the *Book of Common Prayer*, the official prayer book of the Church of England, passed by Act of Parliament in 1571, there is a "collect" or prayer entitled "For All Conditions of Men, to be used at such times when the Litany is not said." The full text is as follows:

> O GOD, the Creator and Preserver of all mankind, we humbly beseech thee for all sorts and conditions of men; that thou wouldest be pleased to make thy ways known unto them, thy saving health unto all nations. More especially, we pray for the good estate of the Catholick Church; that it may be so guided and governed by thy good Spirit, that all who profess and call themselves Christians may be led into the way of truth and hold the faith in unity of spirit, in the bond of peace, and in righteousness of life. Finally, we commend to thy fatherly goodness all those who are in any ways afflicted, or distressed, in mind, body or estate; [especially those for whom our prayers are desired;] that it

3. Lehmann, "Germans as a Chosen People."

4. The official or formal expression of the peculiarly English self-perception, meaning how the civilized and educated, God-fearing English person would like him/herself to be understood is summed up in this prayer. Obviously, most secularized citizens will never have heard of it. Nevertheless, individuals who have been sensitized by the religious culture of Anglicanism manifest the sentiment contained in that "Prayer for All Conditions of Men." One needs to be made aware of its origins at a time when all the nations of Europe were redefining their concept of Christendom; noting, for example, the profound religious-political differences between the English and German reception of the Reformation.

may please thee to comfort and relieve them, according to their
several necessities, giving them patience under their suffering,
and a happy issue out of all their afflictions. And this we beg for
Jesus Christ his sake. Amen.

Here it should be noted that the word "men" in this ancient text is by no
means intended to exclude women, but to be understood as in the sense
of *mankind*, meaning all humanity. The prayer is otherwise explicitly inclusive and encompasses the entire human race regardless of the various
nationalities. The image of almighty God that it projects is one of a father
who loves his creation in its entirety without discrimination; in short, the
prayer is explicitly meant to apply to all dwellers upon Earth. Further to
assuming the unity of humanity in all its manifestations, it prays that all
nations might live together "in the bond of peace," in harmony. It then
moves from the general to the particular in that all persons in whatever
situation they may find themselves might enjoy health and well-being
and indeed live free of deprivation or suffering and should experience a
"happy issue out of all their afflictions."

    In short, this prayer really sums up how Christianity, as the *universal*
religion, should operate and how the church should behave *diaconically*
throughout the entire world. That means that the church consists of people who are the agents within the entire body of Christ *in the service of all
humanity*; we are all responsible for one another because we are baptized
into Christ's body. Christianity is first and foremost a *diaconal* religion; it
prioritizes *being there for others* without discrimination. In any case that
is the ideal toward which Anglicans at least were expected to strive. It is
acknowledged, though, that there have been and are glaring examples of
failure among church leaders and laity to live up to and sustain this goal.
Nevertheless, if all the above is understood, one wonders why Christianity does not have a greater resonance in the world than it has.

    The message has clearly been sent but has not been received and uni-
versally understood. This became most apparent recently when some Roman Catholics in Australia had proclaimed publicly that they were going
to leave the church because of the widespread child abuse perpetrated by
some high-profile clergy. Such responses to spiritual wickedness in high
places indicate that those laypersons, who were understandably disgusted
with what has been happening since time immemorial and who blame
"the church" for the depravity of some of its members, have not really
understood why the church exists. The fact is that everybody from the
supreme pontiff to the simplest layperson is prone to sin of any kind. Even

the apostles themselves showed basic human weaknesses such as greed (Judas) and disloyalty (Peter). And there were many subsequent examples of moral confusion and spiritual wickedness in high places such as in the case of Augustine of Hippo (354–430), who had a great deal of difficulty in coming to terms with his libido. The debauchery and prodigious extravagance of the Medici Pope Leo X (1475–1521) is legendary and is what in part incensed the learned German Augustinian monk Martin Luther so much. Indeed, it was because of that, and the pope's worldliness coupled with his curiously comic and absurd *theology of indulgences*, that led to the Reformation. This turned out to be the greatest political and religious upheaval ever experienced in the West because of its direction-changing impact on human thinking about God. The theological fallout from a corrupt papacy, given over as it was to debauchery, murder, and intrigue, sparked Luther's theology of forgiveness of sins, which he formulated after his intensive study of St. Paul's theology, especially as outlined in the Epistle to the Romans. Indeed, Lutheranism affected the entire church.

Today Rome acknowledges that Luther was correct in pursuing this issue. It should be remembered that had the Council of Trent (1545–1563) voted otherwise than it did, there would have been radical reform in the church without disruption of unity at that time and the world would have been spared the murderous consequences that followed, and which have lasted down to the present time. It should also be recalled that at the third session of the Council of Trent there was several bishops who were convinced that Luther's theology was correct, but these were outvoted by those who harbored scruples about offending the bishop of Rome. History was tilted, one might justifiably say, in the wrong direction. So, while the church is, metaphorically speaking, the body of Christ, it is peopled by fallible human beings who are capable of the most grievous of sins and misguided judgements. The obverse of this fact of life is the teaching of the church that enables people "to turn from their wickedness and live."[5]

5. In the Order for Morning and Evening Prayer, as published in the *Book of Common Prayer*, there is a General Confession said by the congregation followed by a pronouncement of absolution by the presiding priest as follows: "Almighty God, the Father of our Lord Jesus Christ, who desireth not the death of a sinner, *but rather that he may turn from his wickedness and live,* and hath given power and commandments, to his Ministers, to declare and pronounce to his people, being penitent, the Absolution and Remission of their sins: He pardoneth and absolveth all them that truly repent, and unfeignedly believe his holy Gospel. Wherefore let us beseech him to grant us true repentance, and His Holy spirit, that those things may please him, which we do at this present; and that the rest of our life hereafter may be pure, and holy; so that at the last we may come to his eternal joy; through Jesus Christ our Lord."

Forgiveness is assured if there is contrition, and this guarantees that the sinner is not destined to remain forever bound and spiritually immobilized by past sins. As a Christian one is not defined by the sins of the past but by the hope that comes after the knowledge that sins are forgiven and one is liberated to fulfill one's calling as a member of the body of Christ, in which everyone with his/her unique gifts serves the well-being of the whole. All of that exercised the mind and spirit of St. Paul, who had in his original persona as Saul of Tarsus persecuted Christians on behalf of the Jewish authorities. He must have acted like a fearsome chief of the Jewish thought police and therefore been well informed about Christian teaching before any of the Gospels were published. Saul's Damascus road experience must be seen as a defining moment in the history of Christian civilization. Indeed, the Jewish zealot Saul's conversion into the Christian champion Paul was an event of world-changing dimensions. This was "good news" for all humankind.

Essentially, the God whose "nature is always to have mercy"[6] through forgiveness of sins enables humanity to live again. People are not hamstrung by a permanent sense of guilt, which is both soul-destroying and socially corrosive. Christianity thus understood is primarily concerned with the building up of a community of creative and productive human beings to replace the existing world of numerous tribal entities locked in permanent chaotic conflict over how to share the Earth's bounty. But tribal enmity and chaos can be overcome once the nations submit themselves to fraternal cooperation and abandon the Machiavellian power struggle.

As St. Paul had come to understand, the ways of peace are infinitely life-affirming. It is, however, a recommendation that assumes there is a benevolent creator God concerned for the welfare of his creation. The fact that the existence of such a being cannot be proved or easily demonstrated is a problem. Because of that political decision-makers are unable to prioritize the sentiments expressed in the above-cited "Prayer for All Sorts and Conditions of Men," bearing in mind that that prayer could only have been composed by someone who firmly believed that Jesus of Nazareth was/is the human face of almighty God. This is what the church since St. Paul's time had always affirmed. For example, in Philippians 2:5–11 Paul comprehended Jesus as a phenomenon unique in time when he wrote:

---

6. This is another typically Anglican phrase taken from the "Prayer of Humble Access," said by both the presiding priest and congregation just prior to the administration of the Holy Communion at the Eucharist.

Have this in mind among yourselves, which was in Christ Jesus, who, though he was not in the form of God, did not account equality with God a thing to be grasped, but poured himself out and took the form of a servant, being born in the likeness of men and being found in human form, he humbled himself and became obedient to death, even death on a cross. Therefore, God highly exalted him and bestowed on him the name which is above every name, that at the name of Jesus every knee should bow, in heaven and on earth and under the earth, and every tongue confess that Jesus Christ is Lord, to the glory of God the Father.

This is one reason why the faith is still preached and practiced. Colossians 1:15–20 affirmed with great conviction that Jesus is

the image of the invisible God, the first born of all creation, for in him all things were in heaven and on earth, visible and invisible, whether thrones, dominions or principalities or authorities—all things were created through him and for him. He is before all things, and in him all things hold together. He is the Head of the body, the church; he is the beginning, the first born from the dead, that in everything he might be pre-eminent. For in him all the fullness of God was pleased to dwell, and through him to reconcile to himself all things, whether on earth or in heaven, making peace by the blood of the cross.[7]

Without a rationale of this nature, there is no compelling reason why an individual should submit herself to any of the Christian precepts. It all comes down to a leap of faith in what Paul and the creeds say about the person of Jesus of Nazareth, namely that it is better to pursue the ideals of peace and goodwill than to allow self-serving behavior to determine the structure of human society, because such behavior always

7. Cf. Mascall, *Jesus—Who He Is*, 47. It is important to note that among New Testament scholars there is a debate concerning the authenticity of the authorship of Colossians. Burton Mack, for example, in his *Who Wrote the New Testament*, 183–84, is emphatic that both Colossians and Ephesians are not by Paul but by Christian writers who came after Paul. On the other hand Kummel, *Introduction to the New Testament*, supports the authorship of Paul. This debate should not, however, detain us because it is clear from the historical evidence that these texts of Christian antiquity are human artifacts composed by people from various cultural backgrounds. The point is that Jesus is precisely who those writers said he is, namely the presence of God in human form in the world. As Mascall affirms, this is far from being a literalist or fundamentalist assertion; rather it is the conviction that the "historic Christian tradition is a living and growing organism, the voice of Christ, speaking in his Body the Church, constantly reacting to new situations and manifesting new and unsuspected developments but maintaining and preserving all the time its essential homogeneity" (51).

leads to the marginalization and exploitation of the weak. What some theologians call the "Jesus myth" works against this regardless of whether Jesus was literally the Son of God or simply an inspired rabbi with a wider humanistic vision for the world. In short, Christianity in all its precepts produced what is called "civil society." That means it is good for everybody whether they are believers or not. But Christianity is not just about striving for justice and welfare for the world, which it must continue to do; rather it is about recognizing in the life, death, and resurrection of Jesus of Nazareth that humanity is lifted to a new plane of spiritual reality. It is not a mere nostalgic recollection of a courageous social reformer whose teaching is worth preserving, but a realization that he is not a dead and buried phenomenon from around two thousand years ago, but a living reality through his resurrection, and today made tangible in his body, the church.[8]

The precise meaning of "resurrection" is, of course, the neuralgic point at which the convinced Christian and the unimpressed secularist part company. But belief in what is called the "meta-historical" event of the resurrection is, as St. Paul so early pointed out, the keystone to comprehending creation. As Dr. Peter Carnley memorably phrased it:

> The Christian story, which pre-eminently transcends and celebrates the memory of Jesus' and God's revelatory deed in and through his life and death, should lead us beyond itself to a living encounter with the real presence of all that celebrates and rehearses him, whom by story we recall, we know as the living Spirit of the fellowship of faith.[9]

Here it is argued that this is the reason why Christianity survives to this day. Admittedly it is divided and disputatious within itself, but one has reason to hope that Christians are striving valiantly for the most part to recover unity or to tolerate each other's theological peculiarities. And it has survived against the most insidious and violent efforts in the course of human history to obliterate it and in its place to establish imperialistic dictatorships that misguidedly claim to be able to solve the problem of

---

8. See 1 Cor 15:1–58, where St. Paul expatiates on the centrality of Jesus' resurrection, but note verse 17 in particular: "And if Christ has not been raised, your faith is futile; you are still in your sins." The question of what "resurrection" could possibly mean is, of course, a challenging one that invites a variety of explanations. See the next footnote.

9. Cf. Carnley, *Structure of Resurrection Belief*, 364. The resurrection is called a "meta-historical" event because of its uniqueness. Corpses cannot be resuscitated in the "normal" world, but parallel to it is the real spiritual world.

how the diverse nations of the Earth should live. These were principally the twin scourges of Marxist Leninism and National Socialism.

Introduction

THE ARGUMENT

THE TWO MOST AGGRESSIVE movements of our age that aimed to re-
mould human society according to their allegedly infallible perceptions of
the world and human life in it were Marxist Leninism (or Soviet Russian
Communism) and German National Socialism (Nazism). Both proved to
be *murderous utopias* and have been responsible for the greatest catastrophes the world has ever seen. They have now been consigned to the dung
heap of history by most thoughtful people. Communist China, however,
at least outwardly maintains its commitment to Marxism-Leninism-
Maoism. As the world's second superpower, pursuing expansionist policies prescribed by an oligarchy of functionaries who claim to base their
goals on Marxist-Leninist-Maoist principles, it seeks to destabilize the
entire world. These Chinese Communist apparatchiks may or may not
be believed by their people, but the leadership persists in observance of
the ideology externally at least as a justification for maintaining absolutist power over the toiling masses, which are composed by a considerable variety of different cultural groups who inhabit vast sections of the
Asian continent. One may be sure that there is seething opposition to
this notoriously oppressive system, which recognises no rule of law or
basic human rights and acts with the caprice of the proverbial oriental
despot. Any dissidents are summarily dealt with. The world witnessed
impotently as antidemocratic forces dismantled the parliamentary structures and rule of law in Hong Kong. But there is still hope. Such oppressive regimes, as history has frequently illustrated, inevitably implode or

are overthrown by superior military force from outside. During all this turmoil the Christian church in its various manifestations throughout the world continues to exist despite the many internal derailments it has experienced, and the odious scandals perpetrated by its hierarchy in every age. Despite all that, it has still been able to bequeath to the nations those principles by which they should live.

Essentially, these are principles based on the perception that all people are equal because of their filial relationship under the one Creator or heavenly Father, who is sovereign over all creation. One is aware that these are words at which the secular mind bridles. Both the thought and the language used to explain Christianity are not readily or sympathetically received and understood by many people. The fact is, however, that the church has continued to exist through the changing fortunes of history including the shocking moral derailments of its members that still occur. Parallel to this, however, the church seeks to fulfill her mission to bring justice, peace, and reconciliation to all peoples despite instances of curiously misguided policies in some regions.[1] Whenever these things have happened, however, there have always been those Christians who have had the courage and conviction to stand up for the essential gospel of love. This has been graphically demonstrated in our time by the fact that the main resistance to the murderous utopias of both Nazi Germany and the Soviet Union has come from convinced Christian men and women, both clerical and laypersons.

The brutal excesses of the Third Reich were early opposed by Christian leaders such the renowned Swiss reformed theologian Karl Barth and the Lutheran pastor Dietrich Bonhoeffer and their associates, who formed the Confessing Church (*die bekennende Kirche*) in Germany, as well as by various courageous Roman Catholic clergy. Many paid with their lives for their outspokenness and practical resistance or were subjected to inhumane imprisonment and martyrdom. In communist postwar East Germany, Christians coped with so-called "real existing socialism in different ways to survive oppression." For example, while the policy of the minority Roman Church was to go into hibernation, many Protestant pastors doggedly preached against the inhumane absurdities of

---

1. Places where the Christian church has made abysmal errors of judgement in endorsing genocide, for example, included the East African country of Rwanda, where the Tutsi and the Hutu peoples were the victims. See Prunier, *Rwandan Crisis 1959–1994*. See also the policy of Apartheid in Southern Africa, which was also endorsed by the Dutch Reformed Church there. See Ritner, "Dutch Reformed Church and Apartheid."

the regime. Among these was Bishop Albrecht Schönherr (1911–2009), who had been a pupil of Dietrich Bonhoeffer. Schönherr survived the oppression of Communism by standing up for the gospel, which he clearly regarded as a higher authority for humanity than the caprice of the Central Committee of the Communist Party, which was called in East Germany the *Sozialistische Einheitspartei Deutschlands* (SED). Schönherr's conviction that the teachings of Jesus of Nazareth were not only superior to those of Marxist Leninism but of eternal validity was vindicated by the course of history.[2] So the present argument maintains that the Christian church, despite the many lamentable betrayals of its hierarchies throughout the ages, is still the source (*fons et origo*) of civilization.[3] This needs to be better understood.

Finally, it is noted that while the present writer was trained in modern German history, he lays no claim to expertise in critical biblical studies and in this is totally reliant on the discourse of specialists in that field. For example, he is aware that the Pauline authorship of Hebrews, Colossians, and Ephesians is contested, and further that in the compilation of books of the Bible into the very first edition, namely the *Codex Sinaticus*, the attribution of authors to various texts were guided by different rules from those one would expect in modern times. That said, it is noted that the Christian world has inherited in the Bible a source book that has been subjected to various amendments and interpolation by persons who remain historically anonymous. So, for example, if scholars claim to have discovered that parts of the writings of St. Paul were composed by different people, one may wonder whether that really makes any difference to our reception of the world of ideas in Christian antiquity. One may conclude that obviously there were numbers of different Christian authors at that time who contributed their separate versions of the significance of the ministry of Jesus of Nazareth. In short, one must accept that the biblical text has been repeatedly edited, augmented, and revised by unidentified Christians of a variety of backgrounds, all trying to improve their understanding of Jesus of Nazareth just as earnest people do at the present time. It is therefore impossible to regard the biblical texts as literally the Word of God because quite obviously they are human artifacts,

---

2. For Lutherans in East Germany, see Schönherr, *Zum Weg der evangelischen Kirche in der DDR.* For Roman Catholics, see Denzler, *Widerstand oder Anpassung?*

3. Collins, *Birth of the West.*

the contributions of pilgrims on a journey bequeathed to subsequent generations for their edification.[4]

STATEMENT OF PROBLEM

There are two questions to be raised at the outset. First, is there a benign creator God, author of the universe, indwelling and transcendent simultaneously? And second, may Jesus of Nazareth be designated his Son as the Christian creeds proclaim? It is often argued that there is no logical possibility for human beings to know for certain that there is a creator God. As the German philosopher Ludwig Feuerbach (1804–1872) made clear if it had not been established by other thinkers prior to him, everything that humanity has read and learned from previous generations must have been the product of human minds. Prophets such as those in the Hebrew Bible, the Old Testament, merely assumed there was a God or gods. They were men and women whose ideas were recorded for the benefit of descendants of the tribe, and these included their notions about the nature of the creator God and how they imagined she/he preferred the tribe to behave among themselves and toward other tribes. The prophets were obviously not the amanuensis of an old man up in the sky with a long white beard who dictated to them in the isolation of their studies what he wanted to tell people on Earth.

This is just common sense. The prophets in the Old Testament were essentially moralizing storytellers in their time, very politically driven and inspired to admonish both their rulers and fellow countrymen how they should behave in times of crises of either political or climatic causes. If the prophets invoked a spirit, as those of ancient Israel did, whom they called *Yahweh*, that spirit was clearly a product of the collective imagination and *Yahweh*'s characteristics varied from prophet to prophet. So, the Old Testament is a collection of writings that in all probability began life as the stories of a nomad tribe before they were committed to writing by more learned scribes. These writers were responding at various stages during the history of their tribe to the different circumstances in which they found themselves. The Bible contains no uniform history of these events, only fragmentary accounts by different authors over a very long period.

---

4. Aspects of this problem are carefully addressed in a series of essays edited by Dr. Gregory C. Jenks entitled *Cultural Afterlives of Jesus: Jesus in Cultural Perspective.*

Archaeologists continue to add to our knowledge about these questions. Already, however, in the biblical text one may discern a certain progression in the perceptions of *Yahweh* by various authors, ranging from a bloodthirsty warlord or tyrant to a loving and caring father of all creation, such as, for example, from the prophet who wrote the book of Exodus or the one who wrote the book of Joshua. The tribal leaders were all bloodthirsty tyrants. They behaved as military commanders exhibiting the warrior characteristics of their presumed deity. Then much later in the history of Israel we encounter the book of the prophet Isaiah, who was quite the opposite. So, which one is projecting the right image of God? Establishing the true nature of God is clearly a work in progress for those theologians qualified to investigate the question. Some scholars argue that man has made God most certainly in his own image.[5]

Professor Hans Küng, however, argued persuasively in his book *Does God Exist?* against atheism and insisted that only the existence of God enables humanity to make sense of creation. Denial of God or nihilism ultimately cannot affirm the reality of the world.[6] In short, belief in the existence of God is essential for a full life in this world. So, we reject atheism and endorse a life-affirming reality as did Jesus of Nazareth.

Küng conceded, however, that belief in God is not invulnerable from attack by atheists or agnostics. Indeed, belief is continually being attacked by authors of those persuasions. The aggression of some of these antagonists toward champions of belief might well suggest that they are afraid that it might just be true. Human beings are clearly being torn between trust and mistrust, faith and unbelief, service to the well-being of the whole or self-seeking personal aggrandizement at the expense of others.

Against this Küng advanced the proposition that belief in God is a benign and sacred gift. It opens humanity to the ever-expanding reality of creation. In short, God reveals to humanity the origin, purpose, and essential value of life. So, what Küng, like Luther, offered to the thinking Christian is a "mighty fortress," an edifice of thought that can withstand all the nihilistic arguments of the atheists and agnostics. Essentially, he was saying that only with God can we realize our full potential as human

5. O'Grady, *And Man Made God*; and Polkinghorne, *Searching for Truth* and *Science and Religion in Quest of Truth*.

6. The German original is *Existiert Gott? Antwort auf die Gottesfrage der Neuzeit*, translated as *Does God Exist? An Answer for Today*. I am using the German original. Küng's argument is both intellectually challenging and persuasive.

beings. True Christians are the only truly developed human beings, a claim that obviously atheistic humanists find repugnant because it challenges their claim or assumption that humankind has no need of any kind of God.

Christian theologians, however, uphold the concept that only through faith in a creator God can full humanity be realized. When this is internalized, one's faith is strengthened and the limitations of education and life experience have been overcome. Hans Küng, for example, recapitulated his scholarly encounter with all the great thinkers in modern European history since Descartes, Pascal, Kant, Hegel, and further with Marx, Nietzsche, and Freud.[7] All have pursued their own agendas and had given reasons for their separate positions on belief or unbelief. Küng then confidently affirmed that God certainly does exist. In short, Christian faith makes real and abundant life possible, which for Küng was/is the clinching argument for the existence of God.

Further, belief in God is the *raison d'être* for the existence of the three Abrahamic faiths and consequently of central importance to many millions of people throughout the world. That being so, the question arises: how and why did these faiths, namely Judaism, Christianity, and Islam, become the worldwide monotheistic religions that they are? The range of studies devoted to this question is understandably extensive. All this means, however, that even the most faithful Christian will have neither the time nor the requisite ability to investigate this question, but she/he may reasonably enquire about the authenticity of a faith that has no obvious compelling rationale for its beginning.

Not everybody can account for his/her faith as does a learned theologian such as Hans Küng. If one is interrogated for a reason for one's belief or value system, one would logically have to answer that it is because one prefers one over another. Most often one's Christianity is the consequence of having encountered a practicing Christian such as a parent, sibling, friend, priest, pastor, or teacher whom one admires. Then finally it might depend on one's concept of what is better for humanity. Remarkably, many Westerners seem suddenly to have embraced the teachings of Hare Krishna or some other exotic belief system as a viable solution to the world's problems. Again, what is good in one tribal group or culture may not be upheld as equally relevant or good in another. There is also the reasoning that advances the idea that there is already implanted in

7. Küng, *Existiert Gott?*, 767.

every human being regardless of race and culture a universal idea of right and wrong.

In the final analysis, however, what one believes still comes down to a matter of preference. One is, after all, an autonomous being with the ability to make rational choices. That is the main distinguishing characteristic of being truly human. In addition, even though as an infant one may be baptized into the church, one may in adulthood decide to opt out of membership because the creeds and practices appear to be intellectually untenable. This book poses, then, an inescapable question to Christians in particular, namely: why have they chosen to be followers of the teachings of the Jewish carpenter-rabbi Jesus of Nazareth, who himself apparently never wrote a single word about his career at any stage? All we have are reports about him in the New Testament.

By the time of the birth of Jesus of Nazareth, who was perceived to be in the lineage of the house of David (Matt 1)—that is, his ancestry went back to King David, and spiritually he was in the line of the benign prophets preaching universal love and forgiveness—prophecy had reached, if one will, the peak of a humanistic wave. This becomes most evident in the sentiments attributed to Jesus in, for example, the Sermon on the Mount (Matt 5–7), the most comprehensive statement of the ethical content of Christianity in the New Testament. That passage is essentially an updating or expansion of the Ten Commandments, reportedly handed to Moses on Mt. Sinai during the exodus journey of the Israelites in their flight from Egypt. Here the point is that the rabbi Jesus of Nazareth had a new message, namely that God's love is not just intended for one nation or tribe only (the chosen people) but for the entire human race. So, Christianity, the religion propagated by the New Testament, constituted a complete game-changer when its message of universal love and forgiveness was transmitted initially by word of mouth throughout the entire Roman world and then by the texts that eventually, by the end of the third century AD, were assembled into the New Testament.[8]

An important point was made by the German theologian Dietrich Bonhoeffer (1906–1945) already in his days as *Vikar* or catechist in Barcelona in 1928 in an address to young Germans in the congregation there. He told them that there were quite a few other "prophets" prior to the appearance of Jesus of Nazareth who preached earlier versions of what amounted to the Golden Rule. Nevertheless, the entire theological edifice

8. Mack, *Who Wrote the New Testament?*

based on the ethical teachings of Jesus has superseded those forerunners and spread throughout the entire Western world by zealous advocates such as St. Paul. Indeed, without Paul's tireless energy in preaching about Jesus of Nazareth, it is hard to see how Christianity could have grown into the world religion it became. Jesus' "good news" clearly exerted a compelling influence over the thousands of people who heard it when first preached in the Holy Land, Asia Minor, and Greece. By claiming to be the Messiah, the expected one, Jesus had attracted a considerable following. However, in his self-identification as the Son of God, saying, "I and the father are one" (John 10:30–38), Jesus divided the Hebrew nation. In short, Jesus presented himself as the mouthpiece of the Hebrew God, who was also the one God of *all* the nations as well as Lord of all creation. Therein lay both the attraction of his good news to the gentile world on the one hand and the reason for the emphatic rejection of it by the Jewish authorities on the other. This was behind the call of the high priest Caiaphas, who decreed that it was expedient that one man should die for the people (John 18:14).[9]

Consequently, as all educated (as opposed to brainwashed) theologians are aware, the record of the life, ministry, death, and resurrection of Jesus of Nazareth is a human artifact. One chooses to follow it out of personal motives; one finds it preferable to all other ideologies, such as Communism or fascism, which purport(ed) to be able to solve all the world's problems and bring humanity at large to a stage where everything would be peaceful and settled and everyone satisfied, each according to their needs. The problem is that under a ruthless omnipresent and all-powerful regime, the "big brother" State, described by the German Lutheran bishop Otto Dibelius as a regime of robbers and liars, there is no rule of law, only capricious use of force, oppression, and barbarism.[10] Order can only be maintained by the permanent surveillance apparatus of a secret police. It is impossible to speak of such regimes as engendering happiness in the population.

One notes in passing that history is a record of rival solutions to perceived human problems. And these are all about how to survive in this world, which is described in the Bible as a "vale of tears" (see Psalm 84:6), meaning a place of tribulations or unresolved issues that one will

---

9. See the pioneering work of the French literary scholar René Girard, summed up by Cowdell, *René Girard and Secular Modernity*.

10. Dibelius, *Obrigkeit*. See especially the chapter "Römer 13 und der totalitäre Staat 7," and also his "Christ against Tyranny."

only escape when one enters the new life promised after death. Meanwhile the Christian is admonished to follow the way of Jesus of Nazareth, which means there is no blissful utopian end goal in this life; complete healing (salvation) is not promised in the here and now; indeed all that broken humanity experiences is that vale of tears. So human beings are urged to pray for the resilience to survive it. In that case, Christianity is falsely understood if people think it is about the assurance of a happy, carefree, and prosperous existence. This is the false impression conveyed by theological mountebanks like the mostly American TV evangelists, for example Jimmy Swaggart (*1935) and other revivalist preachers who follow the American example. In Australia the Hillsong movement purveys a similar message. The idea that if one takes up one's cross (Matt 16:24–26) and follows Jesus, you can expect to live a carefree life in health and bourgeois comfort strikes one immediately as pie in the sky. That is clearly not what the gospel is about.

The overriding message in the New Testament is that to follow Jesus means to follow the *via crucis,* the way of the cross, because it is nobler to serve than to be served. Obviously, many people calling themselves "Christians" opt out of that and try by theological sleight of hand to bring their comfort-seeking lifestyle into harmony with the gospel. That simply cannot be done. Others, beyond any religion, also opt out to pursue a frankly hedonistic lifestyle, convinced that that is all there is to life in this world. Such is the range of the human perceptions. Even among declared Christians there is confusion as to what it all means. It is therefore unsurprising that there are a variety of interpretations devised to explain what being a Christian really entails.

STATEMENT OF METHOD

In the pursuit of an answer to the above question, various philosophers, historians, and prophets have arisen in their time, such as Karl Marx (1818–1883), the reputed systematizer of "scientific Communism" (as opposed to "utopian socialism"), and Adolf Hitler (1889–1945), the charismatic leader of National Socialist Germany 1933–1945. Both these ideologues had set out to denigrate, marginalize, and ultimately destroy Christianity. They purported to be required to do this either by "providence", as was the case with Hitler, or by the "laws of history" that Karl Marx claimed to have "scientifically" revealed. These two Germans had been most influential in their time and their legacy still lingers on in some countries such as Communist China. As well, there exists a minority of Germans who still dream the dream of world domination[11] pursued by Adolf Hitler and his disciples. Even in the United States there is a neo-Nazi party based in Arlington, Virginia, founded by George Lincoln Rockwell (1918–1967).[12] Similarly, Karl Marx still exercises a residual attraction in various countries beyond mainland China such as North Korea or Cuba. The once small but still quite disruptive Communist Party of Australia dissolved itself in 1991 and left its meager assets to the Australian Labour Party.[13] Its once faithful membership is left wondering why they could have been so deluded as to believe, sometimes most passionately, in a Communist utopia.

The method to be followed here takes the form of an investigation of the spread of Christianity followed by surveys of the rise and fall of the ideologies of Communism and fascism because they were the most powerful threats to the continued existence of the Christian church ever posed. The point is that Christianity, despite the best efforts of the followers of Marxist Leninism on the one hand and National Socialism on the other has survived and is flourishing, though in some places there is a problem with fundamentalism, which inhibits ecumenical outreach and reconciliation as well as interfaith dialogue.[14]

Regarding the two most notorious forms of totalitarianism, Communism and Nazism, it is well known that both have been apostrophized as *false religions*. The question is: on what grounds is it justified to claim that Christianity should be accepted, as it understands itself, as the authentic world religion? This book aims to show precisely what those grounds are. For many people the question of belief in a creator God is just not possible. They cannot make the *leap of faith* that is required because they have a diminished "sense of the numinous."[15] On the other

---

11. Laquer, *Fascism Past, Present and Future*; and Manthey, *On the Pathway to Violence*.

12. On Rockwell, see Goodrick-Clarke, *Black Sun*. There are also several similar right-wing extremist organizations.

13. Fitzgerald, *People's Champion*.

14. Christian fundamentalism strikes one as a form of intolerant ideological bullying akin to both Communism and fascism because it insists on demanding the total submission of the individual to its creed and ostracizes anyone who refuses to submit to it.

15. "Numinous" comes from the Latin word *numen*, which means "divine presence." The term became widely known through the work of the German theologian

hand, if the idea of God is a mere figment of human imagination, it has proved remarkably durable and very important to the lives of millions of people as the existence of Christian communities testifies.[16] The church is still with us despite always having been plagued by scandals and schisms from ancient times up to the present, which have no doubt discredited it in the eyes of the world. Nevertheless, the extensive missionary enterprises sustained by most mainstream churches as well as the charity work throughout the world in all countries testify to a spiritual force that is apparently unquenchable. One speaks understandably of the "mystery" of the church.

CHAPTER DISPOSITION

Effectively introducing the subject is the prologue (see above), intended to orient the reader more closely to the methodology of the book. Then the first chapter recalls the origins of Christianity in the Roman Empire and its spread throughout Europe and the world in general, entitled "From St. Paul via Constantine to the World." Chapter 2, "The Social Problem and Its Solution since the Industrial Revolution," takes a chronological leap forward to survey the impact of industrialization on the world and the rise of various solutions to what was called the "social problem." This functions as preamble to the next chapter, which focuses on the phenomenon of Marxism-Leninism, an ideology that had divided the world from 1917 until the present day. This chapter is entitled "The Destructive Chimera of Communism: The Example of real existing socialism in the German Democratic Republic." The fourth chapter examines the short-lived but enormously destructive phenomenon of fascist/totalitarian dictatorships and is entitled, "The Fascist Lure of Limitless Power." A final chapter, "The Choices Have Run Out," concludes the survey. An addendum reflects on the split Bonhoeffer reception in the GDR. Finally, there is an an appendix relevant to the nature of the church's opposition to real existing socialism.

Rudolf Otto (1869–1937). His famous study *Das Heilige* was translated into English as *The Idea of the Holy: An Enquiry into the Non-Rational Factor in the Idea of the Divine and Its Relation to the Rational.* This work went through eight editions up to 1959.

16. See reflections relevant to this issue in Davies, *Mind of God.*

1

From St. Paul via Constantine
to the World

THE CHURCH UNIVERSAL IS unthinkable without the tireless missionary work of Jesus' apostles, above all of St. Paul, a Jewish tentmaker from Tarsus in Asia Minor who lived from 5 AD to around 65–67 AD. He had been sent to Jerusalem for his further education as a Jew and there he achieved notoriety as a prominent persecutor of Jews who converted to Christianity. Before his own famous conversion on the road to Damascus (estimated to have occurred around 33–35 AD) he was known as Saul of Tarsus. He was the first person to commit to writing a record of what he knew of the life, ministry, death, and resurrection of Jesus of Nazareth, elaborating primarily on the significance of Jesus' sacrifice on Calvary and the mystery of his resurrection. It is important to keep in mind that Paul did this from within a Hebrew worldview, a fact he never tired of stressing.

Leaving aside the mystical Damascus road conversion, Paul had never met Jesus personally. Had he done so at the time he was persecuting Jews for their conversion by Jesus, world history would have not taken the course it did. After Paul's Damascus road mystical encounter he experienced the most dramatic *volte face* to become Jesus' most energetic advocate, known as the "apostle to the gentiles," the one who carried the "good news" beyond the borders of Palestine. So, whatever one believes about God, one would have to acknowledge indebtedness to

Paul as a person of the greatest world-historical significance in spreading knowledge about the ministry of Jesus of Nazareth. More than any other individual Paul went through hell and high water to proclaim his revolutionary message. Paul became transformed into a person convinced of the universal world-changing significance of Jesus' life, ministry, and resurrection, first for fellow Jews and then for the outside world peopled by Greeks and other gentiles, meaning non-Jewish people. In Paul's writings the words "Greek" and "gentile" are often interchangeable.

Further, Paul's writings, being the very first written record of Jesus of Nazareth to survive, are the key to how the Christian tradition, or the "Jesus' myth," was established. We conclude that as Paul never knew Jesus personally, his knowledge of him must derive from an oral tradition. That means the memory that people had of Jesus' activities during his short public ministry. It was all promulgated by word of mouth, in short by vigorous preaching. Jesus' reputation had gone before him and had made the first converts among his kinsmen, obviously in sufficient numbers to alarm the Jewish religious authorities that subversive ideas were being circulated. These had to be stamped out, which is the point in history where the figure of Saul of Tarsus the persecutor appears, the one who becomes transformed into the indefatigable champion we now call the "apostle to the gentiles."

The German Pauline scholars Ferdinand R. Prostmeier and Horacio C. Lona, while examining the spread of Christianity from its beginnings as well as the mystic nature of Jesus, have observed:

> Whoever investigates the scholarly debate in the West concerning the impact of events in the second century AD will be confronted with the phenomenon of the appearance in Antioch of a previously unheard-of Jewish sect known as Χριστιανῶν λαός, that is "Christian people" who had spread themselves among all strata of society by winning supporters and had begun within the Roman Empire to generate discord within the dominant culture. Because of this rapid growth educated foreigners heard the message and were moved to join the movement and these were people who expressed their beliefs in the thought categories of Hellenist-Roman culture.

It is not therefore surprising that the concept of *Logos* played a central role in this ongoing debate. For those in the classical tradition the multifaceted semantic possibilities of the concept *Logos* enabled them to express essential elements of their own tradition, namely the power of

understanding, the primacy of reason, the idea that the world is compre-
hensible; indeed the variety of words, speech, and doctrine among other
things enabled educated Christians to add the specific content of their
faith to the existing mix: the Logos was with God from the beginning
(John 1:1) and the Logos became flesh (John 1:14).[1]

The phenomenon of Antioch that is recorded in chapter 11 of the
Acts of the Apostles is a remarkable example of a diffuse spiritual power
at work in human society. It certainly postulates the existence of a creator
spirit, the Logos, and documents the search for meaning by thoughtful human beings who were products of the Hellenist-Roman cultural
environment. There at Antioch the Christians were apparently in the
forefront of the public discourse. In Acts 11:25–26 we read: "So Barnabas
went to Tarsus to look for Saul; and when he had found him, he brought
him to Antioch. For a whole year they met with the church and taught a
large company of people; and in Antioch the disciples were for the first
time called Christians."

These were indeed events of world-changing significance as we now
can see. Saul's (Paul) unparalleled zeal drove him to spread the message
of his mystical experience of Jesus of Nazareth as far and wide as he
could. His missionary journeys are also events of world-historical significance while the content of his preaching about Jesus established the
essential groundwork for the evolution of the church universal, namely
of communities of converts to the new faith in many places. Everywhere
Paul journeyed and preached there arose a church, making him the pre-
eminent church planter. His point of departure was, as the American
biblical scholar Burton L. Mack formulates it:

> Thus, starting with the revelation that Jesus Christ was the son of
> God and that his death and resurrection marked the great hinge
> of social and epic history, Paul set out on two grand adventures.
> One was what he called his mission to the gentiles. The other was
> constructing a complete theology based on the Christian myth.

---

1. Prostmeier and Lona, eds., *Logos der Vernunft–Logos des Glauben* (translation
by present writer). This section is not to be understood as new contribution to Pauline
scholarship but as a usable summary of Paul's perception of his task as an advocate
of an improved belief system. Obviously he was passionately convinced that he had
discovered in the teachings of Jesus of Nazareth the formula for the healing of the
world. Romans, then, is essentially a compression of Paul's accumulated experience
that he wanted to pass on to the Christian community in first-century Rome, the center
of world power at the time. Its relevance to the twenty-first century is undiminished,
indeed if anything it is heightened.

His quest would be to comprehend the "wisdom and knowledge of God" or God's inscrutable ways (Rom 11:22). His letters to the Corinthians and Romans do not provide us with a complete record of Paul's intellectual quest but they do document major moments in his elaboration of the Christ myth. And in the case of Romans, we have a well-crafted and comprehensive statement of his theological system. Since it was "Christ Jesus," as he said, "who has become for us the wisdom from God" (1 Cor 1:30), it was the Christ myth that focussed and generated his quest to comprehend what he called God's "ways." We should not be surprised, therefore, to find that every feature of Paul's worldview was eventually touched by the symbol of the Christ. That naturally would have some consequences for the shape of the symbol itself.[2]

So then the theological content of Paul's epistles to those various churches are the earliest attempts to systematize the cosmic meaning of the life, work, death, and resurrection of Jesus of Nazareth. Paul's point of departure was that Jesus is the human embodiment of the Logos, the Word. And this is of key importance. He did not mean "word" in the way in which some evangelicals use it, meaning the *text* of the Bible from Genesis to Revelation, because when Paul was preaching there was yet no Bible; rather he meant emphatically that the Logos in its all-encompassing significance is the driving force of the universe. Just how one arrives at this belief exceeds the limits of human comprehension. The experience of the phenomenon of Antioch was clearly instructive, edifying, and profoundly inspiring to many who heard it. In time it would displace most other religions that were competing for the allegiance of people in the first three centuries AD.

That whole episode of history conveys hitherto unexplored intimations of what it means to be fully human. We are not just flesh and blood. There are among "all sorts and conditions of men" those endowed with the spiritual/mental equipment that allows them to envisage, initiate, and implement changes for the better. Christians were called to rise to an existential challenge because under the socialpolitical conditions of the Roman Empire in the first three centuries there was no absolute security of life. For Christians it was an era punctuated by arbitrary and ruthless persecutions. They had to demonstrate that they were no threat to

---

2. Mack, *Who Wrote the New Testament?*, 125. Of key relevance here is the reappreciation of the Pauline legacy by Seidenkop, *Inventing the Individual*; see ch. 4, "The World Turned Upside Down: Paul."

the Roman administration. As pointed out by Uta Heil,[3] Christians in the early Roman Empire had ample opportunity to demonstrate love of one's enemies and to pray for one's persecutors as Jesus reportedly demanded in his Sermon on the Mount (Matt 5–7). The danger of arrest and execution or being thrown to the lions in the Colosseum was an everyday experience whenever persecutions were ordered by the imperial authorities. It was at times sufficient just to be known as a Christian to be accused and sentenced to death for disloyalty to the empire. Political authority in Rome was based on emperor worship and since Christians were committed to the worship of an invisible spiritual being, they could not worship an earthly being even if he was the most powerful person in the world. Consequently, Christians were regarded as the followers of an esoteric and possibly subversive cult that carried out obscure rites all of which aroused the mistrust of the state. The fact that in all other respects Christians within the Roman Empire behaved as exemplary subjects did not shield them from arbitrary persecution.

Paul himself had managed not infrequently to offend the authorities in various places within the empire and was punished by being imprisoned and subjected to torture and other indignities. We are told in Acts that his third missionary journey took him to Jerusalem and there too it was the Jews whom he inadvertently offended and who took umbrage at him. Things had become so bad that a group of Jews planned to murder him before he could be tried in a regular Jewish court for those alleged violations. It was clear to Paul that even if he succeeded in being transferred to the court in Jerusalem from the prison in which he had been confined on the coast at Caesarea, it was unlikely that he would get a fair trial. These dramatic events are recorded in Acts 23–28.

Finally, Paul had one last card to play to escape the vengeance of the Jews and that was his Roman citizenship. He was able to convince the local Roman authorities that he should be sent to Rome for trial, and it was precisely there that he had always wanted to go. The hand of Providence intervened and to Rome he was to be sent, but on a voyage that turned out to be anything but a pleasure cruise on the Mediterranean. After a series of life-threatening adventures his ship finally docked in Rome. Luke's account in Acts ends rather abruptly but in doing so it stresses that Paul lived in Rome for two whole years at his own expense and welcomed all who visited him while preaching the kingdom of God and teaching about

3. Heil, "Menschenliebe im Superlative."

the Lord Jesus Christ quite openly and unhindered, except that he was under house arrest (Acts 28:30–31).

History recounts few adventures in the biography of one man so threateningly dangerous as those experienced by Paul, the apostle to the gentiles. Driven by his intense crusading zeal, his sole aim was to spread the message preached by Jesus of Nazareth. This ability was the very reason why Christianity was promulgated to the world beyond the tiny province of Palestine. And here is the main point of this book: Christianity spread from the Roman Empire and ultimately around the entire world and is still operating despite the crimes and outrageous misdemeanors committed by some of its leaders and the enormous setbacks it has experienced throughout the course of history.

For example, both Communism and National Socialism each in their own brutal way have made it their mission to eliminate or at least marginalize the church and to impose political systems that are aptly described as "murderous utopias." In pursuing this destructive endeavor those regimes have now been totally discredited both by their harebrained economic dogmas and their notoriously inefficient and corrupt administrations. As governments that should have ensured justice and decency to their respective populations, they only spread fear, being agencies of terror and massive injustice, not to mention economic mismanagement on a monumental scale. The result was widespread hopelessness among the subjected populations.

Here at the outset, it is necessary to dilate on the content of Paul's manifesto for Christianity as he recorded it in his famous Epistle to the Romans. First, as recounted in Acts 9:1–22, Paul, because of his conversion, namely the mysterious Damascus road experience, abandons his official task of persecuting those Jews who had converted to Christianity and becomes instead the most dedicated agent of Jesus to carry his name "before the gentiles and kings and the sons of Israel . . ." (Acts 9:15–16). So, the fanatic persecutor of Christians Saul of Tarsus becomes Paul the apostle to the gentiles, a development that is obviously seen as an outrageous betrayal by the Jewish authorities. This conversion experience on the road to Damascus, regardless of the way it is interpreted, was an event of far-reaching world-historical significance.[4] However one attempts to describe it, one is confronted with an out-of-life phenomenon. Paul himself from the New Testament record was obviously convinced that

---

4. Paul spoke of the event in 1 Corinthians 15:5–6 and in Galatians 1:11–16. Further in Luke-Acts it is noted on three occasions: 9:13–19; 22:6–21; and 26:12–18.

it was an event of divine intervention. Whether it was that or something psychological does not seem to matter in the long run because the consequences have profoundly impacted human history ever since.

An investigation of Paul's career and how he came to compose his most famous epistle, namely the one to the Romans, reveals that it is a statement of his beliefs for the healing of the world, concentrating as he does on the significance of Jesus' sacrifice on Calvary and his resurrection. It should be noted that many ideologies have been evolved and implemented with the aim of curing with one formula the problems of human life on this planet. None of these have delivered what they promised; on the contrary, they have rather left human society in a much worse state than before. For example, the two most spectacular examples are Marxism-Leninism and National Socialism; both systems have been designated "false religions" or "murderous utopias" that have tried to stamp out Christianity and depict it as a curious aberration and hence irrelevant to the human condition. Against all that Christianity has survived most noticeably in those countries where people of the faith are are still subjected to persecution, namely in totalitarian states. For the latter Christianity is a permanent thorn in the flesh, indeed an agency of criticism of their claim to have captured the total truth, the so-called *absoluter Wahrheitsanspruch* as it was called in the East German Democratic Republic, which was an uncompromising and brutal Stalinist regime.[5]

CHRISTIANITY'S CLAIM TO POSSESS THE TOTAL TRUTH

Of course, Christianity itself may also be accused of mounting a claim to possess the *total truth*. Certainly Jesus is recorded as having made such wide-ranging claims for himself such as in John 14:6, "I am the way the truth and the life; no one can come to the father except through me."

---

5. For insights into the character of such regimes the widely popular book by the Australian Germanist and novelist Anna Funder *Stasiland* is most helpful. Further, the Marxist-Leninist (M-L) rationale by the infamous leader of East Germany (the German Democratic Republic), namely Walter Ulbricht (1893–1973), expounded the supposedly world-changing "truth" of M-L in a paper published as "Referat zum Grundriss der Geschichte der deutschen Arbeiterbewegung." Ulbricht's summary of the M-L version of human history is followed by a detailed description of the contents of the official multivolume publication of the same name, as "An Outline of the History of the German Working-Class Movement." Ulbricht was First Secretary of the Socialist Unity Party of the GDR from 1950 until 1971. The "Outline" is an ideological propaganda straitjacket and as such a model handbook for political indoctrination in a false gospel.

There is, however, a vast difference between the meaning of the claims of Jesus with those of totalitarianism. For example, Jesus told Pilate in John 18:36 that his kingdom was not of this world. Converts, therefore, must accept Jesus' teaching voluntarily in their heart, because in its essence Christianity abjures the exercise of brachial force and threats of penalty if one does not submit. That said, one notes that history, however, is replete with examples of misguided Christian authorities, popes, bishops, and monarchs who have used force ruthlessly in such military exercises as the Crusades (1095–1291) to force people to submit to the faith.[6] Such phenomena are, however, recognized as tragic errors of judgment on the part of their instigators, indeed derailments of the essential gospel message of love.

Further, it is not possible to justify any kind of violence to others in the name of spreading the gospel. This is not the case in the histories of Communism or National Socialism, both of which justify their terrorist form of government by keeping their subjects permanently dumbed down and intimidated. In practice the ideology is only there to enable the ruling elite, the so-called *Nomenklatura*, the political manipulators of the ideology, to sustain themselves in power.[7]

In Communist China, remarkably, the Christian churches have a legal right to exist, but they are subject to surveillance by the regime and can be arbitrarily closed while clergy and faithful can be arrested and imprisoned at any time. This situation has given rise to a house church movement whereby people meet in secret in private homes. Also, they move locations to avoid where possible the intrusion of state officials. By all accounts Christians in Communist China have put up a stubborn resistance to government policies to contain and suppress them.[8]

Regarding Nazi Germany the trend in current research is to argue that the dominant ideology was a form of religion and that the dictator Adolf Hitler perceived himself as its peculiarly gifted prophet. It is here worth noting that most studies dealing with the history of the Third Reich focus on the origin and implementation of both war aims (militarism) and domestic policy designed mainly to enforce total submission of subjects to the ideology.[9] So there has been something of a seismic shift in

6. Runciman, *History of the Crusades*, 54.

7. On the phenomenon of *Nomenklatura*, see Voslensky, *Nomenklatura*.

8. Lambert, *Chinese Christian Millions*.

9. The list of such works is extensive, but a monumental example is that of Ian Kershaw, *Hitler*, in two volumes: *1889–1936: Hubris* and *1936–1945: Nemesis*.

the efforts to explain the Hitler phenomenon.[10] But first it is necessary to outline what might justifiably be called the "Christian manifesto," namely the content and intention of St. Paul's Epistle to the Romans.

Unlike all the other epistles attributed to St. Paul, the only purpose of Romans was to provide a coherent explanation of the universal and timeless significance of the phenomenon of Jesus so that the miniscule Christian communities in Rome had at their disposal a clear summary of the distinctiveness of the new faith, something that would clarify any misconceptions and bring all the divergent racial outposts in Rome on to the same page. Those communities consisted of some expatriate Jews but also gentiles, so it made practical good sense to bring them into doctrinal alignment. Given that Paul's earlier letters to the other communities in the East Mediterranean world were written to clarify *ad hoc* issues concerning elements of the faith that were either misunderstood or disputed, he deemed it prudent to forewarn the communities in the metropolis of Rome to maintain unity by providing them with a succinct manifesto in advance. Paul's intention had been to visit Rome with the ultimate objective of traveling to Spain, where he had hoped to win converts to Jesus' revolutionary liberating message.

As was the then prevailing custom, the Letter to the Romans was dictated by Paul to his amanuensis before he arrived in the "eternal city," apparently while he was in Corinth. His many previous experiences at cultivating churches around the Eastern Mediterranean had obviously suggested to him to focus now on the West, meaning Spain. And Rome was not only on the way, but it was also the center of the known world. Further, Paul was aware of existing clusters of Christians in Rome of both Jewish and gentile origins and was anxious that they were all of one mind regarding the essentials of the new faith. That, as indicated, seems to have been Paul's motivation in composing arguably his most significant epistle, which is an exposition and rationalization for Christianity's innovative ideas and values. The historic consequence of these was nothing less than a radical reshaping of humanity's perception of itself. For the present purpose, then, what follows is a step-by-step unraveling of the key points that Paul deemed necessary to make. In doing so it must be kept in mind Paul's own Jewish formation, his experiences everywhere he had been over the previous years, and above all the impact of his Damascus road conversion, which triggered the entire adventure.

10. Recent research explaining Hitler as a religious leader is by Heep, "Hitler—das Heilige in Erscheinung?" See the English language summary appended to the issue.

There exists an extensive body of scholarship on Romans by theologians of immense erudition. The present study as stressed above does not aspire to be a contribution to that category at all. Rather it is the work of modern historian of nineteenth- and twentieth-century Germany. This distinction should be clearly understood. In contrast to the biblical scholar the task of the historian is to stimulate public dialogue, which means s/he chooses to address an educated readership from all walks of life rather than exclusively professional scholars. Hence what is said in the following pages about the *Epistle to the Romans* is a communication of relevance to the contemporary reader who is interested in texts that have contributed centrally to the evolution of Western political history. For this reason, historians have perforce to try to be interdisciplinary to explain how the present grew out of the past.

ROMANS: AN OVERVIEW

Right at the beginning of the letter, in verses 1–7, Paul identifies himself as a *slave* of Jesus Christ. His main point is that Jesus is the master who owns him and to whom he, the slave, Paul, is committed to serve unquestioningly for the remainder of his life. He does this, however, with a glad heart because Jesus' message to the world is the best news ever proclaimed. This "good news" (gospel) derives from Jesus' authority, which has two sources, namely a worldly one because Jesus was a physical descendant of King David[11] and a spiritual one because his heavenly father had resurrected him, which is a "meta-historical event"[12] used by Paul to justify naming him the mighty Son of God.

It is instructive to observe that the notable German theologian Rudolf Bultmann (1884–1976) drew attention to the difference between the task of the "objectifying historian," who identifies Jesus as the descendant of the Jewish king of old, namely David (circa 1000 BC), and the theologian, who identifies Jesus of Nazareth as the eternal *Logos*, the Word of God. As Bultmann stressed, however, the latter is an "eschatological" statement outside the categories within which the historian of

11. The biblical sources are: 2 Sam 7; Matt 1:1–16; and Luke 3:23–38.

12. Carnley, *Structure of Resurrection Belief.* "Meta-historical event" means in this context an event outside the normal everyday human perception of cause and effect; in short, something that cannot be explained empirically. It falls under the heading of *psychological* and thus beyond practical explanation, but nevertheless efficacious as in the case of Paul's Damascus road experience.

world history operates. When, on the other hand, the theologian comprehends Jesus of Nazareth as the agent of divine redemption, she/he is operating in an entirely different realm although Jesus' work and destiny that played out in Roman-occupied Galilee happened in world history.[13] What Paul has to say about Jesus of Nazareth, then, is an assessment of his meta-historical or eschatological impact both on him personally and on some contemporary companions of Jesus. So, Paul begins his Epistle to the Romans by identifying himself metaphorically as Jesus' *slave* to make clear to his readership the nature of his relationship to his master. In Paul's writing, then, he amalgamated both history and theology. This process is remarkable since it has had a very long-term impact on the world. One may say with justification that Paul's dramatic ministry was/is a major building block of Western and world civilization. So, the *meta-historical* dimension has been and is still clearly of continuing eschatological edification for humanity while having been physically enacted in the "real world" by real *dramatis personae*.[14] It uses perforce metaphorical language such as that frequently used in the Holy Bible.

As Jesus' slave and apostle, then, Paul and all humanity have received grace, and the role of apostles was to awaken "faithful obedience" to a new set of rules among both Jews and gentiles. Both have been called into divine service. To be a slave of Jesus Christ implies at once a great obligation of love side by side with the honor of a great office. The point is made at the outset that being a Christian means first and foremost being in the world to perform a responsible duty imposed by a loving father. And to do this the servant receives *grace* as a gift of almighty God. God is always, via his Holy Spirit, the initiator. So the servant, as it were, gets the authority or commission to act in this world via the Holy Spirit.

Everybody receives a task, having been equipped with spiritual gifts such as Paul outlined in 1 Corinthians 12 to execute that task or calling. His was to be an apostle to the gentiles. Since the Damascus road experience, Paul was convinced that he had been chosen for a special task, not to elevate his personal status; rather had been given a unique

13. Bultmann, *Jesus Christ and Mythology*, 80. This publication contains the Shaffer Lectures presented at Yale University in October 1951 and at Vanderbilt University in November 1951, when Bultmann was invited to visit some theological faculties at various US universities.

14. People of all cultural heritages practice their religion or cult, which gives them their unique identity. They do so obviously without theologizing about it but because the practice of religion is essential for their understanding of what it means to be human. See Küng, *On Being a Christian*, 602.

responsibility, namely, to bring the news of God's unstinting love to the entire human race. This was underlined by the fact that God had gone to the trouble to reveal himself to humanity in the *incarnation* and then confirmed his identity by the *resurrection*. These facts testified to Jesus' uniqueness, especially affirming that his Holy Spirit still lives among us.

Acknowledged biblical commentators, including those such as Ernst Käsemann, James D. G. Dunn, Brendan Byrne, and William Barclay,[15] for example, have pointed out that Paul wanted earnestly to meet the Christians in Rome and to be an encouragement to them all whether they were of Jewish descent or foreign, highly educated or just ordinary everyday people making a living according to their individual abilities. Being apostles of Jesus of Nazareth Paul implies being totally non-discriminatory, echoing what he had already written to the Galatians (4:27–29) about the racial inclusiveness of Jesus' message to humanity—all being one in Christ Jesus.

Similarly, Paul's message to the Romans was that he hoped to come as a friend to people whom we may justifiably call "all sorts and conditions of men." And this was indeed good news of which one could be proud, "for it is the power of God which produces salvation for everyone who believes, to the Jew first and to the Greek." Being in a right relationship with God is the result of the faith that God has implanted in us: "He who through faith is righteous shall live" (Rom 1:16–17). Again, in such passages one sees that the Christian message proclaims that only being in a right relationship with God enables humanity to approximate being truly human. That is implicit in what Paul was writing to the Romans. And despite all the humiliations he had suffered because of his dedication to Christ, he remains proud of his calling. It had seen him triumph over all manner of adversities. Indeed, this ability to recover from the most extreme setbacks he attributes to the lesson of the cross. Paul is understandably thankful for his survival due exclusively to his great faith in the saving power of the gospel of Jesus Christ.

Paul then perceived himself as *justified*, meaning in this context that Paul was aware of being loved by God regardless of his sinful state, which is the state of all humankind. Christ's salvific act on Calvary meant that humanity is enabled to enter a new relationship with God. And this is a relationship of close amicable confidence that replaces any sense of remoteness from or fear of God that had formerly been a problem for the

15. Wright, *Paul for Everyone: Part 1*, chs. 1–8; Dunn, *Romans 1–8*, liv–lvii; Byrne, *Romans 8–12*; Barclay, *Romans*; Käsemann, *Epistle to the Romans*.

Jews. In short, Paul assures us if we needed assuring that now God accepts us as we are. But this new relationship comes about not because Paul has fulfilled the Jewish Law but because in total faith he has cast himself, the slave, on the boundless compassion of the Creator. Consequently, God is not a stern, punishing father but an all-forgiving friend. In the history of salvation, then, Paul is teaching his readers that via Jesus of Nazareth a revolution in the human understanding of God has occurred.

The Wrath of God

Having made this key point, Paul then confronts the issue of the *wrath of God*. This may surprise in the light of what has just been observed about God's all-forgiving love. One needs, however, to comprehend what is meant by "wrath." In the Old Testament it is understood as part of the covenant between God and his chosen people, the Jews. Their relationship was/is governed by the Law. If this Law was broken by any of his people, God was justly angered and there would be consequences. And right here Paul, who had previously lived strictly according to that Law, formulates a creatively new insight as to the true nature of God's *wrath*. In short, the Jewish idea of God's wrath is modified or refined as follows: Since God is the embodiment of all virtue, he is in his very nature the antithesis of evil. So, people who are evil, disobedient, and ignore what they know to be right automatically suffer separation from God. That separation or alienation is what "wrath" means.

Paul naturally comprehends that the world, meaning humanity, survives on moral foundations. If these are violated, the moral order suffers and the malefactors are cut off automatically from the love of God. As the Old Testament is clear, the moral order is the *wrath* of God at work.[16] That means the world is made in such a way that if the Law is broken, the consequences will be dire. That would mean the end of everything for violators of the Law; they would be automatically consigned to oblivion.

16. Wright, *Paul*, 2:51–68; Barclay, *Letter to the Romans*, 26–28; Byrne, *Romans*, 63–66; Dunn, *Romans*, 51–70, emphasize also that God is both righteous and wrathful. The two "revelations" are related, even causally in the sense that the revelation of God's wrath means that the final reckoning is underway and that human beings are being found wanting. One needs to remember that there is no indwelling righteousness in human beings. If there is to be any rescue at all, it can only come from almighty God. It is graciously offered to humanity as a gift through faith. God's wrath, on the other hand, indicates the way of God's righteousness, appropriated through faith, and is the only path possible toward salvation. In this sense there can be no escaping the wrath of God.

That is simply the way it was. There could be no salvation as the Law was explicit on this. But with the advent of Jesus and his sacrifice on Calvary that dispensation is overcome. The gospel has revised/revoked that Jewish concept of *wrath* because *the gospel prioritizes the love of God for all creation*. God through his Son Jesus of Nazareth has shown a new way for humanity at the center of which is *forgiveness*. Even from the cross itself, Jesus forgives the penitent thief and pronounces forgiveness upon those who crucified him (Luke 23:34, 43). The consequence of past sin is painfully evident in the continued sufferings in the world. That is inevitable. If the rules that enable life to flourish are violated, the outcomes will be disastrous.

This is what happens when God is left out of human decision making and humanity chooses to deviate from the will of God. In history it was seen dramatically in the many wars and in the Holocaust. It is also tragically evident in the causes of climate change and the conflicts that still rage unresolved. If human beings continue down a path of their own devising and ignore the nature of the universe, namely God's creation, the outcomes are always hugely catastrophic. This, then, is the definition that Paul chose to explain the wrath of God. The message is that humanity needs to prioritize the will of the Creator and not exalt ill-conceived human priorities, which are a form of idolatry that is putting the egoistic ambitions of mere men above those of almighty God. Paul has effectively, through insights derived from Jesus of Nazareth, opened an expanded vision of God's relationship to the world for the benefit of all humankind.

By raising these issues at that very time Paul was letting the flock in dissolute Rome know what they were up against. The dominant social culture was one of such extreme decadence that even non-Christian writers such as the Roman philosopher and statesman Seneca (4 BC–65 AD) fulminated against it as did other contemporary non-Christian observers. For Paul with his newly acquired vision of creation the world needed to be returned to reality, meaning to be so ordered that it complied with the true nature of things, namely as prescribed by almighty God himself. For the Jews their reality had been bequeathed to them by the Law beginning with the Decalogue, the Ten Commandments. Jesus had, however, very substantially revised and up graded the Law by his Sermon on the Mount (Matt 5–7). What Paul is now recommending to the Roman Christian community is precisely the ethics contained therein. The only way to overcome degeneracy and the disasters consequent upon such depravity as manifested in Rome is to adopt a new paradigm of values. Standards must change and the reward for that change as promised by Jesus is that humanity "will have life and have it more abundantly" (John 10:10).

In his Letter to the Romans, Paul had already projected his view of what the world should look like if humanity were obedient to a God whose nature is both loving and at the same time intolerant of all forms of abuse. And for those who succumbed to degeneracy in any of its repugnant forms there awaited the inevitable wrath of God. And here is a key point related to human free will: one can "turn from his wickedness and live" as the above-cited prayer affirms. It is a case where the sinner makes a choice to live as though God did not exist and to accept the consequences. In that situation one is apparently so alienated from God, so spiritually brutalized and bereft of remorse, that one no longer cares; *one is impenitent.* But there is a way back; forgiveness is promised to the genuinely penitent. The past can be buried, and the sinner can look forward to a creative and fulfilling future. In short, one chooses life over everything that is life-denying.

The Fallacy of Racial Exclusivism

So far in this epistle Paul has focused on wider issues but then he gets down to the tortuous subject of where he finds that the Jews with their insistence on the Law were embarked on what had to seemed to him a false path. He does this by pointing out that the rigidity of the Jewish Law does not allow for the growth of a genuinely humanized multicultural society. Here in the second chapter of Romans Paul takes his countrymen to task for believing themselves better than all other nations for claiming exclusive access to God and the benefits that flow from that. His stance no doubt made Paul especially suspect among observant Jews. Paul for his part found them guilty of an anti-humanitarian racism by believing themselves to be specially privileged by God. How could the Jew believe that everyone was destined for judgment *except himself?* The question is posed: how could one be immune from judgment simply because he is a Jew?[17]

The absurdity of such a claim clearly offended Paul, who had mentally digested what Jesus had preached. For Jews to argue that they were exempt from the judgment of God was to impute to God the characteristics of a capricious tyrant because the rest of humanity was consigned

17. Barclay, *Letter to the Romans,* 41; Dunn, *Romans,* 144–60.

to the pit. All non-Jews were "lesser breeds without the Law," to adapt Kipling's famous phrase, and this did not tally with what Paul had learned from the preaching of Jesus. One cannot read into the New Testament any form of racial intolerance. Paul emphatically rejects the concept of Jewish exclusivity.[18]

Conscience and the Civilized Person

Since we are now looking at the text of Romans as a *Christian manifesto,* we need to get clear also what Paul has to say about *good works.* These are essential for humanity because as Jesus proclaimed, "I am among you as one who serves," which means one who so shapes his/her life to be of service to others, for the common good, that is, for the "love of neighbor."[19] Civilized human society must be based on "good works." Paul's insight is that a faith that did not produce good works was a travesty, in fact no faith at all.[20] It is by deeds that men are judged. Further, Paul insisted that people should be judged according to what they know. If they know the Law, then they should be judged by it; if they are ignorant of the Law, judgment must take that into account, although Paul is convinced that in everyone there is a conscience that informs them what is right and what is wrong, the unwritten law within. That being so, Paul was no different from the philosophers of the ancient world. Conscience was an essential characteristic of being human.

Paul's Critique of Jewish Law

As the earlier mentioned German theologian Rudolf Bultmann averred, Christianity must be seen as a revolt against Judaism, that is, against the Judaism as it had come to be practiced in Jesus' day.[21] Nowhere is this more emphatically spelled out than in Paul's Epistle to the Romans. Here the Jewish Law is subjected to a blistering critique because it is demonstrably unworkable in practice. The reason for that is its rigidity. Jews were people who perceived themselves to be the light of the world,

18. Gal 3:23–29.

19. Luke, 22:27; Matt 20–28; John 13:12.

20. Barclay, *Letter to the Romans,* 44.

21. Bultmann, *Jesus,* translated as *Jesus and the Word.* In this context the work of the American Pauline scholar Paula Fredriksen is relevant; see her *Paul: The Pagan's Apostle.*

the chosen ones of God, who claimed to be saved regardless of whether they had lived blameless lives. However, it was very unlikely, rather impossible, that people could remain steadfastly or inerrantly observant. And as Paul makes abundantly clear the Jewish system in which he was raised produced hypocrites, meaning people who violated the Law but who at the same time condemned others. The mere fact that one is a circumcised Jew does not ensure one from hypocrisy. As Paul says, "Do you suppose, O man, that when you judge who do such things [that is, violate the Law] and yet do them yourself, you will escape the judgment of God?" (Rom 2:30).

Understanding what Paul says about his "observant" compatriots, meaning the Jewish race, is of key importance. Above all the Jews did and do have a special relationship to God as they continue to believe. Paul, however, took the view that their special relationship implied a *responsibility* while the Jews themselves believed that it was one of special *privilege*. They had forgotten that the "oracles of God" (the Ten Commandments) were just that, *commandments*.[22] Some Jews were convinced that being special or chosen did give them *carte blanche* or license to do anything they pleased. Obviously not all Jews behaved like that because there was always a faithful remnant. They were the true Jewish race. Nevertheless, Paul had come to believe that God was justified in condemning the Jews, but that judgment was not final. The door was open through which under the new dispensation gentiles were enabled to bring Jews back into the fold. And that is what the new dispensation meant: Jew and gentile would both be reconciled in Christ.

This reasoning has been confirmed by none other than the German theologian Dietrich Bonhoeffer in his fragment known as *Ethics*.[23] The tragedy of the Jews was that the great task of evangelization of the world that had been entrusted to them by God was refused and subsequently inherited by the gentiles. And so, "God's plan was, as it were, reversed, and it was not as it should have been, the Jew who evangelized the gentile, but the gentile who evangelized the Jew—a process which is still going on."[24] Understandably it appears that Jews who still do not take on board what Paul had long pointed out are living in a parallel universe. Paul went

22. Barclay, *Letter to the Romans*, 52.

23. See Bonhoeffer, *Ethics*, in *DBWE* 6, especially on p. 105 and the chapter on "guilt," pp. 124–45.

24. Barclay, *Letter to the Romans*, 53.

so far as to charge them with having lost the fear of God: "There is no fear of God before their eyes" (Rom 3:28).[25]

Paul's tirade against the Jews can, understandably, elicit the charge from them that he was being anti-Semitic—a Jewish anti-Jew—and that Christianity is by its very nature anti-Semitic.[26] But this would be a complete and tragic misunderstanding; Paul steadfastly believed in the special calling that the chosen people had from God, and acknowledged that Christianity was a wild branch grafted on what was already a cultivated tree, saying in Romans 11:24: "For if you have been cut from what is by nature a wild olive tree, and grafted contrary to nature, into a cultivated olive tree, how much more will these natural branches be grafted back into their own olive tree." The Jew has indeed a special part in the economy of God, so the signs of the times, meaning right now in the twenty-first century, perhaps as never before, urge the necessity of an even more intense Christian-Jewish dialogue.[27] As far as Paul was concerned the door was always open, and that speaks for both the rigor and sensitivity of his thinking.

In modern parlance, Paul in his Epistle to the Romans was promoting a paradigm change that had both deep theological and political implications. He had come to see as the rabbi Jesus had already made clear that the Jewish paradigm of the Law and Jewish exclusivity, in short, aloofness towards non-Jews, could not possibly accord with the mission with which they had been entrusted by a just and loving God. Jesus had spelled this out in such New Testament passages as Matthew 5–7 (The Sermon on the Mount) and in his parables, especially the Prodigal Son and the Good Samaritan.

The Prodigal Son teaches about the limitless love of God for all humanity no matter how far individuals and tribes have drifted away from him. Its central theme is the unconditional acceptance of the penitent sinner and thus it is about *forgiveness*. Without that both personal

---

25. Cf. Barclay, *Letter to the Romans*, 54.

26. Byrne, *Romans*, 106–11, the section following "Gods' Faithfulness to Israel Still Stands."

27. There have been some outstanding instances of promoting Christian-Jewish dialogue in the twentieth and twenty-first centuries. See the pioneering work of the Anglican Judeophile priest James Parkes, *Jew and His Neighbour*, *Jew*, *Conflict of the Church and the Synagogue*, and *Judaism and Christianity*. Parkes's work laid the foundation of the Council of Christians and Jews in 1942 by the then archbishop of Canterbury, William Temple, and the chief rabbi of the UK, Josef Hertz. See Simpson and Weyl, *Story of the International Council*; and Simpson, "Jewish-Christian Relations."

relationships as well as international relations become impossible. In the Parable of the Good Samaritan the point is that mercy and compassion are not meant to be restricted and applied to one's own tribe but applied to *all* humanity without discrimination. Consequently, the terror of God is banished; one does no longer live under a shadow of fear of retribution; one is indeed liberated from all that. But that is by no means a license for human beings to do whatever they like in a self-centered way and the reason is that now people are constrained to act with decency toward everybody by *the law of love*. This is the key concept that Paul is at pains to get accepted by all humanity. Christianity is namely *applied decency* to all and that is a concept far removed from the Judaism of Paul's time and that of Israel today, at least for elements in the Likud Party. The Palestinians yearn for decent treatment from their Israeli masters.[28] But the Israel of today is far from being a one-party state. It is peopled by a mixture of citizens of various political, secular, as well as religious persuasions and has a liberal democratic constitution.

This means that Israel is a state locked in a struggle between unbending, backward-looking people on the one hand and liberal, modernizing citizens on the other who genuinely accept the modern pluralist society that Israel has become, to be a role model for the entire world. What is remarkable are the ultra-conservative religious elements today who derive their inspiration from the history of King David, who flourished circa 1000 BC and extended the kingdom of Israel over the Fertile Crescent.[29] That the history or legends of past imperial greatness can inspire tribes and nations still thousands of years later is well known. It is, however, politically fraught because it ignores the movements of peoples during the intervening centuries. History has moved on and so today the Palestinian question in the Holy Land remains tragically unresolved. A better illustration of the need for sober Christian-Jewish dialogue removed from all fundamentalist assumptions could scarcely be imagined. The preconditions for this to take place are not yet foreseeable, given the Old Testament fundamentalist convictions of Israeli conservatives. The relevance for the twenty-first century of Paul's ancient critique of Jewish Law and political practice cannot be overstated.

In his Letter to the Philippians, chapter 3, Paul recalls his Jewish heritage with harrowing frankness: "circumcised on the eighth day of the

28. On the case for decency in the treatment of Arabs by the State of Israel, see Victor, *Voice of Reason*.

29. See 2 Sam 5:6–10 and ch. 8.

people of Israel, of the tribe of Benjamin, a Hebrew of Hebrews; as to the law a Pharisee, as to zeal a persecutor of the church, as to righteousness under the law blameless. But whatever gain I had, I counted as loss for the sake of Christ." These distinguishing marks or attributes and experiences are a classic example of a paradigm of belief to which Paul adhered prior to his Damascus road conversion and then perceptively and creatively revised. This crucial paradigm change can be traced through all his epistles; the Jewish paradigm was replaced by a Christian paradigm, and the concise summing up of that is in the Epistle to the Romans.

Therein is the unmistakeable message that the Christian law of love overtakes and displaces the Hebrew Law, rendering it obsolete in almost every respect, and Paul goes to great lengths to make this clear, especially about the obligation for males to be circumcised. He makes the point that the ancient ritual is meaningless as a badge of loyalty and commitment to almighty God and Law if, as inevitably happens, the Law is repeatedly breached and God is expected to absolve and accept all Jews but not gentiles. In short, Judaism became discredited in Paul's experience as a kind of religious sleight of hand, lacking integrity and credibility, demonstrating that the Jews had betrayed their initial covenant with almighty God. And this was precisely what Jesus' preaching highlighted. See again the Sermon on the Mount (Matt 5–7). The gospel replaces the Jewish Law. Obviously, this made Paul highly unpopular in rabbinic circles. But nothing could dissuade Paul from preaching that all humanity is ruined by sin but is rescued by Christ.[30] It is the graciousness that comes from God that has made the Law superfluous and irrelevant.[31] A new spirituality for human beings is here being advanced.

All Nations Are One Family.

So far Paul has been at pains to enlighten the individual Christians living in Rome about where each one stands in relation to God. In addition to that, however, one is now a member of a *family* governed by new rules of behavior. The father of this new family is none other than God himself and that makes the entire human race joint heirs with Jesus Christ, God's own Son. In short, through the love and mercy of God the "lost, helpless, poverty-stricken, debt-laden sinner" has been adopted into the family

---

30. Barclay, *Letter to the Romans*, 82; Byrne, *Romans*, 62–114; Dunn, *Romans*, 666–69.

31. Rom 6:12–14.

of God.[32] There is only one precondition, namely that to join and stay in the family the individual must love God. Considering the benefits, that is a devotion one should be overjoyed to give. And this is a great innovative idea of world-historical significance: all peoples could be linked in a filial relationship and that has immense political implications. These become starkly apparent when through pride people and nations become disobedient, refuse God's gracious invitation—which, of course, no one has a right to expect—and pursue selfish and worldly objectives that end in such crimes as genocide and warfare.

If Paul had been a news commentator in the twentieth century, we would know already what his views would be. Peoples and individuals who reject God inevitably have replaced the love of God with an idolatrous love of the *Volk,* for example, as in the case of Prusso-Germany, or also in those countries that had embraced the seductive but equally false ideology of Marxism-Leninism.[33] In countries governed by the latter ideology it was/is imagined that via a so-called *command economy* a classless society could be established in which each individual would be recompensed according to their separate needs.[34] How that was supposed to work will be dealt with in chapter 3. For the moment suffice it to note that the new Pauline paradigm has endured to the present day whereas those of the two murderous utopias have been rejected, though it is recognized that there are still some countries in which the party in power appeals to the authority of Marxism-Leninism or a Maoist variation of it.

Returning to Romans, the reader cannot help but be impressed by Paul's thoroughness in the way he has introduced and explained his new paradigm to the Christian communities in Rome, who of course stand for all the human races. Through Paul they are getting the best advice for life. Whereas the Jewish Law seemed to have a completely unrealistic understanding of the power of sin over humanity, Paul came to the full realization that what Jesus was saying and accomplished on Calvary, by his resurrection and ascension, had opened an escape route from the

32. Barclay, *Letter to the Romans,* 107.

33. *Jingoism* of which the British once stood accused and now the Americans also.

34. Cf. Deut 31. See especially the reference to "whoring after the gods of strangers of the land . . ." in verse 16 (KJV). The irony of Marxism-Leninism is that while Marx had believed his analysis of history had been "scientific" and hence scrupulously objective, he and his disciples seem to have forgotten that throughout history human beings were driven by emphatically self-centered goals. The challenge was how to get disparate social groups to work together humanely for the welfare of the whole, and that is still today the elusive goal of all national communities who inhabit planet Earth.

crushing consequences of sin. Indeed, Paul cannot state more strongly how his encounter with Christ and the gospel has changed him. It also has the capacity to change the world, which is in thrall to sin; now the grace of God through the salvific acts of Christ has made humanity free from that bondage. A new and very different image of man has been projected from that which prevailed under the Jewish Law. That means human beings everywhere are liberated to become agents of God's will both for themselves and for service to others. And this is crucial because it is all very well for one to feel elation, say experiencing a masterly performance of a Mozart Mass in a great cathedral; that experience must issue in a Christian becoming a conscious agent of God in the outside world, where the struggle between good and evil is palpable.

All this is very encouraging, but the reality is that sin always gets in the way preventing people from becoming the joyous slaves that God wants them to be. Temptation in many guises appears and seduces the individual as Paul himself well knew from his own experience. Human beings are all creatures of flesh and blood and hence subject to the power of sin as the following famous passage affirms:

> We know that the law is spiritual; but I am carnal, sold under sin. I do not understand my own actions. For I do not what I want, but what I do not want, but I do the very thing I hate. Now if I do what I do not want, I agree that the law is good. So, then it is no longer I that do it, but sin which dwells within me. For I know that nothing good dwells within me, that is in my flesh. I can will what is right, but I cannot do it. For I do not do the good that I want, but the evil I do not want is what I do. Now if I do what I do not want, it is no longer I that do it but sin that dwells within me. (Rom 7:14–20)

The Fateful Human Dilemma

Here Paul recognized frankly that he and all humankind were faced with a dilemma: one knew what was right but nevertheless was seduced by baser instincts and did what was wrong. Paul attributed this to what he called the "body of this death" or this "fatal body," which all too readily submits to sin. Indeed, the lures of temptation are the warp and woof of literature as Oscar Wilde cynically wrote: "The only way to get rid of temptation is to yield to it. Resist it, and your soul grows sick with longing for the things it has forbidden to itself, with desire for what its monstrous laws have made monstrous and unlawful."[35] Human beings find out soon enough in life that they are up against a virtually invincible enemy who resides within them. But Christians also know that the only release from this bondage is provided by Jesus Christ as reported in the Gospels.

As modern writers such as Hans Küng have pointed out, the way to salvation is not by signing off on a list of rules relating to morality but by acknowledging the *person* Jesus of Nazareth as the "captain of one's soul." That means literally to submit oneself to the Holy Spirit in all things. Küng asks the question:

> Who is a Christian? Not the ones who say 'Lord, Lord' and subscribes to a fundamentalism be it of a biblical-protestant or an authoritarian Roman Catholic or a traditionalistic eastern Orthodox character. Rather a Christian is one who on his or her personal path through life (and every human being has their own) is striving practically to orient themselves on the person of Jesus Christ. Nothing more is demanded.[36]

Even more pointedly he concluded his earlier book *On Being a Christian* with the following sentence: "By following Jesus Christ man in the world today can truly humanly live, act, suffer and die in happiness and unhappiness, life and death, sustained by God and helpful to men."[37]

These insights mirror those of St. Paul made some two thousand years ago. The longevity of Christ's teaching as promulgated by Paul testifies to the inexplicable convincing power (*Überzeugungskraft*) of the gospel. There is no doubting its power even if it remains outside the realm of comprehension of most people. As Paul in 1 Corinthians 3:18–19 formulated it, "Let no man deceive himself. If anyone among you thinks he is wise in this age, let him become a fool that he may become wise. For the wisdom of this world is folly with God . . ."

And a little further, in 4:9–11, Paul reiterates, "For I think that God has exhibited us apostles as last of all, like men sentenced to death; because we have become a spectacle to the world, to angels and to men. *We are fools for Christ's sake*, but you are wise in Christ. We are weak but you are strong. You are held in honor, but we in disrepute" (RSV, emphasis added). The reader is left with a seeming inanity yet precisely

---

35. Wilde, *Picture of Dorian Gray* (1890).

36. Küng, *Jesus*, 10. Translation by present writer.

37. Küng, *On Being a Christian*, 602.

this exerts an inexplicable attraction on human beings. Only those who love God and who are willing to enter his universe are in the real world after all. People who prefer to remain in a condition dominated by self-centered objectives find themselves in a fantasy world, a parallel universe going nowhere. This is an observation of that enables us to see what really matters at all. An excellent illustration of this is what happened to the German people because many had become deluded and threw all their hopes on the seductive but empty promises of a false prophet. And Dietrich Bonhoeffer observed this in his book *The Cost of Discipleship* (1936); only Christ's way would lead the German people out of their bondage to National Socialism and the wickedness into which Adolf Hitler had lured them. If anyone ever became a *fool for Christ's sake*, it was that courageous young German pastor whose gifted insights proved by the course of history to have been the right ones.

The modern restatements of Paul's preaching in the examples of Bonhoeffer and Küng underline that by formally submitting oneself to Christ, as every pastor does at ordination, one is entering a spiritual-intellectual universe in which a separate set of values apply. They are certainly very different from the selfish, materialistic values of the world in which baser instincts predominate. A dichotomy is established that sees good confronting evil; and when it comes to putting the world right or fighting against the atrocities perpetrated by wicked men, the church has always produced martyrs who have fearlessly witnessed for the truth. The path of the foolishness of God has turned out after all to be the most humane path to follow. And further, Paul goes on to show that by submitting to Christ the individual is no longer dominated by past sins but by the prospect of a creative future in service both to God and humanity, and this hope overcomes all despair.[38] The affirmation comes in Romans 8:31–39:

> For I am convinced that neither death, nor life, nor angels, nor principalities, nor the present age, nor the age to come, nor powers, nor height, nor any other creation will be able to separate us from the love of God which is in Christ Jesus our Lord.[39]

Here Paul proclaims with burning conviction that the love of God overrides all the efforts of cosmic powers that strive to separate us from the Creator. The extent of this paradigm change is immense.

---

38. This is the thrust of Romans 7–8. William Barclay says in his study of Romans, "The penalty of the past is removed and strength for his future is assured" (*Romans*, 103).

39. Cf. Wink, *Naming the Powers*, 1:48–49.

Paul's Jewish Problem

Paul's paradigm change requires him to relocate the chosen people in God's plan. The reason for this was because on Calvary the Jews had emphatically rejected Jesus. This is covered in chapters 9–11 of Romans. The theological ideas contained here are key to unraveling the issue of how almighty God could seem to reject his chosen people and embrace the gentiles. First, it is essential to grasp that God is unchangeable and steadfast in his plan to redeem the entire human race. Therefore, the way the Jews had chosen to follow, which ended with their rejection of Christ, placed them at odds with God. They needed to find a way back into the fold. Paul in Romans and elsewhere wrestles with how this might be accomplished. And the answer is the fact that a *remnant* of Jews did not reject the drama enacted on Calvary and did accept Jesus as the new "way." The first Christians were obviously Jews. They had embraced the gospel, which means they willingly and gladly accepted the *other*, meaning the non-Jewish world. Now the process of Jewish-gentile negotiation for reconciliation could take place. Summarized, the process looks like this:

Israel is the chosen people, but Israel is not a racial concept; rather it means all those people, irrespective of blood or color, who open their hearts and minds to trust God implicitly. To achieve this trust, one must be willing to see that the way of the Law as discussed above is irresolvable and problematic. It does not lead to reconciliation with God. One must really accept what the "sovereignty of God" implies. In St. Paul's judgment many Jews had made the mistake of exalting their own works as prescribed in the Law and this was unachievable.[40] The individual had to be shown that the only way to approach God was by having complete trust like that of a child in its relationship to its father. The gentiles as wild olive trees for their part must henceforth humbly remember that they through the grace of God have been grafted onto the true olive stock.

The beauty of that imagery is that in the end all humanity will be saved. Paul wants with every fiber of his being for his countrymen to be included but he is alienated by their attitude to religion. He is insistent that they learn to abandon their legalism and accept what Jesus

---

40. It must be noted that it was God who had "hardened their hearts," since nothing is outside of the control of God. The question of why God allowed this (as a theologian might respond) is answered in saying that he had to demonstrate that the Law was not the way as it seduced the chosen people into thinking that they could by their own human efforts merit salvation. See Barclay's discussion of this in his *Letter to the Romans*, 119–23; and also Byrne, *Romans*, 87–101.

had taught, namely that all that is necessary is for the individual soul to abandon her/himself to the limitless grace and mercy of the one creator God. Indeed, this insight was already present in their prophets, such as in Joel 2:32, "All who call upon the name of the Lord shall be delivered." No restrictions or exclusiveness are evident here. But that is not the way in which Jewish history developed.[41] Nevertheless, in the fullness of time, as Paul pointed out, as the prophet Isaiah (59:20–21) proclaimed:

> And he will come to Zion as Redeemer, to those in Jacob who turn from transgression, says the Lord. And as for me, this is my covenant with them, says the Lord: my spirit which is upon you, and my words which I have put in your mouth, shall not depart out of your mouth, or out of the mouth of your children, or out of the mouth of your children's children, says the Lord, from this time forth and for evermore.

God, being God, does not renege on his word so his later rejection of the Jews cannot be permanent and so they too will be saved. That was God's unchangeable purpose, namely salvation and not destruction.[42] But it was still a work in progress. God in the end will present humanity with the solution. The duty of mortals is to try to the extent of human intelligence to grasp the mind of God, which of course is impossible as we are reminded by such a scholar as Karl Barth, who wrote:

> For when we have clearly perceived that, if divinity be so concreted and humanised in a particular department of history—the history of religion or that of the history of salvation—God has ceased to be God, and there can be no relation with him, then we are able to see that the whole occurrence of the known world derives its content and significance from the Unknown God.[43]

---

41. Therefore, Old Testament studies are essential for all ordinands. They illustrate the tentative way in which the writers sought to arrive at a true image of the creator God. While the prophets tried to influence Israel's behavior in their day without success, their pronouncements did alter the course of history and that is valid for the present day; conservative Israelis wish to re-establish Jewish control of the Middle East, disregarding the claims of Palestinian Arabs, who have occupied the land for hundreds of years. Useful in this regard is Perlman, *Propheten*.

42. Barclay, *Letter to the Romans*, 153. This was Israel's situation in the first century AD and it is still the case in the twenty-first century. The Jews have fought perversely against God and continue fighting. Despite that, however, God's love is still extended to them.

43. Barth, *Epistle to the Romans*, 79.

All one can do in the final analysis is to love and follow the divine precepts to the best of one's ability. And this is expressed in Paul's thought when he wrote:

> I appeal to you therefore, brethren, by the mercies of God, to present your bodies as a living sacrifice holy and acceptable to God which is your spiritual worship. Do not be conformed to this world but be transformed by the renewal of your mind, that you may prove what is the will of God, what is good and acceptable and perfect. (Rom 12:1–2 RSV)

The wisdom of this admonition is manifest in all human activities in which one is tempted to overindulge. A dissolute and undisciplined life ravaged by desires of the flesh inevitably ends in wreckage. The answer is provided by Paul in his Letter to the Philippians, 4:5–6 (RSV):

> Rejoice in the Lord always; again, I will say rejoice. *Let all men know your forbearance.* The Lord is at hand. Have no anxiety about anything, but in everything by prayer and supplication with thanksgiving let your requests be known to God. (emphasis added)

Here is an admonition to be *Christ-focused* in everything one does, and all will be well. Achieving that level of discipline will, however, always be a struggle. But one does not struggle alone because one is a member of the Body of Christ and as such one experiences a sense of solidarity and encouragement in collaboration with others. Each person with their separate gifts exists as a fellow worker in the vineyard contributing to the welfare of the whole Body of Christ. Indeed, within the fellowship of the Body everyone can focus his actions on what really matters and offer to contribute to the wellbeing of all by means of the unique abilities with which one has been bestowed.

Paul is very strong about personal gifts, a subject he especially addressed in 1 Corinthians 12, where he listed them. And here in Romans 12:6–8 (RSV) he stressed:

> Having gifts that differ according to the grace given to us let us use them; if prophecy, in proportion to our faith; if service, in our serving; he who teaches, in his teaching; he who exhorts, in his exhortation; he who contributes, in liberality; he who gives aid, with zeal; he who does acts of mercy, with cheerfulness."

In this way the Body of Christ serves a world in need of stability; Christ is manifest among us in the ethics of everyday practice. Above all, though, our behavior must be genuinely sincere, not simulated. The practicality of the advice given is from one who really understands how the world works. Paul has been through it all as graphically illustrated by this famous passage of 2 Corinthians 11:23–29 (RSV):

> Are they servants of Christ? I am a better one—I am talking like a madman—with far greater labours, far more imprisonments, with countless beatings, and often near death. Five times I have received at the hands of the Jews the forty lashes save one. Three times I have been beaten with rods, once I was stoned. Three times I have been shipwrecked; a night and a day I have been adrift at sea; on frequent journeys, in danger from rivers, danger from robbers, danger from my own people, danger from Gentiles, danger in the city, danger in the wilderness, danger at sea, danger from false brethren; in toil and hardship; through many a sleepless night, in hunger and thirst, often without food in cold and exposure. And apart from other things there is the daily pressure upon me of my anxiety for all the churches.

This is the picture of a man driven by superhuman will trying to remain steadfast to his calling. He yearns for an ordered life in which decency can prevail, but it eludes him. Nevertheless, he still perseveres.

Paul's Vision of Order for the World.

It does not take much reflection to appreciate, as Martin Luther had done much later, that a world without order is the devil's inn (*des Teufels Wirtshaus*) or playground in which life is chaotic and "solitary, poor, nasty, brutish and short," as Thomas Hobbes had observed in his study of state power, *The Leviathan*.[44] Martin Luther's worldview was exactly the same since he also had been very much influenced by St. Paul's writings on the subject, especially the content of Romans 13. There it says in the King James translation: "Let every soul be subject unto the higher powers. For

---

44. On Luther's understanding of secular authority see Moses, "Church and State in Post-Reformation Germany." Interestingly, Luther's imagery of the world was that of a medieval inn where a cross section of human society came together. There were the usual drinkers plus law-abiding travelers spending the night, but also thieves, cutthroats, and prostitutes just waiting to ensnare the innocent. It was a microcosm of the real world. To keep order, however, there were the police, a necessary adjunct in all human society to ward off crime, protect the innocent, and punish the criminals.

there is no power but of God; *the powers-that-be-are-ordained-of-God.* [emphasis added] Whosoever therefore resisteth the power, resisteth the ordinance of God: and they that resist shall receive to themselves damnation" (verses 1–2). In the more modern English of the Revised Standard Version, verses 1–10 are rendered as follows:

> Let every person be subject to the government authorities. For there is no authority except from God, and those that exist have been instituted by God. Therefore, he who resists the authorities resists what God has appointed, and those who resist will incur judgment. For the rulers are not a terror to good conduct, but to bad. Would you have no fear of him who is in authority? They do what is good, and you will receive his approval, for he is God's servant for your good. But if you do wrong, be afraid, for he does not bear the sword in vain; he is the servant of God to exert his wrath on the wrongdoer. Therefore, one must be subject, not only to avoid God's wrath but also for the sake of conscience. For the same reason you also pay taxes, for the authorities are the ministers of God, attending to this very thing. Pay all of them their dues, taxes to whom taxes are due, revenue to whom revenue is due, respect to whom respect is due, honour to whom honour is due.
>
> Owe no one anything, except to love one another; for he who loves his neighbor has fulfilled the law. The commandments, "You shall not commit adultery. "You shall not kill; you shall not steal. You shall not covet," and any other commandment are summed up in this sentence, "You shall love your neighbor as yourself." Love does no wrong to a neighbor, therefore love is fulfilling the law.

Paul was very conscious of the fact that the sovereignty of God was reified or made manifest in ordered and humane relationships. What else would one expect from a deity whose chief characteristic is love for his creation? It was logical that there had to be governance through civil authority. Without a regulating agency there would be chaos, confusion, and disorder. Not only would criminal tendencies have free reign but also fanatical groups within the nation could go around marauding and wreaking havoc among fellow countrymen, terrorizing peaceful and law-abiding subjects.[45]

---

45. A contemporary example of organized crime at work in the world is the Sicilian and American mafia, on which there exists a vast literature. For an introduction, see Lupo, *Two Mafias.*

The Legacy of Romans 13

This chapter of Romans is arguably the one section in the entire epistle that has had most obvious and enduring relevance to *public life*, as opposed to spiritual guidance for people at the personal and social level, because it points to the central importance of the body politic. Here indeed the spiritual and the political are intertwined. For this very reason it was picked up by none other than Martin Luther at the beginning of the Reformation and it surfaced again in the writings of another Lutheran pastor, Dietrich Bonhoeffer, when during the Third Reich he redefined what true, (godly) as opposed to barbaric, governance really means.[46] Not surprisingly, also during the notoriously capricious rule of the Communists in East Germany, 1945–1989, the Lutheran bishop Otto Dibelius (1880–1967) confronted the issue of the true role of political authority in a polemic against the East German regime of Walter Ulbricht (in power 1945–1973) entitled *Obrigkeit*, that is, "The-Powers-that-Be."[47]

The question of how a humane government should behave has been at the center of public debate for many centuries and as late as the 1960s in West Germany it was the focus of both academic and public discussion. For example, the then leading Reformation historian, Walther-Peter Fuchs (1905–1997), at the University of Erlangen in 1963 ran a path-breaking seminar on the question of "Resistance to the Powers-that-Be" (*Widerstand gegen die Obrigkeit*). The political-pedagogic intent of the seminar was to explain to German students at that time how the political culture of their country had been perverted by a false interpretation of Romans 13. Professor Fuchs even went so far as to designate that section of the New Testament as the most important document in modern German history.[48] It was therefore essential to understand exactly what Paul was advocating in the first century AD under the rule of the Roman Empire. Why did Paul think so highly of the empire? The answer is that it was a bulwark against chaos; it was an instrument that conformed to

---

46. See his *Ethics* in *DBWE* 6.

47. Dibelius, *Obrigkeit*.

48. In 1963 the present writer was a member of Professor Fuchs's seminar. It only much later became known that Herr Fuchs during the Third Reich had been a Nazi supporter, but because of the Allied victory over Germany in 1945 he began to reflect on the differences between the liberal democratic political culture of the Western powers and that which had taken root in authoritarian, anti-democratic Prussia-Germany. That had been the matrix out of which the barbaric dictatorship of Adolf Hitler had emerged.

the will of almighty God to maintain law and order. If it lost control, the insurgent elements within it such as the turbulent Jewish Zealots, besides other elements of tribal unrest, would cause it to disintegrate, thus making the reproduction of civic order impossible. Paul was adamant that the Christian dispensation would create the conditions out of which good citizens would emerge.

Further, there were great advantages to being a Roman citizen. One had the protection of the state, a legal system to dispense justice, and as well the state built and maintained amenities in communication, water supply, and sewage, which fostered community, commerce, and social intercourse. Above all the state ensured security. One could no more opt out of the state any more than one could opt out of the church. Clearly, Paul understood the concept of the social contract without the need to formulate it. This implied duties on the part of the citizen and obligations in addition to paying taxes. Male subjects, for example, would have the obligation of military service and this encompassed Christians in the empire.[49] If one was a male citizen, one could be recruited into the army regardless of whether one felt any patriotic compulsion. This situation obviously introduced a tension for Christians between Jesus' prioritization of peace-making on the one hand and the duty to serve the state, on the other.[50]

In this regard it should be kept in mind that Jesus himself uttered ambiguous statements, such as in Matthew 10:34, "Do not think that I have come to bring peace on earth; I have not come to bring peace but a sword." Nevertheless, the thrust of the New Testament is that Christians should be at the forefront of peace-making and behave as reconcilers, promoting a just and peaceful society domestically and international harmony abroad, all for the good of humanity at large. It is therefore of interest to note that Paul was adamant about obedience to the emperor even to the extent of submissiveness to such a barbaric and capricious ruler as Nero (37–68 AD), under whose jurisdiction during the persecutions that occurred after the great fire of Rome in 64 AD Paul was martyred.

Finally, on the question of the state in Paul's thinking, he saw it as a divinely sanctioned instrument for preserving the world from chaos. As William Barclay observes, "Those who administered the State were

---

49. Harnack, *Militia Christi*.

50. Cf. Matt 5:9: "Blessed are the peacemakers . . ." in the Beatitudes of the Sermon on the Mount. There are many other New Testament references to military service, and these are listed by Harnack in *Militia Christi*, 108–9.

playing their part in that great task. Whether they knew it or not they were doing God's work, and it was the Christian's duty to help and not to hinder."[51]

The Final Admonitions in Romans

After having expounded upon the public duties of the Christian as a citizen, Paul returns to preaching about the centrality of *faith*. He repeatedly reminds his readers that it is a Christian's duty to think about the world, not simply as circumstances affect oneself but also as it affects one's neighbors, and he gives specific examples such as the dietary laws. Being over-scrupulous in such matters can give offense to others. Pedantry and ostentation are unbecoming of a Christian also. While Christians perceived themselves dispensed from Jewish laws and rituals, there was still the obligation to show consideration for the deeply held convictions, customs, and practices of others. In short, one must be strong and confident enough in one's own position to be able to cope with the weaknesses of others and not to embarrass them for their inadequacies. One must foster fellowship and avoid discord that could arise from being judgmental. Toleration is a priority. And one must be versed in the Scriptures, that is, know the sources of one's beliefs.

Further, one's belief in God gives one strength of character and lends one *hope*, and bearing in mind the above virtues, one never gives in to despair because the human spirit and goodness of heart derive from God and so in all human relationships one will prioritize harmony over self-righteousness, which inevitably produces division. Indeed, one must be sure to infuse one's dealings with others with a generous spirit that praises God. The main thing is to be aware of the obligation to serve rather than to be served, and to strive for and maintain unity. Both Jew and gentile are intended to be reconciled. If one gets one's values right, there is great hope for the community at large, no matter how dismal the circumstances at a given time and place may seem. And out of hope comes joy and out of joy comes peace and out of peace comes the power to surmount all difficulties, because that power derives from the life pattern set by Jesus Christ. "By ourselves we can do nothing: but with God all things are possible" (Matt 19:26).

---

51. Barclay, *Letter to the Romans*, 174.

The foregoing recommendations or advice were proffered in the most tactful way to the Roman Christians. Paul had gathered valuable experience in his dealing with "all sorts and conditions of men" over three decades and so he knew how important it was to avoid offending others. It is always better to be encouraging in contrast to carping in dealing with people. *Meekness*, rightly understood, should always be the defining characteristic of the Christian. William Barclay elsewhere in his writing defined "meekness" as having two connotations, one derived from the Hebrew and the other from the Greek. Neither suggests spineless submissiveness or subservience. The Hebrew implies a person committed to God in perfect obedience and in total trust. The Greek defines it as that quality in a person who is in complete control of his passions and instincts, in short, a very self-disciplined individual. Barclay, however, points out that this can only mean the person who is *God-controlled*.[52] He defines "meekness" as used in Matthew 5:5 (the Beatitudes) as follows: "O the bliss of that man who has so committed himself to God that he is entirely God-controlled, for such a man will be right with God and will be right with self and will be right with men and will enter into that life which God has promised and which God alone can give."[53]

Paul's Letter to the Romans, then, is a summing up of what he had learned and experienced since his conversion on the road to Damascus, a time span of some three decades. In that period Paul had developed a new "image of man" that he projected piecemeal in all his writings and rounded off in the Epistle to the Romans. That "image" differs radically from that projected either by the *Jews* or the *Greeks*, by which latter term he meant the gentile world of his day. Both had fallen far short of what Paul believed was God's intention for creation. The Jews were blameworthy because they were/are God's beloved or chosen ones who were entrusted to bring God's Law to the entire world. In this they had demonstrated that the Law was unworkable. The Jews had become self-centered and nationalistic and thereby forgotten their vocation.[54] The rabbi Jesus of

52. "Controlled" here cannot mean that a person is under God's control, behaving like a kind of robot who can only do what the controller signals. That would eliminate free will. Instead, it must mean someone whose yardsticks for behavior are those derived exclusively from God.

53. Barclay, *Plain Man Looks at the Beatitudes*, 42–43.

54. The behavior of successive conservative Israeli governments since the foundation of the state of Israel up to the time of the Gaza invasion during October 2023 is instructive in this regard. The conviction that the Jewish state is to be understood as the executor of Old Testament predictions and restorer of political achievements such as at

Nazareth had preached to refocus his countrymen on their divine calling. He was fired with the ambition of teaching both Jew and Greek what true human beings should be like in all respects. But Jesus' mission had been rejected by the Jews except for a small remnant, and Christian Jews were persecuted for their alleged disloyalty. Paul had initially been among the chief perpetrators of these persecutions until his dramatic conversion on the Damascus road. Thereafter he became Jesus' most dedicated and vigorous apostle. Theologians in modern times such as Dietrich Bonhoeffer and Hans Küng have echoed all this in their perceptive writings as well as actions. In Bonhoeffer's case what he did during the Third Reich led to his martyrdom.

Paul appears, then, as the very first Christian theologian and expounder of the content and implications of Jesus' teaching of the good news. It was he who was primarily responsible for laying the foundation of Christianity as a world religion. Due to his faith and energy, his dynamism and courage, it grew from being a persecuted sect considered to be hostile to the state to become by the year 313 under Emperor Constantine the *official state religion of the Roman Empire*. The so-called Constantinian Age had been initiated.

WHY WAS CHRISTIANITY PERSECUTED AND HOW DID IT BECOME THE OFFICIAL RELIGION OF THE ROMAN EMPIRE?

Ordinarily within the Roman Empire local religions were tolerated; a cultic pluralism prevailed. Jews, however, were troublesome because they fought among themselves. And initially Christianity was considered a kind of separate Jewish cult. It was tolerated if it was law-abiding. However, at some undetermined point by the end of the first century emperor worship became a distinct problem of conscience for Christians. They could be put to death for refusing to worship the emperor or for simply being identified as members of the sect that had allegedly set fire to Rome under Emperor Nero. If a Christian refused to curse Christ and worship the emperor, she/he could be literally thrown to the lions. St. Paul's admonitions for good citizenship expressed in Romans 13:1–4 did not save

---

the time of King David some two thousand years ago persists and must be considered as a major factor in shaping the political will of many Israelis today. This is obviously rejected by sections of the Arab world.

them, so the cult of emperor worship had to result in the persecution of Roman citizens who had become Christians.[55] Emperor worship was a device for securing religious uniformity (read: political subservience) throughout the empire. This enabled many local cults to coexist under one overriding and all-embracing quasi-religious practice. Obviously, that had to affect the conscience of Christians. The cult of Christ and the cult of Caesar were manifestly incompatible.[56] However, for purely political reasons it was often only the church leaders who were targeted while their congregations were left unmolested. In this way the church was able to sustain itself, go underground literally (catacombs), and by the turn of the second to the third century the spread of Christianity was such that Tertullian (c.160–225), the African church father, commented that martyrdom had to be accepted and that the blood of the martyrs was the seed of the church.[57]

Persecutions continued sporadically during the second century but later they became more systematic punctuated by long periods of peace under various emperors until about 250 AD. Then with the accession of Emperor Decius (r. 249–251) all subjects regardless of local religious usage were commanded to make sacrifices to the state and obtain certificates of their obedience. Those who refused were designated as Christian and suffered accordingly.[58] That ceased with the death of Decius in 251 AD. However, with the accession of Valerian (r. 253–260) the new emperor soon found excuse to resume persecutions by issuing two decrees. As it was a time of political instability it was deemed prudent to appease the panoply of Roman gods by insisting on appropriate observance of pagan Roman religious practice. Here again the Christians were thrown into a crisis of conscience because they could not perform any acts of obeisance to a multiplicity of deities. So, the first decree or edict was directed against higher clergy, forbidding Christian services and even funerals. The second edict imposed the death penalty on bishops and the confiscation of the property of well-to-do lay Christians. None of this, however, prevented the continued spread of the new religion. It is noted in passing that Valerian has the distinction of being the only Roman emperor to

---

55. Bainton, *Early Christianity*, 21–22.

56. Bainton, *Early Christianity*, 23.

57. Bainton, *Early Christianity*, 26; and *Oxford Dictionary of the Christian Church*, s.v. "Tertullian."

58. *Oxford Dictionary of the Christian Church*, s.v. "persecutions."

have been captured by the enemy, in this instance the Persians, suffering the indignity of death at the hands of his captors.

Valerian's successor was his son Gallienus (r. 253–268 AD). He reversed his father's edicts, thus ushering in an era of peace that lasted until the reign of Emperor Diocletian (r. 284–305). Towards the end of his reign, however, Diocletian reaffirmed the principle that it was politically expedient to appease the Roman gods and so demanded religious conformity and made examples of Christian personages in the army and the court. It was, however, possibly under the influence of Galerius (r. 305–11), who had been appointed Diocletian's coadjutor (or *Caesar*), that widespread and draconic persecutions were resumed. Mercifully when Galerius finally succeeded Diocletian as emperor, he issued an edict of toleration.

All this vacillation was the product of the peculiar Roman worldview, which assumed that mortals were watched over by a panoply of gods who had to be appeased in times of political crisis. Consequently, Christians were endangered because at such times their loyalty came under scrutiny and so they were subjected to exceptional laws resulting in persecution. This did not necessarily take the form of the death penalty but often the destruction of churches and the desecration of their scriptures occurred. In addition, the right of assembly for Christian subjects could be abrogated and legal disabilities imposed. When, however, it was rumored that Christians were plotting against the state, edicts were issued leading to the arrest of clergy and consequent punishment. It was a dire situation for believers with only the prospect of living as marginalized and hunted subjects of a capriciously tyrannical state. Providentially, though, the exceptional status of the Christian church was soon to change dramatically and that occurred with the conversion of Emperor Constantine, who reigned from 306 to 337 AD.

THE CONVERSION OF CONSTANTINE AND THE USHERING IN OF THE CONSTANTINIAN ERA IN CHURCH-STATE RELATIONS

The administrative or bureaucratic history of the struggle for the leadership of a united empire resulted from that fact that the Roman Empire was divided by a Byzantine administration in the East and an another in the West based on Rome, each region being ruled by a so-called *Augustus* assisted by a Caesar. In the course of time the Augusti were replaced by a Caesar. This bureaucratic solution resulted in Constantine becoming emperor in the West. It was, however, an arrangement not destined to endure because of rival dynastic tendencies, which were finally overcome by Constantine, the son of the former Caesar of the West. The latter had died shortly after the abdication of Diocletian, leaving the way open for Constantine to wrest the office of Caesar for himself. Theodor Mommsen (1817–1903), the renowned historian of ancient Rome, records that this marked the triumph of the dynastic over the bureaucratic principle of leadership.[59] Constantine's move, however, was not uncontested because it unleashed wars of succession that lasted some twenty years. The confusion of the era is illustrated by the fact that there had been some seven rival contestants for the right to rule the empire. As Roland Bainton (1894–1984) whimsically formulated it,

> The rivals in the West and in the East reduced the aspirants to one for each region and these played off in the finals [sic]. From the point of view of the history of the church, the significance of this turmoil is that Christianity had assumed such political importance that every contestant sought to advance his prospect by persecuting or tolerating the faith, depending on its strength in given localities.[60]

Consequently, throughout the turmoil Christian communities naturally endorsed an aspirant who would be tolerant of the church, so finally when Constantine triumphed, he was regarded as an instrument of the providence. He had entered Rome with his forces on October 29, 312 amid the jubilation of the populace. The defeated Maxentius had drowned himself in the Tiber, but his body was retrieved. In the barbaric fashion of triumphalism of the time the corpse was decapitated and the head flaunted throughout the city. Constantine's victory gave him complete control of the West while Licinius, Constantine's brother-in-law, commanded the East. In 313 AD a joint statement by the two, entitled the Edict of Milan, was promulgated, according to which Christians and all other religions from then on enjoyed the protection of the state. The exceptional status of Christians had been at last removed. This meant that Christians could practice their religion without fear of oppression, and by 330 AD Christianity had been proclaimed the official religion of the Roman Empire.

59. Cf. Mommsen, *Geschichte Roms*; and Bainton, *Early Christianity*, 61.

60. Bainton, *Early Christianity*, 61.

Remarkable is the fact that Constantine, while being the acclaimed champion of Christianity, did not himself receive baptism until he lay on his death bed in 336 AD. He was apparently relying on the general absolution from his sins that accompanied baptism so that he could without spot of sin enter his heavenly reward. Be that as it may, the fact remains that under Constantine a new era of world history opened. Christianity flourished and laid the foundation for a world that at least in theory prioritized mercy, justice, and forgiveness of sins. Rulers had become princes by divine right, monarchs who, while lord of their realms, were nevertheless all subject to the one true God, the creator of the universe. The Roman world and beyond had become *Christendom*.

Commenting on these momentous events, the eminent church historian Roland Bainton wrote in 1960, "The entire relationship of the Church to the State had become profoundly altered when the world ceased to be hostile to the Church . . . under Constantine Christianity became the favored religion of the empire."[61]

This was indeed a turning point in world history of enduring significance, especially when it is appreciated that the toleration came immediately following an unprecedented wave of the most horrendous persecutions. The extermination policy of Diocletian's time was brought to a dramatic close and guaranteed the church the freedom to expand without fear of brutal intervention by the state.

Finally, as the German founder of the discipline of modern history Leopold von Ranke (1795–1886) affirmed, the first obligation of the historian is to show as impartially as is humanly possible how the past in each era essentially or actually (*eigentlich*) was. For the present subject one does not have to be a believer to investigate the history of Christianity, but one must try to comprehend the mindset of the then Christians and their rulers (the powers-that-be) within the social-intellectual universe they inhabited. There is a world-historical reason for doing this, because the subsequent history of Europe cannot be related without investigating the history of the Christianity; not only the record of the early Patristic Era, that is, the first three centuries after the ministry of St. Paul, but also the subsequent eras leading up to the late Middle Ages, when the Reformation occurred to form the complex matrix out of which Western civilization emerged. Church-state relations took center stage in world history. And out of the Reformation in the sixteenth century the modern

---

61. Bainton, *Early Christianity*, 59.

world evolved. One cannot write European history with the church left out. In a word, what we are pleased to call the "West" is the product of an amalgamation of various European tribal histories with the history of the church that had been implanted, fertilized, and nourished in the womb of the Roman Empire. Knowledge of this huge phenomenon, one would have thought, should be obligatory for all who would consider themselves civilized, but people today inhabit a decidedly post-Christian era. With the resurgences of faith, who knows when it will change.

2

The Social Problem and Its Solution since the Industrial Revolution

THE END OF THE CONSTANTINIAN ERA[1]

WE ARE INVESTIGATING THE historical roots of a long running political crisis. If one wanted an illustration of the continuing effects of ancient historical events and movements on the contemporary world, here is a striking example.

In the Synod of the Evangelical Church of Germany (EKD), held in Berlin in 1956, pastor Gunter Jacobs, with an eye on the church policy of the Stalinist regime then ruling in the eastern part of his divided country, proclaimed that Christians were now witnessing the end of the Constantinian Era. He meant that the state no longer protected the church but instead it was persecuted by the Marxist-Leninist-Stalinist regime.[2]

---

1. Berger, "Ende des Konstantischen Zeitalters," and *Evangelisches Staatslexicon*, 1374–75.

2. In German the distinction between the words *Regime* and *Staat* is perhaps more pointed than in English. A *Regime* has something of a decidedly inhumane, brutal, and reprehensible connotation, certainly lacking in integrity. A *Staat* is supposed to be the embodiment of godly order, which connotes justice, humanity, and decency expressed by a rational and accountable administration.

The church policy of the party[3] was dictated by the so-called *absoluter Wahrheitsanspruch* (claim to absolute truth).[4] In short, since 1945 the revolutionary ideology of Marxism-Leninism-Stalinism was meant to be the new point of reference for all humanity. The consequence was that Christian churches in the entire so-called eastern bloc were subjected to various forms of persecution. God in triune form never existed, although in the constitutions of all these countries freedom of religion was supposed to be guaranteed. There was, however, only one authority in the state and that was the *revolutionary committee of the proletariat*. Only they knew how the course of human history unfolded, so it was claimed. It was remarkable how dogmas like that were apparently swallowed by reasonably intelligent people. All other worldviews were in practice denigrated, especially Christianity. It is observed here that the church with its creeds may be also accused of mounting a claim to possess the absolute truth. Certainly, the church makes that assertion in all its creedal statements, but it does no longer persecute others for their refusal to accept the truth of Christianity. In short, in the twenty-first century the church accepts the right of all individuals to decide for themselves whether to submit to the teachings of Jesus Christ. Christianity is present in the marketplace of ideas of most countries, competing for the allegiance of all free peoples without fear or favor. This, however, was not the case under the either the National Socialist regime in Nazi Germany or that of the Communist regime in postwar East Germany.

There the church was effectively persecuted with varying degrees of barbarism from 1945 until the implosion of all the regimes within the Communist bloc in 1989.[5] For over four decades the Cold War domi-

3. The Communist Party in power was officially named Die Sozialistische Einheitspartei Deutschlands (SED, that is, the Socialist Unity Party, an enforced union of the old KPD (Communist Party of Germany) and remnants of the old Social Democratic Party in 1946.

4. This is explained by Sidney Hook in the *Dictionary of the History of Ideas*, 3:153: "As a state philosophy, Marxism-Leninism became an all-inclusive system in which social philosophy was presented as an application and expression of the ontological laws of a universal and objective dialectic. . . . It professed to prove that the laws of dialectic guaranteed the victory of communist society, that no one could subscribe to the ontology of dialectic materialism without being a communist and more fateful, that no one could be a communist or a believer in communist society without being a dialectical materialist."

5. Regarding the two main "confessions" in Germany, namely the Protestant on the one hand and the Roman Catholic on the other, the regime applied different policies. This is explained by the two different forms of ecclesiastical organization with which it was confronted. In the case of the Roman Church, Vatican policy toward Communist

nated world politics, so the present chapter traces the evolution of the ideology of this murderous utopia from its beginnings in the Industrial Revolution, when a so-called social or labor problem was experienced throughout Western Europe.

And here the focus must be on Germany because it was there that Karl Marx (1818–1883) and Friedrich Engels (1820–1895), having studied the class struggle occurring in early industrializing Britain, began to record the origins of the class struggle that shaped the internal history of the Prusso-German Empire, and which had such dire consequences for Europe and the world. This era of Prusso-German history has had the most far-reaching and deleterious impact on humanity for reasons that will be made clear in the following pages. Policies were adopted by successive governments in nineteenth- and twentieth-century Prusso-Germany that issued into the formulation of the two most catastrophic ideologies ever to emerge in the history of human civilization. It comes down to the following observation: if the administration of Bismarckian-Wilhelmine Germany had been able to find a humane solution to the social problem, the world would have been spared not only the two most fateful world wars in human history but also the Holocaust and finally the Cold War.

It is noted that the Weimar Republic in the years 1919–1933 made a valiant attempt to align Germany constitutionally with the liberal West but that was eventually frustrated by the dual hostility of the Communist and the Nazi parties to all ideas of "liberty, equality or fraternity."[6] What follows is an account of how the German social problem became the fertile soil out of which emerged two political systems, the first being Marxism-Leninism-Stalinism and the second National Socialism—*the two murderous utopias.*

---

regimes was for the church in each Eastern bloc country to go into hibernation. This meant the church adopted a passive stance toward the ideologically hostile state and simply carried out its liturgical and pastoral functions, avoiding where possible any confrontation with the regime. It simply waited for the regime to wither away, which of course it did. The Protestant churches on the other hand were divided between those dioceses that simply conformed to the wishes of the powers-that-be and others where individual bishops and pastors showed a determination not to be intimidated by the regime. This subject is examined in greater detail in later chapters.

6. Apelt, *Geschichte der Weimarer Verfassung* and *Hegelscher Machtstaat oder Kantischer Weltbürgertum.*

THE RISE OF REVOLUTIONARY OR "SCIENTIFIC" SOCIALISM IN GERMANY

In the German Democratic Republic, that is, the former East Germany from its inception with the inauguration of the constitution of October 7, 1949 until its collapse in December 1989, we have an example of how the leaders of the revolutionary working class used their peculiar form of historical pedagogy to educate the population about how the representatives of the working class arose to seize power with the objective of creating a new society in which every individual received the true value of their labor power. A society would evolve where the owners of the means of production, distribution, and exchange, that is, the capitalist class, would be forcibly expropriated and their property socialised/nationalised, meaning that all property would now be owned collectively by the nation. The result would be that everyone would be rewarded each according to their needs. Such a utopian solution to all human problems as devised by Karl Marx, Friedrich Engels, Vladimir Ilyich Lenin, and Josef Stalin would change the world, but before that could happen there had to be a series of revolutions. First, however, the question must be answered as to how this ideology germinated and spawned revolutionary Communist parties in countries all over the world. To do so it is necessary to go back to what historians call the Germany of *die Vormärz* (literally: pre-March), meaning the period between 1815 (the Congress of Vienna) and the revolutions that occurred on the continent in 1848, the "turning point that failed to turn" (Namier).

What is called modern Germany came into existence in 1871 when the so-called Iron Chancellor of Prussia, Otto von Bismarck (1815–1898), created the second German Reich after his three "wars of unification" (*Vereinigungskriege*), first against Denmark in 1864, then against Austria in 1866, and finally against France in 1870. It was called the Second Reich because the "First Reich," founded by Charlemagne in the year 800 AD, had been extinguished by Napoleon I in his conquest of central Europe in 1806. That entity had become a conglomeration of petty states known as the Holy Roman Empire of the German Nation (HRE), putatively the successor to the ancient Roman Empire. It was, however, a loose, ineffectual *Staatsgebilde* (association of principalities) that became a plaything of European power politics. Goethe (1749–1832) had observed that he knew of a German language, literature, and art but did not know where to find a body politic called Germany.[7] Indeed the HRE had suffered from petty state particularism (*Kleinstaaterei*), having been effectively dominated by the rivalry between its two main components, Austria and Prussia, known as the German Dualism (*der deutsche Dualismus*).

Napoleon I had tried for a time to influence the "German question" by creating a Federation of the Rhine (*der Rheinbund*) out of sixteen Rhenish provinces, proclaiming himself Protector of the Confederation, which coalesced in 1806 (after his victory at Austerlitz) and lasted until 1813, when the Battle of the Nations at Leipzig in October of that year saw the demise of French power in central Europe. The outcome of the Napoleonic defeat proved to have long-term consequences for the growth of an all-German nationalism. Dreamers of the founding of a greater German nation-state had been aroused from their slumber and subsequent disillusionment with Napoleonic imperialism (*Fichte*).

Various intellectuals sensed the dawning of a new era in Europe. First, however, peace had to be restored and that occurred at the Congress of Vienna in 1815. This event is often referred to in German historical works as the "Restoration," not to be confused with the Restoration of the English monarchy after the republican interlude under Oliver Cromwell (1649–1660). In June of 1660 the Stuart dynasty had been restored under Charles II, who reigned until his death.[8] A sideways glance at these events will prove instructive.

THE CONSEQUENCES OF THE ENGLISH RESTORATION

This English Restoration is mentioned here to highlight the radical difference between its consequences and the post-1815 situation in Germany. In England the period following the Restoration under Charles II saw considerable constitutional change. The monarchy was no longer "absolute," if it ever had been since the Magna Carta in 1215, because new arrangements made it impossible for the sovereignty of Parliament ever again to be challenged by any attempts by royal personages to reintroduce the old royal prerogatives under such concepts as the *divine right of kings*. When Charles II attempted to do so, it provoked a parliamentary crisis the outcome of which was the installation at the behest of parliament of the dual monarchy of William and Mary of Orange. It

---

7. Goethe, *Werke*, 5.1:218.

8 Cf. Clark, *Later Stuarts 1660–1714*.

was thus the power of Parliament that decided the line of succession in a series of decisions and events known as the "Glorious Revolution" of 1688. From that time parliamentary-based authority could be gradually extended eventually to ensure the principle of *popular* as opposed to the *monarchical* principle in Great Britain. In a real sense Britain had become a "disguised republic" because the executive powers of the monarch had been relocated in Parliament.[9]

Significantly, the process by which the British monarchy had given way to increasingly democratic institutions and practices was a lesson not lost on some of their German cousins who favored the same kind of liberal modifications to the German monarchies. They, however, were to be sadly disappointed with the course of nineteenth-century Prusso-German history.

THE RESTORATION IN CENTRAL EUROPE

The "Restoration" of the German monarchies after the Napoleonic invasions that occurred at the Congress of Vienna ushered in what became known as the *Metternich System*, so named after Count (later Prince) Clemens von Metternich (1743–1859), the foreign minister and chancellor of Austria. His aim was to preserve the various Germanic monarchies *by divine right* against the growing tide of liberalism and social unrest. In September 1819, then, the Germanic Confederation held a month-long conference in the spa town of Carlsbad.[10] A series of repressive anti-liberal decrees were proclaimed there. Student fraternities (*Burschenschaften*) were outlawed, and the censorship of the press was enforced, including bans on the publication of liberal ideas or the advocacy of German unification.

As well the Carlsbad conference had taken place against the background of anti-Semitic unrest known as the "Hep-Hep riots." Under Metternich's chairmanship these reactionary decrees were rigorously enforced but they only succeeded in provoking and intensifying opposition to the system by various intellectuals comprising writers, poets, and academics. Great social political and cultural changes were destined to result also from stirrings of industrialization. So, the period in German

9. Bagehot, *English Constitution;* Dicey, *Introduction to the Study of the Law.*

10. At the time Carlsbad was part of Austria. Today due to subsequent historic border changes it is in the Czech Republic.

and Austrian history between 1815 and 1848 witnessed the fertilization of various political ideologies and movements that would grow to change the course of world history to an unimaginable degree.

THE DUAL LEGACY OF G. W. F. HEGEL (1770–1831)

Nineteenth-century Germany produced thinkers whose teaching and political activism ignited movements unprecedented in the world. The political cultures they seeded produced atrocities and damage with which the world is still coming to terms in the twenty-first century. The two main figures were Georg Wilhelm Friedrich Hegel and Karl Heinrich Marx. Hegel inspired followers from both the right and left of politics. Those on the right were called "Old Hegelians" and those on the left "Young Hegelians." Right-wing Hegelianism had a range of influential advocates, both philosophers and historians throughout the nineteenth and twentieth centuries, whose teachings led eventually to National Socialism, the most brutal form of authoritarianism and racism in human history. The left-wing Young Hegelian movement took another direction led by none other than Karl Marx. Both these adaptations of Hegelianism claimed to be able to abolish oppression and usher in a utopian world order of justice, peace, and freedom. However, to accomplish that all putative enemies would have to be forcibly eliminated, by genocide if necessary. This section deals first with the *right-wing Hegelians*.[11]

Hegel and His Time

The unavoidable question here is whether it is ideas that change the course of history or whether efficacious ideas emerge in the mind of thinkers who have been influenced by the social-political circumstances of their age. It is a variation of the chicken-and-egg question. Indisputable, however, is that the ideas of right-wing Hegelianism have been catastrophically efficacious in molding the values of generations of Prusso-German subjects since Hegel's death in 1831 until the present day, as evidenced by the writings of some ultra-conservative German historians in the early twenty-first century.[12] Older historians such as the aforemen-

---

11. Kiesewetter, *Von Hegel zu Hitler*; Sherratt, *Hitler's Political Philosophers*.

12. Major examples in the German historiographic hierarchy are the Berlin political scientist Professor Herfried Münkler (*1951) and the much younger Professor Sönke

tioned Franz Schnabel had even prior to the Nazi seizure of power in 1933 already reflected on the fateful role that Hegel had played in sabotaging the heritage of the Enlightenment in Germany. He explained first how Hegel's teaching about the nature of the state as *autonomous power* (*Der Machtstaat*) functioned. It was not beholden to any elected popular assembly and could thus pursue any policy it chose regardless of the consequences for any other states or indeed even for the welfare of its own subjects.

This was a conscious rejection of Enlightenment liberal thinking that was based on the concept of the value and inalienable rights of the individual person, that is, human rights enshrined in law and constitution. When Hegel separated the state from the community it was presumed to serve, he claimed to have identified the "march of God on Earth," a metaphor that is freighted with peculiar religious-ideological convictions. A translation of the source of this is:

> The march of God in history is the cause of the existence of states [*Es ist der Gang Gottes in der Welt, dass der Staat ist*]. Their foundation is the power of reason realizing itself as will. Every state, whatever it be, participates in the Divine Essence. The state is not the work of human art; only Reason could produce it.[13]

The state, then, in Hegel's philosophy always acted autonomously, disregarding any other inhibiting moral precepts as Machiavelli in the sixteenth century had proclaimed. It could pursue any policies whatsoever that ensured the continued existence of the state. *This was essential for the unfolding of history*, but in contrast to the Italian Roman Catholic Machiavelli, the German Protestant Hegel taught that this was how almighty God intended it to be. Hegel had devised a theologically focused philosophy of history to demonstrate that God works out his purposes for humanity precisely via the institution of the state. This is a crucial insight that puts historians who have not taken account of Hegel at a considerable disadvantage when it comes to understanding any form of

---

Neitzel, who is currently chair of War Studies at the University of Potsdam. Both are internationally eminent scholars though of decidedly conservative persuasion, which means they represent a quasi-Bismarckian comprehension of foreign policy for Germany as the leading European power. Theirs is a mindset not shared by other leading German scholars such as the Social Democrat Heinrich August Winkler (*1938), who also occupied a chair of political science at Berlin's Humboldt University.

13. Hegel, *Philosophy of Right*, paras. 257–58; Avinerni, *Hegel's Theory of the Modern State*, 176–93.

totalitarianism. There exists an undeniable naiveté among some social scientists that blocks understanding how German intellectuals and the bourgeoisie comprehended the state during the late nineteenth and twentieth centuries. In short, a curious ignorance prevails about the reception of Hegel's teaching about the nature of the state and how it seduced generations of Germans into an uncritical acceptance of the inhumane policies that the custodians of the state conceived and implemented.[14]

As Franz Schnabel in his heroic attempt to counter the all-pervading influence of Hegel pointed out, the state for Hegel was the realization of the moral idea; it was reason materialized, indeed the physical manifestation of the Divine Spirit, worldly and holy at the same time.[15] If this is not grasped, then the ability to comprehend the course of Prusso-German history is seriously compromised at the outset. Hegel's teaching was paradigmatic for right-wing Germans even if they did not expressly articulate it. Liberals and Social Democrats vigorously contested this and still do.

THE LEGACY OF FREDERICK THE GREAT (R.1740–1786)

In practical terms the character of the German state was presumed to be defined for all time by the legacy of arguably the most successful absolutist prince (*Fürst*) in German history, namely Frederick II of Prussia (1712–1786). He had ascended the throne in 1740 and so had reigned for an unusually long period. This redoubtable monarch by virtue of his efficient bureaucracy and legendary conquests had captured the imagination of most educated Germans, to the extent that with Bismarck's Prussianization of Germany in 1871 one could justifiably affirm that the "Iron Chancellor" had rescued Frederick's ideas of statecraft into the nineteenth and bequeathed them to the twentieth century. The bureaucratic-authoritative ethos was sustained and bore particularly noxious fruit as the course of Prusso-German history has shown.

Admittedly, in Bismarck's federal constitution of 1871, which lasted until 1918, there were concessions made in relation to the voting system according to which a version of adult male suffrage was introduced for the Reichstag. This, however, was merely a concession to the broader electorate, who wanted a unified Prusso-German Empire. The lower house of the

---

14. Cf. Stern, *Failure of Illiberalism*, "The Political Consequences of the Non-Political German," 3–25.

15. Schnabel, *Deutsche Geschichte*, 3:12.

Reichstag was intended to remain essentially a debating chamber because the Reich chancellor was not obliged to select his cabinet from it as in the Westminster system. The Reichstag did, however, retain *das Budgetrecht*, that is the right to vote the budget. During Bismarck's long period in office as Reich chancellor from 1871 to 1890 he was able to rely on the conservative parties to support his policies, so the presence in the Reichstag of social democrats and liberals, even when they together secured a parliamentary majority, posed little threat to the quasi-authoritarian rule exercised by the Reich chancellors from Bismarck's time onwards.[16]

It is instructive here to rehearse what Schnabel had already formulated about the influence of Hegel on Prusso-German political culture, bearing in mind that his criticism was formulated well before Hitler's seizure of power. Hegel had indeed, in his Berlin lectures from 1818 until his death in 1831 as well as in his voluminous writings, successfully reversed the Enlightenment doctrine that the state was separate from the person of the monarch, that is, the idea of the sovereignty of the people was replaced by the concept that it was the state that was indisputably sovereign. In short, the monarch in his or her person was the manifestation of the state. That meant in practice the apotheosis of the state bureaucracy and there was no limit placed on its power or efficacy. It is summed up in the sentence: "every value which a human being has; all spiritual reality derives solely from the state."[17] Further, the liberal Roman Catholic Schnabel observed that the precursor to this ideal was to be found in the post-Reformation Lutheran principalities within the Holy Roman Empire. Hegel had systematized Luther's ideas about the state as being essential for human governance. It was as St. Paul in his Epistle to the Romans had long before affirmed but the nature of the state was essentially a dictatorship of the monarch

Hegel, one may not forget, was a committed Lutheran, which meant that he was convinced of Prussia's protestant German mission. Consequently, he had read history through a Lutheran lens and so believed implicitly that the papacy was the Antichrist, to be opposed at all costs. Hegel had indeed apotheosed the Reformation settlement in world history as the triumph of reason (*Weltvernunft*) for the well-being

16. The subject of Bismarck's imperial constitution has been widely discussed by transatlantic scholars over many years. See Steinberg, *Bismarck—A Life*. The standard work in German on the constitution is by Erst Rudolf Huber, *Deutsche Verfassungsgeschiche seit 1789*, vol. 3, *Bismarck und das Reich*.

17. Schnabel, *Deutsche Geschichte*, 3:12–13.

of humanity. The fact that it had spawned a multiplicity of often short-lived sects alongside enduring national churches each with a prince as its head was a necessity of providence because they replaced the diabolically enthralled papal church with a purified ecclesiastical order. The prince was from then on termed in German *Notbischof* (literally: emergency or substitute bishop). In Luther's reformed understanding the prince was both head of state and head of the church. The secular realm had been merged with the spiritual. The implications of this change in European history were revolutionary.

The monarchs of post-Reformation Christendom had become little *de facto* popes in their own realms. Whereas previously there had been two realms, namely church and state, ruling the spiritual and secular spheres respectively, now there was only one overarching source of power, namely the absolutist monarch, who may or may not be benevolent. As Hegel correctly observed three centuries after the Reformation, a governance had been created that saw an unprecedented intertwining of church and state. Reformed Christianity became in German an *Obrigkeitsreligion*, meaning that the princes determined the religion of the people, and for the Lutherans this was confirmed, as noted above, by referring to St. Paul's Epistle to the Romans chapter 13. Further, it is documented in the Confession of Augsburg of 1530.[18] Its significance for the future course of German history cannot be overstated. It meant that any idea of pluralism, meaning the toleration of alternative systems of authority, was at best irrational sentiment while at worst it was treason or sedition, and its advocates and adherents could be persecuted accordingly. It sounded the death knell of liberalism while it was for Hegel the pinnacle of the Lutheran concept of *Obrigkeit*. The moral autonomy of the state was thus established for all time, as it seemed for many Germans.

Franz Schnabel has designated this development as heralding a new idea of the state, which he called the *Kulturstaat*. He observed that it exercised a monopoly over the education of all subjects through the power of the highly professional bureaucracy; it was in fact a veritable pedagogic dictatorship. Under the Hohenzollern dynasty in Brandenburg-Prussia, as Schnabel noted, every vocation from the lowly milkmaid to the monarch himself formed part of an organic whole with all subjects united in

---

18. The Augsburg Confession was presented by twenty-eight German princes and the representatives of the "free cities" of the HRE to Emperor Charles V on June 25, 1530. This document summarized in twenty-one theses the essential Lutheran versus papal claims at that time.

service of the state. And this state functioned like one extensive army establishment. In fact, as Schnabel illustrates, the state really was the creation of the army. Prussia was not a state with an army; it was the army that built the state.

It must have seemed rational to the dynasty and the General Staff that this should be the case since Prussia was very much a land-locked kingdom, sandwiched as it was between France in the west and Russia in the east, while in the north and the south lay the Scandinavian kingdoms and the Austrian Empire respectively. In such a situation military preparedness really was the highest priority. The consequences, however, for the community were dire. As everything was regulated by a tight bureaucracy, Schnabel observed that

> All human relationships as well as social and economic differences disappeared in the face of a hierarchy of duties, and in Prussia that meant the hegemony of military rank. The arrogant tone of command guaranteed the certainty and uniformity of all procedures so that the machine functioned smoothly. As well, the insularity of the army and its officer corps erected a barrier against outside influences while the commanding officers always had at their disposal a reliable and ever ready instrument with which to answer all questions of civilian life strictly in accordance with their military priorities.

The elegance of Schnabel's portrayal of Prussian society under the Hohenzollern dynasty scarcely disguised his profound abhorrence for the system. He reiterated:

> So, if the tone of the barrack square predominated it was to be expected because the state was one big military camp. The rattle of weaponry permeated the atmosphere as accompanying music witnessing to a predominantly martial mentality which was inevitably transferred to the bourgeois population.[19]

One needs to appreciate here that the Prussianization of Germany that took place after Bismarck and had unified the nation under Prussian hegemony in 1871 was at first not universally welcomed, especially in the southern German principalities, where subjects were accustomed to a more liberal political atmosphere. In time, however, gradually even those regions came to accept the Prussian solution: Hohenzollern militarism was endorsed as quintessentially German. And this was arguably

---

19. Schnabel, *Deutsche Geschichte*, 1:95–97. Translation by present writer.

the chief intellectual source of the suspicion and later outright hostility of many Germans toward the liberally disposed parliamentary democracies of the West. It also accounts for the anxiety of the German educated bourgeoisie and upper classes, especially towards liberals and social democrats within Germany, whom they tended to regard as virtually disloyal; indeed they railed against them as "vagabonds without a fatherland." (*vaterlandslose Gesellen*).[20] What Bismarck had bequeathed to the German bourgeoisie in the name of Prussia certainly gave the assurance of security both against domestic unrest and any threat from neighboring realms, especially France. The great bonus was that the united Germany had achieved parity with its surrounding neighbors and Great Britain; certainly a magnification of international prestige. The Prussianized Germany had entered the ranks of the "Great Powers."

What was still missing, however, was the so-called internal or domestic foundation of the Reich (*die innere Reichsgründung*), meaning inward acceptance by the non-Prussian German states of life under Prussian hegemony. This took some time to achieve. Centuries of regionalism could not be swept away with the stroke of a pen. Consequently, both historians and Protestant theologians at the universities worked energetically to overcome this by teaching generations of students that the Prussian solution to the German question was providentially preordained. This was the doctrine of *Borussismus*. That, however, was to prove to be an ideological delusion of catastrophic magnitude for both German and world history. Arguably most Germans from the time of liberation from National Socialism in 1945 until the present day have come with the passage of time to accept the need to unlearn the legacy of Bismarck and his professorial harbingers in addition to the many theological apologists, to realign Germany spiritually and intellectually with the transatlantic community of nations.[21] The debate about this prospect for Germany continues between the genuine liberals on the one hand and those on the other hand who still endorse a more nationalist stance in the twenty-first century for the reborn European great power. The nineteenth-century roots of this development need to be understood.

---

20. *Vaterlandslose Gesellen* was a term of abuse originally used by Kaiser Wilhelm II against the Social Democratic Party and left liberals for their opposition to government policies such as the great naval build-up (Tirpitz Plan) when it was launched in the late 1890s.

21. There is a burgeoning literature on this subject. For example, see Decker et al., *Dynamics of Right-Wing Extremism.*

The Industrial Revolution on the continent of Europe that began at that time characterized the era by not only the stirrings of unprecedented social change but also growing political ferment when the so-called German question was posed and not yet satisfactorily answered. People were exercised by the question of whether there should be a unified Germany under Austrian leadership, the so-called *Grossdeutsche Lösung*, the "greater German solution," or the *Kleindeutsche Lösung*, meaning German unification under Prussian leadership, which meant the exclusion of Austria from the German Confederation. It was, as we have seen, the Prussian solution that finally prevailed but with hindsight one cannot speculate whether the alternative "greater German solution" under conservative Austrian leadership would have led the European countries and the world into more peaceful relationships. All one can reliably say is that the future Germany would have been decidedly different from what finally materialized under Prussian hegemony. That question has haunted historians of rival ideological persuasions particularly since 1945, when pondering the so-called *continuity thesis* concerning the course of German history. At least they are agreed that the investigation of the various ideological solutions that exercised the various protagonists in the era 1815–1848 is the place to start.[22]

The present task is to clarify some of this confusion. The outcome is well known because what became Prusso-Germany (*Preussen-Deutschland*) succeeded in alienating itself from both the rise of liberalism in the West and reactionary Slavdom in the East.[23] A singular Prusso-German self-perception (*Selbstbewusstsein*) had developed, albeit chiefly among the ruling classes and the educated bourgeoisie (*Bildungsbürgertum*). This alienation could be sheeted home to the way in which the Reformation of the fifteenth and sixteenth centuries played out because thereafter in Germanic territories absolutist monarchical power had been firmly established while in Britain it spawned a variety of religious-political ideologies and out of these crystalized the rival political movements of the

22. Srbik, *Deutsche Einheit*. See also Schnabel, *Deutsche Geschichte*. Further, the numerous works of the late Walter Grab (1919–2000) on this period are of key importance and are listed in the bibliography.

23. The classic summing up of this was formulated by Thomas Mann during the Great War (1914–1918) in his celebrated work *Die Betrachtungen eines Unpolitischen*, in which he recorded his then firmly held conviction that Germany had every right to defend her unequalled *Kultur* against the decadent West and the barbaric East. See pp. 39–40 of the Fischer Taschenbuch edition. See also the English translation, *Reflections of a Nonpolitical Man*.

Whigs and the Tories, which led to the strengthening of the parliamentary system. In France the struggle between the monarchical-absolutist
institutions and the rise of anti-authoritarianism issued in the Revolution
of 1789. And from then on the so-called ideas of 1789, namely liberty,
equality, and fraternity, inspired many writers to espouse more liberal
democratic positions.

Eastward across the Rhine there was similarly no shortage of champions, mainly poets and writers, who saw Germany's future in terms of
the ideas of 1789. All that, however, was anathema to the Prusso-German
power elite and their aristocratic and bourgeois supporters, who remained firmly wedded to the idea of monarchical sovereignty.[24] Germany
lacked sufficiently far-sighted princes and aristocrats who could read the
signs of the times and implement liberalizing reforms. Consequently
the pre-March era in Germany resembled an arena in which various
factions advanced rival solutions to the *German problem*. It was against
the background of this largely verbal wrangling that Otto von Bismarck,
the minister president of Prussia from 1862 and later chancellor of the
united Germany, made his famous "Blood and Iron" speech in the Prussian *Landtag* (parliament) on September 30 of that year: "Not through
speeches and majority decisions will the great questions of the day be
decided—that was the mistake of 1848–1849—but by iron and blood."[25]

This speech reveals both the contempt and fear that the Prusso-German ruling classes had for liberal democracy. The fact that the selfsame
classes in Germany as late as August 1914 were able to force through

24. It needs to be kept in mind that all the German princes since Luther's Reformation at the latest saw themselves exercising their role by divine right (*Königtum durch
Gottessgnaden*). As indicated, this was re-enforced by the Carlsbad Decrees.

25. Steinberg, *Bismarck—A Life*, and the East German Professor Ernst Engelberg,
Bismarck—Urpreusse und Reichsbegründer, 527. The speech was held during the budget
committee on September 30, 1962 soon after Bismarck's nomination by the king as his
chief minister. In it Bismarck unmasked himself as an unreconstructed autocrat who
had no time for liberal ideas. He fulminated: "*Nicht auf Preussens Liberalismus sieht
Deutschland, sondern auf seine Macht . . . Preussen muss seine Kraft zusammenfassen
und zusammenhalten auf den günstigen Augenblick, der schon einige Male verpasst ist;
Preussens Grenzen nach den Wiener Verträgen sind zu einem gesunden Staatsleben nicht
günstig; nicht durch Reden und Majoritätsbeschlüsse wereden die grossen Fragen der Zeit
entschieden –das ist der grosse Fehler von 1848 und 1849 gewesen—sondern durch Eisen
und Blut*" (p. 527). Translation: "Germany is not looking to Prussia's liberalism but to
her power . . . Prussia's borders that were set by the commitments entered at Vienna
are not favorable to a healthy political existence; it is not by speeches and decisions of
majorities that the great questions of the age are decided—that was the big mistake of
1848 and 1849—*but by iron and blood.*"

illiberal decisions in the Reichstag to facilitate the war effort was based on the doctrine of monarchical absolutism that Bismarck had enshrined in his federal constitution for the nation in 1871. One cannot fail to observe that this constitution was the seedbed of all of Germany's subsequent social and political disasters both domestically and internationally.[26] The fateful repudiation of liberalism represents the culmination of *folkish* and very anti-democratic aspirations that took root during the Napoleonic campaigns in Germany and flourished afterwards in the pre-March era. Notably Johan Gottlieb Fichte (1762–1814) via his publications in 1807–1808, entitled *Reden an die deutsche Nation* (Addresses to the German Nation) fostered an upsurge of German national consciousness. He and the father of the German mass gymnastic movement Friedrich Ludwig Jahn (1778–1852) led an unprecedented wave of enthusiasm for German unification. This alarmed the ruling classes, especially the rise of the above-mentioned politicized student fraternities. Events such as the Wartburg Festival in 1817 and the Hambach Festival in 1832 and a repeat of the Wartburg Festival in 1848 were symptomatic of the ideological turmoil that was to divide the German peoples for decades to come, indeed up to the present day.

A major factor in this development was that pre-March era coincided with the Industrial Revolution in Germany, that resulted in marked social change generated by population shifts from villages into the centers of industrial development. There was even a migration of British workers with their families to Germany in this period because of the demand for trained mechanics and other craftsmen required for burgeoning new enterprises. As well, England, the home of the Industrial Revolution, began to attract German entrepreneurs, who traveled to the island kingdom to learn more about the latest technological advances.[27]

26. Willms, *Bismarck: Dämon der Deutschen*. Most of the biographies of Bismarck by German authors prior to the Second World War are adulatory. This one by Willms benefits from the postwar reflections among educated Germans who could perceive the accumulated dire consequences of the Iron Chancellor's policy-making both domestic and foreign.

27. Franz Schnabel (1887–1966) was especially well qualified to research this phase of German enterprise as he had after his training as a historian in Berlin completed his "habilitation" (postdoctoral thesis) at the Technical University of Karlsruhe, where he served as a professor from 1922 until his dismissal by the Nazi regime in 1936. Franz Schnabel's career resumed after the Second World War in 1947 when he was appointed to head the re-established, de-Nazified Department of History in Munich by the United States occupation authorities. The point of highlighting Schnabel's career is to underline the fact that he stood out from the phalanx of German modern historians

Germany was being transformed from a largely agrarian to an industrial economy. This resulted in long-term social changes. There occurred a flight of unemployed and largely unskilled agrarian workers from the country to the centers of industrial development, especially in the Rhineland, where coal mining had made a quantum leap forward. Germany in this era was discovering how the sinews within the economy and bureaucracy would put on the muscle of future industrial and political power. The question is: did the outcome have to be so anti-democratic as it was?

ACCOUNTING FOR THE ANTI-DEMOCRATIC TURN IN PRUSSO-GERMAN HISTORY

As reported above, the Roman Catholic liberal historian Franz Schnabel argued that the major factor leading to Prusso-German rejection of the liberalism of the Enlightenment was the intellectual legacy of the Protestant idealist philosopher G. W. F. Hegel.[28] What needs urgently to be internalized is that Hegel's doctrines sanctioned war as a necessary factor in human progress and these certainly displaced the peace-promoting philosophy of Immanuel Kant (1724–1804). Discredited as well were the democratic ideas of the "general will" as advanced by the French philosopher Jean Jacques Rousseau (1712–1778). The rise of Hegelianism, then, contributed fundamentally to what later became known as Prusso-German peculiarity. After the failure of the 1848 revolutions to establish parliamentary governments to replace the system of rule by absolutist princes, leading German historians and social scientists began to embrace the doctrines of Hegel, who gained the reputation of being the "Royal Prussian State Philosopher" with increasing conviction. It was an intellectual movement that ebbed and flowed and lasted effectively until end of the Third Reich in 1945. Hegel's legacy had been less that a salutary one. For him, the existence of the state took precedence over any claims to inalienable civil rights to which an individual subject might feel entitled. The state, indeed, existed to advance its own priorities above all other considerations. Apart from denying inalienable rights to the

---

precisely because he was both a Roman Catholic liberal (through his French mother) and through his deep interest in technology was willing and able to research this subject. See vol. 3 of his *Deutsche Geschichte*. His detailed reportage of this era is therefore a source of inestimable historical value.

28. Schnabel, *Deutsche Geschichte*, 3:1–35.

individual subject, it was also impossible for the state to enter into any binding international agreements with other states.

Consequently, that meant there could be no international community of states and therefore no possibility of "eternal peace" as postulated by Immanuel Kant. Such a utopian idea was regarded as unrealizable in the actual world because in Hegel's philosophy the conflicting interest of two states could only be resolved through war, as history had repeatedly demonstrated. This meant that a neighboring state was never a potential friend but always a potential enemy. Expansionist tendencies in each state would ensure friction leading inevitably to hostilities. For this reason, preparedness for war was a question of the highest priority.

The statesman's first duty was to prioritize the claims of the state over both the considerations of the individual subject and the claims of rival states. *Raison d'état* always superseded private morality. For a statesman the only morality that could prevail was that which ensured the security of the state. In Hegel's worldview this was a preordained priority because that is how the world spirit (*Weltgeist*) operated, the state being an extension of the will of almighty God beside which no other sectional or personal justification rated consideration. Ethics as hitherto understood in Christendom had been discarded and with that went any notion of eternal peace as advocated by Immanuel Kant. In short, religion was relegated strictly to the private sphere and the church reduced to the status of being the mere handmaid of the state.

Franz Schnabel's acid critique of the triumph of right-wing Hegelianism in Germany was first mounted in the 1920s. In doing so he ventured to break the intellectual mold or dominant paradigm of conviction about the nature of the state in Germany.[29] He noted regretfully that it had captured most of Germany's leading historians and philosophers well before the end of the nineteenth century, so Hegelianism was the seedbed of Prusso-German notions about both social policy and international relations, that is, about *Weltpolitik*. It was certainly the justifying intellectual framework for Wilhelmine armaments policy, and it was undeniably the ideology behind both Kaiser Wilhelm II's naval build up (*Flottenpolitik*) and Pan-Germanism in the last decade to the nineteenth century.[30]

29. Other leading German liberals such as the historian Veit Valentin (1885–1947), the jurist Hermann Kantorowicz (1877–1940), and the Social Democrat Karl Kautsky (1854–1938) were among the leading outspoken anti-Hegelians.

30. *Flottenpolitik* means "naval policy." As well there was also an energetic German *Kolonialpoltik* at the same time. See the works of Roger Pickering in the bibliography.

In summing up his critique of Hegelianism Franz Schnabel observed:

> Much of that to which the Prussian monarchy, aristocracy and
> bureaucracy aspired had been underpinned by what Hegel had
> taught, namely the rejection of natural law, the anti-revolution-
> ary national spirit (*Volksgeist*), the doctrine that states have a
> unique personality, the monarchical principle and the power
> state (*Machtstaat*), the notion that freedom is not an innate
> right of the individual subject but rather in the latter's fulfilment
> of the will of the powers-that-be, and that the German spirit is
> reflected in Prussian discipline (*preussische Zucht*). All of that
> was to be heard repeatedly in the lectures and orations of profes-
> sors during the 19th century. It was the synthesis of Weimar and
> Potsdam . . .[31]

Further, Schnabel noted that Hegel had written at a time when poets and
thinkers were publishing in the expectation that a new age was dawning;
the Napoleonic Era had been traversed, the Great Powers at the Congress of Vienna were seeking to pioneer their way to a golden future for
Europe, and the professors were caught up in a new turbulent spirit of
nationalism. How should all this work out? The great question of the age
was whether the answer was to be found in the implementation of liberal
ideals or those of power politics, namely *Realpolitik*. The latter course
eventually won out because it was espoused by Otto von Bismarck, who
could be described as the quintessential statesman of destiny.

It is recalled that many of the bourgeois members of the 1848 Frankfurt National Assembly had been established academics and occupied
chairs at various universities. After the final collapse of the Assembly in
1850 they returned from their venture into practical politics and assumed
the role of planning or adumbrating national politics via their lectures
and publications. In short, the professors were outlining national policy
for the politicians and statesmen to put into practice, literally crystalizing
national policy in advance: *die Politik im voraus denken*. This phase of
German intellectual history is particularly important because many of
the professors in the Frankfurt National Assembly had gone there in the
hope of forging a liberal constitution for a united Germany. They were

---

31. Schnabel, *Deutsche Geschichte*, 19. The reference to Weimar is to the humanism of the great German poets and thinkers (*Dichter und Denker*), such as Schiller
and Goethe, while the reference to Potsdam is a genuflection to the military spirit of
Prussia. Prusso-Germany was celebrated by conservative patriots as a combination of
these two traditions. Schnabel's assessment is echoed by his successor to the Munich
professorship, Thomas Nipperdey, in *Deutsche Geschichte 1866–1918*, 2:201–49.

not, however, revolutionaries and when the king of Prussia rejected the draft constitution, a conservative political reaction set in. The initially liberal-minded professors at Frankfurt had hoped the king of Prussia would underwrite a liberal constitution but he imperiously discarded the proposal with the excuse that it was incompatible with his position as monarch by divine right.

The effect of this was at first massive disappointment among the liberal-minded deputies but once they saw that Prussia was not going to modernize the constitution, they adopted a policy based on the recognition of realities. What developed next was a process from 1850 onward that amounted to the abandonment of Enlightenment ideas by leading academics and replacing them with agitation for the practical achievement of Prussian hegemony to establish German unity. In short, an intellectual movement called *Borussianismus* arose led by influential German historians advocating *Realpolitik*, the politics of realism.[32]

In doing so, Franz Schnabel observed, its professorial advocates evinced an unprecedented intellectual arrogance and thereby fell victim to the foolish belief that they had attained the highest level of the intellectual-spiritual development of humankind.[33] Indeed, professorial

32. Faber, "Realpolitik als Ideologie." The foremost professorial advocate of a Prussian solution to the German question was Karl-Gustav Droysen (1808–1884). See his study in fourteen volumes, *Die Geschichte der preussischen Politik*, published 1850–1856. He was consequently the founder of the post-1848 dominant school of Prussian-German historians, which had done so much to mould German political ideas and peaked in the work of the extreme nationalist Heinrich von Treitschke (1834–1896). Professor Schnabel in Munich at the time I was his student (1961–1962) conducted a popular seminar on Droysen with the pedagogic aim of informing the postwar generation of how Prusso-German *Kultur* became derailed from the development of genuine liberalism in Germany. See Schnabel, *Deutsche Geschichte*, 3:108; and Srbik, *Geist und Geschichte*, 2:355–400 (ch. 12, "Der kleindeutsche nationalstaatliche Realismus"). On page 372, regarding Droysen, von Srbik observes that the appearance of his multivolume work must be regarded as the foundation and main source of the Prussian legend of the Hohenzollern dynasty's mission to unite the nation under its unique militaristic-bureaucratic tradition. Its educational impact on German students was intensified by subsequent generations of professorial mentors.

33. Schnabel, *Deutsche Geschichte*, 3:20. If one has studied the humanities, especially history, at a German university, this criticism by Schnabel appears totally justified. That arrogance was still perceptible during the decade of the 1960s in both West and East Germany. However, it soon began to change with the practice of German academics accepting fellowships to spend a postdoctoral semester at universities abroad, chiefly in the UK and the USA. The former pretention to superior wisdom was gradually replaced by recognizing the need to consider the liberalism of the West. That was in part the consequence of the Cold War. However, professorial pretentions of this nature are indeed well known in Australasia. There are numerous examples, especially in the

arrogance is a phenomenon not unknown even in putatively egalitarian countries to this day such as Australia, but what happened in Prussia-Germany was of an especially virulent character with catastrophic consequences.

THE ALL-IMPORTANT YOUNG HEGELIAN MOVEMENT AND ITS LONG-TERM CONSEQUENCES

The notable Polish scholar of Marxism Lesek Kolakowski[34] defined the young Hegelian movement as follows:

> Young Hegelianism was the philosophical expression of the re-publican, bourgeois-democratic opposition which criticised the feudal order of the Prussian state and turned its eyes hopefully towards France. Prussia's western provinces, the Rhineland and Westphalia, had been under French rule for the best part of two decades and had benefitted from the Napoleonic reforms—abolition of feudal estates and privileges, equality before the law. After their annexation to Prussia in 1815 they were a natural centre of lively conflict with the monarchical system.[35]

There the original German discontents consisted of a group of literary, philosophical, and theological scholars who were known as *Junges Deutschland*. Among whom were such internationally famous names as the poet Heinrich Heine. The movement extended from the Rhineland provinces to Berlin itself, where many of the group had heard Hegel lecture. Among the Berliners was the theologian David Friedrich Strauss (1808–1874), who had gained notoriety for his book *Das Leben Jesu* (*The Life of Jesus, Critically Examined*; 1835). In this work Strauss had debunked the miracles attributed to Jesus, thereby arousing considerable debate, and out of the polemics thus generated emerged the group known as the "Hegelian Left." These men were exercised by a range of philosophical and political issues, beginning first with the critique of religious

---

post–Second World War era, when personalities arose who, while affecting a pose of Antipodean egalitarianism, manifested a behavior more consistent with the blarney of their more egocentric, bullying Continental colleagues.

34. Kolakowski (1927–2009) was a Polish-born academic and faithful Roman Catholic who in 1968 because of his anti-Communist position migrated to England and found refuge at All Souls', Oxford, where he died at age eighty-one. His most notable work was *Main Currents of Marxism*.

35. Kolakowski, *Main Currents of Marxism*, 1:83.

orthodoxy and moving further to form a radical opposition to the existing monarchical political system, that is, monarchy by divine right or the grace of God. Above all they rejected Hegel's conclusion that the Prussian state was the embodiment of historical reason.

The most prominent member of this group was Arnold Ruge (1802–1880), who from 1838 to 1841 edited the Young Hegelian philosophical journal, *Hallische Jahrbücher*. In this publication is reflected the intellectual turbulence of the age and the crystalizing of more oppositional democratic ideas such as freedom of speech, the abolition of privileged estates, and the opening of public office to all strata of society; in short, a bourgeois egalitarian state based on Enlightenment ideas. Curiously and rather paradoxically, they admired the administrative ideas of Frederick the Great and believed in a particular Prussian sense of mission in world history. The latter was characterized by a non-pietistic, militantly anti-Roman Catholic Protestantism. Indeed, popery to them was a tyrannical abomination that exalted dogma over reason.[36]

What should be noted, however, is that the bureaucratic administrative apparatus of Prussia continued to exert a powerful influence on Prusso-German political culture for decades to come. Its rigorously authoritarian spirit has endured indeed until recent times and was particularly evident in both East and West Germany 1945–1989. Traces of it can still be experienced in the early twenty-first century. Its roots reach back to the 1830s at the latest under the reign of King Fredrick William III of Prussia (r. 1797–1840), when he showed no inclination to implement any liberal changes in the bureaucracy or the introduction of any other Enlightenment principles. Instead of modernization he determined to uphold the historic principles of monarchical absolutism. The existing bureaucracy functioned to enable this, and it was this administrative culture that was maintained by the next monarch, Frederick William IV (r. 1840–1861). The radicals at the time of the revolutions of 1848 had pinned great hopes on him so they were greatly disappointed when the expected liberal changes to the class-ridden bureaucratic system and the divine right Prussian hereditary monarchy were retained. The hoped-for political freedoms remained illusory as before. Radicals were frequently

---

36. Kolakowski, *Main Currents of Marxism*, 1:92–93. A consequence of King Frederick William IV's church policy was the migration oversees of many Protestant parishes in Prussia, for example to South Australia. See Iwan, *Um des Glaubens Willen nach Australien*. The English translation is titled *Because of Belief: Emigration from Prussia to Australia*.

arrested, imprisoned, or forced into exile. As well, a conservative church policy remained unchanged.[37]

The ensuing disappointment among the radicals was palpable. Their faith in Hegel's notion that Prussia was the citadel of reason was henceforth shattered and the Young Hegelian movement appeared to be in disarray. While they had done much in arousing new forward-looking political ideas, it had become clear already by 1843 that it had ceased to be a viable movement of reform, frustrated as it was by the actual political circumstances. Its once enthusiastic leaders were unable to build a bridge between their theories and the practical challenges of the politics of the day.[38] Indeed, they were literally at their wits' end.[39] Then, most dramatically in retrospect, the circuit breaker and pioneer to the future strode on to the world stage. It was fortuitous for some but in the long term disastrous for the world. That circuit breaker appeared in none other than a young German law student named Karl Heinrich Marx (1818–1883).[40]

History provides numerous examples of dynamic personalities who for good or ill captured the international spotlight and by virtue of their individual talents became game changers.[41] Karl Marx was certainly one of these. His hypercritical enquiring mind, after years of probing the history of what he perceived of the real, *materialistic* world, overturned the Hegelian *idealistic* paradigm. The long, adventurous, and tortuous path

37. Kolakowski, *Main Currents of Marxism*, 1:92–93. This period is coterminous with the ultra-conservative administration of the Chancellor of Austria Clemens von Metternich (1821–1848).

38. For information about the demise of the Young Hegelian movement or left-wing Hegelianism, see Kolakowski, *Main Currents of Marxism*, vol. 1; Breckman, *Marx, the Young Hegelians.*

39. The German idiom is more colorful: *Sie waren am Ende ihres Lateins* (literally: They had exhausted their knowledge of Latin), meaning that intellectually they had nowhere to go until Karl Marx arrived to provide the circuit breaker and the route forward into the future.

40. Marx was born in Trier, where his father had become a senior public servant, having converted from Judaism to Lutheranism to qualify for the post. His children were subsequently all baptized in the church.

41. In this book, the careers of both Lenin in Russia and Hitler in Germany exemplify this observation. In retrospect, circuit breakers or game changers have appeared at crisis times in human history. The most notable are Jesus of Nazareth, son of a local carpenter, and of course Paul of Antioch. Following him in the church are Francis of Assisi (1181/2–1226) and Martin Luther (1485–1546), and in politics Abraham Lincoln (1809–1865) and Mahatma Gandhi (1869–1948). This list is by no means exhaustive. Such personages appear throughout history and their careers can have a dramatic effect on the course of events.

traveled by Marx to achieve the unprecedented influence may not detain us long here. The chief concern is to flag the political impact of his thought, known as he was as the messiah of materialism.[42]

The student Marx arrived in Berlin from the University of Bonn in 1836, where he had been enrolled in the humanities faculty to study philosophy and literature, but at the insistence of his father had switched to law. However, after some undergraduate mishaps in Bonn it was decided that Marx would transfer his studies to Berlin, where he became involved with the Young Hegelians. They counted some very thoughtful and energetic adherents among their membership such as Ludwig Feuerbach (1804–1872), Bruno Bauer (1809–1882), as well as Adolf Rutenberg (1808–1869), who became Marx's closest friend in Berlin.

As Young Hegelians these men had become highly critical of Hegel's metaphysical assumptions while at the same time they adopted his notion of "dialectic" progress in history. This merits closer explanation. Hegel's aim had been to provide a "scientific" justification for the Prussian monarchy at a time of revolutionary upheaval. His argument was designed to end all political debate by advancing the idea that history had evolved as the expression of God's will for humankind. If one were a believer, one would be content to see it as the result of the divine spirit (*Weltgeist*) in the process of revealing its will to humanity. Such argumentation seemed quite logical if one accepted the idea of a divine Creator, as many leading scholars did. Hegel was after all a convinced Lutheran Christian. As such he had a fervent belief in God and in particular the Lutheran Reformation that had purified the church by overthrowing the corrupting influence of Rome. So, the motor of human history was God, whose will could be discerned in the historical process that was dialectic. This means that events occurred in the world that provoked a counter-action and via the subsequent interaction a resolution would be arrived at. In Hegelian terms a *thesis* was enunciated, presumably engendered by the will of the *Weltgeist*, which provoked the *antithesis*. Out of the ensuing turmoil a resolution crystallized, namely the *synthesis*. In this way the will of God was made known in history.

Hegel was convinced that the process had reached its peak in Prussian history. With its monarchy and highly structured bureaucracy it marched at the forefront of human civilization. As has been seen, this

---

42. A bibliography of the works on Marx is extensive, but see Nowlan, ed., *Karl Marx: The Materialist Messiah*; Carver, ed., *Cambridge Companion to Karl Marx*; and McLellan, *Karl Marx: His Life and Thought*.

schema attracted many enthusiastic pupils in Germany, especially among Protestant theologians and historians. They came to endorse the idea that Prussia had been singled out by almighty God to impose its superior culture on Europe and the world, by force if necessary. God certainly did not shrink back from employing human violence in the furtherance of his will.

Certainly Hegelianism became and remained most influential among conservative circles in Germany. On the other hand Marx, as with the other Young Hegelians, had a problem with the *theistic* assumption on which the edifice was based. The atheist Marx could, however, run with the idea of the dialectic provided it rested on a *materialist* base. Theology was banned from the enterprise. There had to be an atheistic dialectic and this Marx eventually identified in the process of producing goods needed for human survival. He therefore developed his idea of *materialist dialectics*, a concept that appealed to many people skeptical of religious dogma.

So, for Marx the atheist the primeval driving force in history was the basic need to produce goods of all kinds needed for human survival. In a real sense, Marx despiritualized Hegel. And so after decades of study he concluded that the development of productive forces was the *causa causans*, meaning the real effective origin of everything that unfolded in history. It was a revolutionary breakthrough in thinking about the world and human society that had unprecedented conversion potential. Many came to see that the fate and development of humanity are determined by the forces of production of goods (wares) for human consumption and ultimately survival.[43] The persuasive power of this assertion led to the mobilization of the toiling masses and changed the course of world history. However, before Marxist theory was adopted by a cadre of industrial workers in Germany the process of industrialization on wage earners had engendered the formation of what became *trade unions*. These organizations were essentially defensive mechanisms against the exploitation of wage earners. As Friedrich Engels showed in his book *The Condition of the Working Class in England* (1845),[44] the only leverage that workers had to improve their conditions was to organize into associations that could collectively withdraw their labor and thereby force the employers

---

43. Federn, *Materialist Conception of History*, 6.

44. The original title was *Die Lage der arbeitenden Klasse in England*. The English-language translation by the American social reformer Florence Kelley appeared in 1885.

to negotiate for improved wages and conditions, in short, to initiate strike action if necessary.

Engels's book really disclosed the process of worker initiatives all over industrializing Europe. In Germany, where the Industrial Revolution had taken off with such speed, the first worker organization as distinct from guilds (*Zünfte*) of craftsmen had begun before the 1848 revolution and an organization was formed in that year by a typesetter named Stefan Born (1824–1893).[45] Born was an archetypal autodidact and agitator, such as are individuals both male and female who are very conscious of a need to improve the lot of both themselves and that of their co-workers against oppressive socioeconomic conditions. Born became the driving force that led to the formation of *Die allgemeine deutsche Arbeiterverbrüderung*, that is, the General German Brotherhood of Workers.

This organization, founded in Berlin in 1848, had quickly taken off and become very active during the March revolutions in most German industrial towns. Further, Born had joined the *Bund der Kommunisten* (Association of Communists) and is thus remembered as the first leader of a militant trade union organization, albeit of a non-revolutionary character. Despite its short-lived existence it had a long-term impact because it was essentially the practical human response of the working class to exploitation. Born had through his meeting first with Engels and then with Marx clearly declared his colors but he was far from being a radical revolutionary. Nevertheless, his movement was the first German labor organization dedicated to the improvement of conditions for industrial labor within the existing state. Although its membership dwindled in the aftermath of the 1848 revolutions, it had succeeded in politicizing an element within the working class because those workers resurfaced in the following decades, leading to the formation by 1862 of what became the world's first genuine labor party, namely the German Social Democratic Party (SPD). It was the result of the agitation of the trade unionists and amalgamated both the political and industrial labor movements. The history of German democratic as opposed to Communist labor is one of frustration and later ruthless betrayal. Coinciding with the spread of the Industrial Revolution on the continent, Marx's ideas had begun to crystalize and by the time of the revolutions in 1848 he with the collaboration

45. Stefan Born was Jewish and originally named Simon Buttermilch. For information on Born's activities, see Todt, *Gewerkschaftliche Betätigung*; Todt and Radant, *Frühgeschichte der deutschen Gewerkschaftsbewegung*; Hermann, *Kampf von Karl Marx*; Noyes, *Organization and Revolution*.

of his friend Friedrich Engels began to gain attention. A phase of German history had opened that explains how it became separated from the liberal parliamentary West.[46]

THE RISE OF SOCIAL DEMOCRACY IN GERMANY

The social and political consequences of the spreading industrialization of the Germanic sates, especially along the extensive banks of the river Rhine, were to have long-term world-political impact. A region of Europe renowned for it its brilliant architects, artists, and craftsmen since the Middle Ages, as the great cathedrals from that era testify still today, was inevitably driven into the Industrial Age. The reactionary monarchical regimes then in control of the Germanic principalities were mentally ill equipped to cope with this great social change. Nowhere in Europe at that time was the emancipation of the working classes a current concept. Indeed, it was as alien to the entrepreneurial class and governments as the possibility of flying to the moon. In short, the ruling classes had little idea how to deal with what became increasingly known throughout the second half of the nineteenth century as the *Arbeiterfrage* (labor question) or *Arbeiterproblem* (labor problem) even though it had been raised already during the revolutions of 1848. Indeed, it was labor relations during the second half of the nineteenth century within the capitalist states of what became the Bismarckian empire that impacted upon the world. It is a phase of modern history that needs to be better understood.

To begin with, the mental formation of the capitalist class made it very difficult for its members to envisage negotiation with representatives of organized labor over questions of working conditions. Factory owners were dominated by the conviction that they were masters in their own house (*Herr im eigenen Hause*) and therefore were not obliged to listen to the grievances of their servants to whom they so magnanimously offered the privilege of work. Such a mindset was obviously not a German peculiarity; it was shared by the capitalist class in all industrializing countries. In Germany, however, it endured for a very long time and eventually led to the industrialists throwing their support behind the Nazi movement during the end phase of the ill-fated Weimar Republic, 1928–1933. That is why a clearer understanding of German labor history is crucial for comprehending the political evolution of the fateful twentieth century.

46. Recounted in Moses, *Trade Unionism in Germany*, ch. 3.

History evolves out of the social structures in the different regions of the world and how they grind against each other. Out of this mix are formed the *mentalitiés* of the various social classes, racial groups. and religious institutions. These are consequent upon the so-called *Wechselwirkung*, that is, the reciprocal relationship between existing social structures and the ideas of thinkers who perceive a vocation to change them. All this was certainly happening in the Europe of 1848–1850. The reaction that followed the revolutions prepared the seedbed for a turbulent future.

In Germany, as has been seen, Karl Marx had founded the *Bund der Kommunisten* but this movement inevitably fell afoul of the post-revolutionary reaction and so Marx was obliged to flee, first to France and finally back to England, where in a more tolerant atmosphere he began to systematize his world-shattering reflections. Meanwhile in Germany itself the drive among the burgeoning working classes for a degree of emancipation picked up again. Workers needed to be politically organized and there emerged a remarkable agitator named Ferdinand Lassalle (1825–1864). This largely forgotten figure in the history of German labor has had arguably an even more significant impact on the launching of an organized working-class movement than had Karl Marx even though they were separated by profound differences on economic theory. It is one of the curiosities of the intellectual history of the labor movement how these two men representing two mutually exclusive ideological positions exerted such an enduring influence within the one party and trades union organizations. Here the answer will be provided, first by outlining Lassalle's economic theory and his reasons why there had to be a popular working-class political party to enable a modern German democratic state to emerge.

FERDINAND LASSALLE'S ECONOMIC THEORIES

Lassalle's biography belongs in the history of remarkable autodidacts. He was a man of acute intelligence and was well versed in the law, and he felt called to champion lost causes and fight for them with the passion of an enraged terrier. He knew Marx but had in addition imbibed the economic ideas of the English economists Thomas Malthus (1766–1834) and David Ricardo (1772–1823), and out of them developed his theory of the "iron and cruel law of wages." He explained it as follows:

The iron law of wages, which under present day conditions, under the domination of supply and demand for labor determines the workers' wages, is this: That the average wage is always reduced to a level necessary for subsistence, i.e., a level which a people usually accept as necessary for the eking out of an existence and the reproduction of the species. This is the point about which the real daily wage gravitates in the pendulum swing all the time neither being able to raise itself above the same or not being able to fall below the same. It cannot raise itself permanently above this average—because then there would arise, by means of the slightly improved conditions of the workers, an increase in the working-class marriages, and thus an increase in the working-class population, an increase in the supply of hands which would force down the wages back to their earlier levels. Again, the working wage cannot fall permanently below the necessary subsistence level because then emigration increases, there is a reduction in marriages, a falloff in the reproduction of children, and finally a reduction in the number of workers caused by the general pauperization which thus reduces the supply of hands still more, and therefore brings back the wages again to the previous level. Thus, the real average working wage floats in the movement constantly around it centre to which it always must sink back, circle around, sometimes above it (periods of prosperity in all or individual branches of industry), sometimes a little below it (periods of more or less general depression and crisis). The restrictions of the average wage to a level within the population which is required for maintaining an existence and for reproduction—that is, I repeat, the iron and cruel law which controls the working wage in today's conditions.[47]

For Lassalle this was the unchangeable law of *laissez faire* economics, the result being that wages always hovered around the very limit of that which at a given time was necessary to the basic subsistence of a worker and his family, sometimes a little above, sometimes a little below. There is, however, a problem with what is superficially a very seductive argument: if it were true, then the cultural progress of the toiling masses could not be explained; the working class would remain in a constant state of virtual *immiseration* or *pauperization*. Sometimes and only briefly an increase in productivity could occur that coincided with a period of demand for certain goods. The labor market was required to supply the necessary workers so that goods could be produced in such quantities to

---

47. Cited in Bernstein, *Ferdinand Lassalle as Social Reformer*, 123–24.

meet demand. In such conditions prices became so unusually cheap that they became regarded as items of necessity in each society. In short, they became established as the minimum for a subsistence level existence. Workers' living standard remained hovering at this point, thus ruling out any real cultural progress. For Lassalle the wage laborer and his family were condemned to life-long penury.

That seemed to be the dismal reality, in which case the efforts of workers to organize themselves into trade unions to fight for higher wages was pointless; it would avail them nothing in the end. Indeed, within the existing system of political economy there appeared to be no way out of this vicious circle. Consequently, Lassalle's proffered solution was to organize the workers into their own political party so that via the ballot box they could gain legislative power in the various state and national parliaments with a view to changing the laws governing the production of goods. In short, workers should be legally enabled to set up their own productive cooperatives, and if they could gain parliamentary majorities, they could change the law to require the state to provide it. So, the main objective of the labor movement was to capture the state's bureaucratic apparatus and that could conceivably be done by means of manhood suffrage, that is, by giving the vote to working men. The focus of the labor movement had to be on the state. Nothing less than a dramatic change in political culture was being demanded. The question was: would the existing owners of the means of production, distribution, and exchange voluntarily concede such a change?

Lassalle remained confident that not only was change possible, it was the only path that workers could take. He even managed to consult with the Prussian chief minister, Otto von Bismarck, outlining his ideas. And while the Iron Chancellor reportedly listened patiently to Lassalle's ideas, he was not moved by them.[48] The labor champion's success lay rather in his ability to reach the masses. They were at least persuaded that the "iron law of wages" made sense to them. It was not only the very persuasive basis of Lassalle's agitation, but also the touchstone of real concern for the welfare of the working class, which after all was the source of the labor power upon which the success of industry and the national economy ultimately depended. If politicians did not recognize

---

48. Lassalle has attracted several biographers. One of the earliest was the English historian William Harbutt Dawson, *German Socialism and Ferdinand Lassalle*; more recently David Footman, *The Primose Path: A Biography of Ferdinand Lassalle*.

this and were not prepared to respond to these undeniable realities, they were just blowhards, not to be taken seriously.

The message that Lassalle had been so successful in proclaiming began to bear fruit; he was responsible for laying the foundations of the very first working class *political party*, that is the party that eventually became the Social Democratic Party of Germany (SPD).[49] That was indeed a singular world-historical achievement, but what turned out to be problematic was the fact that it had virtually no place for the role of trade unions. The dogma of the iron law of wages simply made their efforts to improve labor conditions ineffectual. Indeed, for Lassalle if they had any value at all in the workers' struggle for emancipation, it was as recruiting agencies for socialist voters; if anything was going to effect change, it was only going to be through the ballot box at election time. Remarkably, Lassalle's doctrine of the iron law of wages remained a fixed part of the SPD platform until 1891. That fact, however, did not seriously inhibit the pragmatism of workers from responding to their environment, so they continued despite the theory of the iron law of wages to expand union organizations.

Karl Marx's Refutation of Lassalle

In contrast to Lassalle, Marx emerged as a staunch advocate for trade union activity, doubtless because he had acquired a much wider knowledge than Lassalle about the actual work of organized labor in Britain and the USA. Consequently, Marx was able to refute Lassalle in the pages of the socialist newspaper *Der Social-Democrat* on February 13, 1865 as follows:

> Combinations, with the trade unions which grow out of them, are not only of the most extreme importance as a means of organising the working class to fight with the bourgeoisie—this importance shows itself in other things in that even the workers of the United States, in spite of their voting rights and republic cannot do without them—but in Prussia and Germany at large the right of association, in addition to making a breach in the rule of the police-state and bureaucratisation, destroys the

49. Berlau, *German Social Democratic Party, 1914–1921*. The party was initially called the Allgemeiner Deutscher Arbeiter Verein, that is, the "General German Workers' Association."

master and servant regulations and controls of the feudal nobility in the country.

This was a shrewd observation. Marx by virtue of his wider knowledge of the outside world noted that workers must not only organize themselves to resist pauperization at the hands of the bourgeoisie, but they also needed to express their political discontent and fight for emancipation from wage slavery. Trades unions facilitated these objectives. In addition, Marx distanced himself from Lassalle in his famous London address, "Wages, Price and Profit," which was communicated to the General International Congress in September 1865 in support of trade unions. Therein Marx observed:

> Trade unions work well as centres of resistance against the encroachment of capital. They fail partially from an injudicious use of their power. They fail generally from limiting themselves to a guerrilla war against the effects of the existing system, instead of simultaneously trying to change it, instead of using their organised forces as a lever for the final emancipation of the working class, that is to say the ultimate abolition of the wage system.

Obviously, for Marx, unions were not an end in themselves, but they were indispensable for initiating the politicization of the working class, without which that class could not become the source of revolutionary potential required to change the system. This idea was expressed more forcefully by Marx in his instructions to the delegates of the Provisional General Council before their attendance at the First Congress of the International Association, September 3–8, 1866. They should not forget the importance of trade unions because:

> Trade unions originally sprang up from the spontaneous attempt of workmen at removing or at least checking the competition [among themselves], in order to conquer such terms of contract as might raise them at least above the condition of mere slaves. The immediate object of trade unions was therefore confined to everyday necessities, to expedience for the obstruction of incessant encroachments of capital, in one word to questions of time and labor. This activity of trade unions is not only legitimate, it is necessary. It cannot be dispensed with so long as the present system of production lasts. On the contrary, it must be generalised by the formation of the combination of trade unions throughout all countries. On the other hand, unconsciously to

themselves, the trade unions were for many *centres of organisation* of the working class, as the medieval municipalities and communes did for the middle class. If the trade unions are required for the guerrilla fights between capital and labor, they are still more important as *organised agencies for superseding the very system of wage labor and capital rule.*[50] (emphases added)

Nothing could document more clearly that Marx regarded the existence and struggle of trade unions as not only most effective but the essential aspect, indeed the *conditio sine qua non* of the labor movement. Their activity was where the class struggle began and without it there was no chance of success. Trade unions were the indispensable weapon of the labor movement against capitalism. The only proviso was that they never should be satisfied only by winning strikes for better wages and conditions; they must always be alive to the main objective, which was the *ultimate elimination of the wage system.* This was because they were struggling against the effects of a disease, and only functioned as a palliative without being able to conquer the disease within the limits of their regular activity. To this extent, at least, Marx and Lassalle agreed.

What the foregoing has illustrated about Marx is the development in his understanding of the industrial class struggle since the 1848 revolution up to the mid-1860s. In 1848 there existed no viable workers' party; the need for social change was only heeded by a few radicals, while most liberals who demanded parliamentary reform in Germany had been intimidated and had abandoned the struggle, ceding defeat to the forces of reaction. So, by the dawn of the 1860s there had arisen the flamboyant figure of Ferdinand Lassalle, whose historic contribution to the labor movement was the creation of a genuine workers' party. He gave the German working class their own political identity.

It is always rewarding to investigate the evolution of historic movements like social democracy and Communism and to evaluate them throughout the course of history from the standpoint of the present. Out of Lassalle's organizational efforts emerged the modern democratic labor movement, which had essentially transferred class struggle from the violence of the streets to the more serene atmosphere of parliamentary legislatures. On the other hand, since the Marxian formula stipulated that history could only be advanced by the "dictatorship of the proletariat," the nature of the state had to change to allow the aspirations of the working

50. Marx, "Instructions for the Delegates," 347–48.

class to be achieved. The wresting of worker control of the state could not take place without violent confrontation. History has demonstrated that the latter path has led to disastrously inhumane consequences while the moderate ideology of social democracy has led to peaceable outcomes as happened in the history of the rise of the Labour Party in the United Kingdom. So, what was/is at work when the toiling masses chose/choose to follow the path of revolutionary class conflict that was supposed to lead to the dictatorship of the proletariat?

On close observation the decades of oppression (wage slavery) engendered in the working class a deep sense of grievance and the urge to burst out of the shackles imposed by capitalism. Marx and Engels had perceptively highlighted this in the *Communist Manifesto* of 1848, hence the initial appeal of revolutionary socialism to the toiling masses. The subsequent violence and party dictatorship that manifested itself first in Lenin's Bolshevik Russia, which had swept away the old order, inspired similar party dictatorships around the world to the present day. The consequences have been anything but edifying. Immediately, however, historians must observe that without the massive Stalinist contribution to the defeat of Germany in the Second World War, the liberation of the world from the scourge of Nazism would have taken much longer than it did. While that is recognized as indisputable, the result was that the world was then confronted by the threat of Communist infiltration, resulting in the costly and emotionally unsettling era of the Cold War.

Communist parties throughout the world were encouraged to follow the Moscow party line and promote revolutions by politicizing the working class. The following chapter now investigates the record of "Communism in power" (Ernst Nolte) in the former East Germany from 1945 until the implosion of December 1989, when the infamous Berlin Wall was finally torn down. That history represents a case study in the incompetence of Communist regimes to enable civil societies to reproduce themselves. The high-sounding ideology of Marxism-Leninism revealed itself to be a formula for the self-aggrandizement of an oligarchy of unscrupulous party bosses whose chief concern was to sustain themselves in power at the expense of the toiling masses. It was a massive and inhumane deception perpetrated on ordinary people by unscrupulous men who sustained themselves in power for decades by ruthlessly disregarding all standards of human decency and justice.

3

The Destructive Chimera of Communism

The Example of Real Existing Socialism in the German Democratic Republic

IF ONE HAS MET and conversed with card-carrying Communists, one will have often found them initially agreeable and reasonable people. However, when the discussion focuses on the questions of basic human rights, such as freedom of conscience, the right to read whatever one chooses, freedom from capricious police intrusion into one's personal life, especially how one's children are educated, and freedom to travel wherever one decides, then one encounters stony opposition. Communists always insist that the "state," meaning the central committee of the Communist Party, must be obeyed. One is confronted with the ultimate big brother state. Freedom as understood in Western liberal parliamentary democracies simply does not exist. People, for example, in East Germany 1945–1989 had to accustom themselves to a continuation of life under conditions not dissimilar to those experienced under the Third Reich, though the Communist form of totalitarianism, called "real existing socialism" by the postwar regime, manifested certain different peculiarities. For example, there was a constitution that allowed different political parties and it appeared to endorse freedom of religion, but the reality was nothing like the words of the East German constitution seemed to mean. To quote from that document, Article 21:

74

1. Every citizen of the German Democratic Republic has the right to participate fully in the political, economic, social and cultural life of the socialist community and the socialist state. The principle "work with, plan with, govern with!"

2. The right to co-determination and co-shaping is guaranteed by the fact that the citizens elect all organs of power, participate in their activities and in the planning, management and organization of social life; can demand accountability from the representatives of the people, their deputies, the heads of state and economic bodies about their activities; using the authority of their social organizations to express their wishes and demands; to address their concerns and proposals to the social, state and economic bodies and institutions; express their will in referenda.

3. The realizations of this right of co-determination and co-shaping is at the same time a high moral obligation for every citizen. The exercise of social or state functions is recognized and supported by society and the state.[1]

There were indeed elections held to what was called *die Volkskammer*, the German Communist word for a "people's chamber" or national parliament. There, however, the similarity to a real parliament ended. The representatives of political parties from the time of the Weimar Republic were called the "block parties"[2] and they could stand for election, but they never won any seats because on every occasion the Communist Party (KPD) won with breathtaking landslides at the polls. It was common knowledge, however, that the exercise was a sham. Voting statistics, inevitably doctored, were published to show that the KPD candidates always massively outvoted any rival parties. This was part of the reason for bishop Dibelius's designation of the system as one of "robbers and liars." In short, the GDR was a police state controlled by the KPD through the secret state police, the *Stasi*, and the ideological justification for this was derived from the fiction that Marxism-Leninism was the revelation of absolute truth about the course of human history and how modern

---

1. Constitution of the German Democratic Republic, translated on *Wikipedia* from the 1968 updated version of the original constitution of October 7, 1949.

2. The block parties were the non-Communist ones that traced their origins back to the Weimar Republic such as successor to the Centre Party, which became the Christian Socialist Union, and the Free Democratic Party, the successor to the former German Democratic Party.

industrial society should be guided toward a situation of complete domestic social harmony and peaceful coexistence with all neighboring countries.[3] The history of the four decades of the existence of the GDR reveals the complete opposite. It was a mirror image of a Stalinist dictatorship ruled over by an oligarchy of self-serving party functionaries known as the *Nomenklatura*.[4]

THE GDR REGIME AS INSTITUTIONALIZED CRIMINALITY

This fraudulent regime, however, was destined to implode, essentially because it could not enable "bourgeois society to reproduce itself."[5] This is a key statement that needs to be unravelled. The term "bourgeois society" simply means a society under the rule of law in which there is freedom of conscience and where there is a free economy and there is no specifically privileged class of people, and anyone who is sane can stand for election to a freely elected parliament out of which a constitutional government can be formed. It is the opposite to a police state or a dictatorship.

Industrially, the Communist system everywhere was enmeshed in what was known as "command economies," meaning that the regime established what the economic priorities were, the very opposite of *laissez faire* or free market economies. The latter's function on the principle of free enterprise with minimum government intervention has been and is spectacularly more successful at fulfilling human needs than command economies.[6] The question of to what extent governments need to be involved in ensuring the employment, health, and welfare of their citizens challenges all political parties in open societies may, of course, be answered differently from country to country. However, the way in which Communist regimes dealt with these issues shows how inept, inefficient

---

3. See the graphic revelations about the reality of life in the GDR by Anna Funder, *Stasiland*.

4. Voslenski, *Nomenklatura*. The word describes a group of people who were appointed to key positions in the government bureaucracy, industry, agriculture, education, etc. by the Communist leadership in all East European, Soviet-dominated countries. They were a privileged, *de facto* elite.

5. Mason, "Primacy of Politics."

6. Governments in Western societies scarcely any longer operate under an old-fashioned *laissez faire* system and pay attention to welfare issues to ameliorate the effects of unemployment and other issues that arise in the day-to-day management of industrial societies.

and arbitrary they were. The fiction was maintained in all Communist bloc countries that there was no unemployment and that under "socialism" all health problems were more than adequately dealt with. The reality was that even every day essential pharmaceutical products, especially for women, were never reliably available. The reason for this was that the regimes established the production priorities, which were dominated by the need to earn foreign currency. In many ways, although the GDR boasted the strongest economy in the Communist bloc, it was notoriously inefficient compared to its highly successful West German neighbor, with whom it conducted rewarding commercial relations despite each side working within very different social systems, namely capitalism in the West and Communism in the East.[7]

German Protestantism as Key Factor Intra-German Relations

It is recalled that the existence of Lutheran and Reformed churches in East Germany constituted an ongoing problem for the Communist regime on several levels. The first was purely ideological. Any regime that lays claim to possess the absolute truth about human existence must inevitably oppose the existence of Christianity, which is a religion that upholds the gospel of Jesus of Nazareth as the criterion of all truth.[8] The continued existence of churches within countries of the Soviet bloc was a challenge to their respective ministries of culture, whose aim was to instill in the population total subservience to Marxism-Leninism by producing people known as the "new species being."[9] This mythical creature was a figment

7. Egon Bahr, *Was Nun?* Bahr (1922–2015), a confessed Lutheran, was a member of the SPD and close associate of Chancellor Willy Brandt (1969–1974) in the implementation of *Ostpolitik*. In this role Bahr sustained a fruitful dialogue with the East German regime. It was largely due to him that the East German economy was able to sustain itself through commerce with the West. For studies on how the non-Roman churches coped with the atheistic authorities see Goeckel, *Lutheran Church and the East German State*; Henkys, *Gottes Volk im Sozialismus*; Barth and Hamel, *How to Serve God in a Marxist Land*; Moses, "Collapse of the GDR."

8. Moses, "Collapse of the GDR," 154.

9. The *Kultusministerium* is the German term for what would normally be called the "ministry of education" in Western countries. In totalitarian regimes the goal of education is to enforce mental and spiritual submission to the "absolute truth" of the regime's ideology. There can only be one truth that when followed will eventually produce the Marxist concept of the "new species being," that is, a human being molded in the Communist image. Such a being would not be alienated from their work but rather the individual's unique talents would be used for the general good and not to produce "surplus value," which is

of Marx's mental reflections. Indeed, it is hard to imagine the possibility of such a human being ever existing given the universal experience of human behavior. It resembles the hope that one day in human beings the qualities of pride, envy, gluttony, lust, anger, greed, and sloth, distinguished from time immemorial, could be eliminated. That is, the traditional seven deadly sins identified by the church from antiquity would miraculously disappear. All these desires and emotions have been and are manifested in human beings in every culture on planet Earth up to the present day. The idea that Marxism-Leninism would be able to transform human nature was an illusion, a deception projected by Communist parties throughout the world. Whatever they were/are in the fraudulent ideology is propagated to benefit the lifestyle of the *Nomenklatura*.

It does not take much reflection to see that the objective of creating an autonomous and selfless creature that would function according to the Marxist schema was a wish-dream even if it may have been genuinely believed by some. As now can be seen, the entire Marxist-Leninist enterprise was a kind of counter-religion to replace the hitherto dominant religions in Western and Eastern Europe and then the entire world. Marx certainly understood the power of religion over human beings, referring to it as the cry of an oppressed people for liberation and as such representing the "opiate of the people." He likened it to opium administered to individuals for relief from the pain and suffering of an incurable disease.[10]

While Marx's critique was directed mainly against the Christianity of the West, he refused to believe that what he was advocating as a remedy for the ills of capitalist society was tantamount to an alternative religion, and one based on a fallacious assumption that human behavior could be remolded by the imposition of a new set of rules that governed how goods were produced. These rules were supposed to be behind the Communist government's so-called command economy. That meant the governing elite of Communist parties under the general direction of the party secretary specified what kinds of goods would be produced and in what quantities.

---

what workers are supposed to do under capitalism, a system that benefits only the factory owners. See Mezaros, *Marx's Theory of Alienation*.

10. This oft-quoted phrase by Marx comes from the introduction to a text entitled *A Contribution to the Critique of Hegel's Philosophy of Right*, begun in 1843. The introduction was published separately in Marx's journal, *Deutsch-Französische Jahrbücher*, in 1844 together with Arnold Ruge.

No doubt the once unrestricted capitalist system was subject to abuse and inevitably was responsible for the class struggle between the owners of the means of production, distribution, and exchange and the work force required to make society function. This gave rise to the Communist assertion or dogma that the workers were really the source of all value since without their input no goods would ever reach the marketplace. That was the labor theory of value, which as Marxists argued gave the working class a moral right to rise and expropriate the capitalists, who kept the working class in a state of penury or wage slavery. As already seen, Marx had spelled this out in a most persuasive way in his famous pamphlets, which had a great impact on workers, especially trade union organizers, who constituted the vanguard of organized labor against capital. A select few intellectuals among them may have "read, marked, learned and inwardly digested" the daunting three volumes of *Das Kapital,* which appeared in 1865, 1885, and 1894. Translations into English followed piecemeal and were published first in the United States in 1872. A complete edition in English only appeared in 1906.[11]

Bearing that in mind, once circumstances had changed after the working class had wrested political power, as was initially the case after the Bolshevik revolution in Russia, the so-called revolutionary party of the proletariat assumed the responsibility for managing the national economy. However, instead of developing procedures that could realize the projected goals of Communism after the 1917 October revolution in Russia, the Communist party functionaries in all countries, not surprisingly, lost the plot literally. They were generally proven to be incapable, mainly because of incompetence and corruption in their ranks, of rigorously pursuing the putative goals. Such incompetence was, of course, endemic and hence irradicable. The result was the evolution of a doctrine or system called "real existing socialism" (*real existierender Sozialismus*) or "actually existing socialism." Stripped of its rhetoric, this was a system of exploitation of the working class by the above mentioned *Nomenklatura.*

In short, the central committee of the Communist party came to exercise a rigorous dictatorship over the toiling masses. This was the case in all Eastern European countries "liberated" by the Soviet Union after the end of the Second World War. The regime in the German Democratic Republic (East Germany) prided itself as being the parade ground example of this kind of regime. It was the most successful economy of all the Communist

11. Philip S. Foner, "Marx's Capital in the United States" *Science and Society* 31 (4) 1967, 461–66 and Harvey, *Companion to Marx's Capital.*

regimes in the world at following guidelines from Moscow. The GDR flag was very much like that of the Soviet Union, whose ensign featured a hammer and sickle on a red banner. The East German one by subtle contrast displayed a compass over a hammer, circled by a wreath in the center of a banner of black, red, and yellow stripes. These colors were taken from an ancient Teutonic banner that had been reintroduced during the Weimar Republic (1919–1933). So, the recent republican past was recalled as well as an emphasis on the technical superiority of the German worker, hence the compass surmounting the hammer.

The GDR regime was very adept at projecting the right symbolism as well as the cultivation of ideologues whose task it was to produce publications that justified the triumph of Communism in the eastern part of Germany. But all that really availed very little when compared to the economic superiority of then West Germany, which was due to the incorporation of the postwar Federal Republic of Germany into the economies of Western Europe and the transatlantic communities originally via the Marshall Plan.[12] It could also be argued that East Germany's proximity to the West served to prop up what was a totally corrupt and inefficient regime because it received economic aid from the Bonn government and the Evangelical Church.[13]

The Protestant Churches and Lutheran Culture as Challenges to the Regime

Further, a key factor in intra-German relations in the period of postwar division from 1945 to 1989 was the Lutheran territorial churches. At the end of the Second World War in Germany all denominations sought to reorganize themselves on a German-wide basis. Initially they hoped to be able to disregard the political division between the Communist regime in East and the liberal-oriented West, where there existed a so-called public sphere in which all citizens were free to openly discuss anything provided it was not criminal or seditious. This was called by the noted German sociologist

12. The Marshall Plan was an ambitious aid program from the USA offered to sixteen European countries that aimed to kick-start their depressed post-1945 economies and thereby strengthen liberal democracy. It was even offered to Soviet countries, but these predictably rejected it on doctrinaire grounds. Officially it was known as the European Recovery Program, or ERP, but normally called the "Marshall Program" after the US secretary of state George C. Marshall, who announced it in 1948.

13. Maul, *Egon Bahr*.

Jürgen Habermas (b. 1929) the "open speech situation," which describes societies in which citizens were allowed to assemble and debate any issues that concerned them.[14] However, in the eastern Communist-dominated section of the former German Reich the regime could not in practice allow an "open speech situation" since the fraudulent regime projected itself as the embodiment of the infallible laws of history, indeed of all truth.

In short, all regimes of Marxism-Leninism were legitimized by the inexorable (but fictitious) laws of history as identified by Karl Marx and put into practice by Vladimir Ilych Lenin. That meant that all citizens in the GDR were subjected to these laws as the party executive stipulated. However, the edicts of the party secretaries were made to extend their own power via loyal functionaries. These constituted a corrupt elite who behaved more in accordance with human avarice than any desire to promote the welfare of ordinary people. It was, as bishop Otto Dibelius had correctly identified, a "regime of robbers and liars" who ensured that all subjects submitted without question to the criminal "authorities."[15]

Consequently, the idea that their Christian subjects could be directed by an agency outside the Communist state was untenable; hence the status of both the Protestant (mostly Lutheran) and the minority Roman Catholic dioceses was ideologically anomalous. How could there be a section of society that drew their values from an outside agency that was not under the control of the party that was the custodian of absolute truth? So, Christians found themselves beleaguered and isolated, and subjected to close surveillance and harassment by the secret police. The outcome was a church struggle in Communist East Germany that paralleled that in Nazi Germany, namely the *Kirchenkampf*. In both instances the powers-that-be claimed to represent the absolute truth, which was naturally a direct challenge to the churches. How were they to survive under such conditions?

As noted above, the constitution of the GDR enshrined freedom of conscience and belief but that was not in fact allowed. The secret police (*Stasi*) ensured that there was no public sphere, and they could perpetrate all manner of violations of human rights with the sanction of the regime. The Ministry of Culture stipulated what was taught in schools and exercised a veto over the publication of books, especially on history as well as in all facets of literature. In short, it was of paramount importance to all Communist regimes to extend their ideological hegemony throughout the

14. Habermas, *Theory of Communicative Action*.

15. Dibelius, *Obrigkeit*. See also his "Christ against Tyranny," as well as Fritz, *Otto Dibelius*, 500.

population. Under these circumstances the churches and their clergy were often subjected to random intrusions from *Stasi* officers to ensure that nothing critical was preached about the virtues of "real existing socialism."

An atmosphere of psychological oppression permeated the entire country, heightened by the fact that regular consumer goods and everyday items for personal hygiene, especially for women, were often unobtainable because of the arbitrarily imposed priorities on production by the command economy. In addition, the goods that were produced, especially clothing, were often of a very low quality compared to what was the norm in the West. And the small sedan produced by the Communist automobile industry, named the *Trabant* and designed to be an updated people's car (*Volkswagen*), was nothing more than a notoriously underpowered vehicle whose chief characteristic was the foulness of its putrid exhaust fumes.

A further negative feature of the marketplace in the GDR was that luxury goods, especially comestibles, were made secretly available in restricted outlets only for the *Nomenklatura*. The contrast between the flourishing economy in the Federal Republic in the West and that of the GDR in the East was the subject of innumerable bitter jokes.[16] Before the Berlin Wall came down the population lived in a permanent state of anxiety about the arbitrariness of the regime.[17] The breaching of the wall on December 9, 1989 and the subsequent incorporation of the GDR into the Federal Republic were events celebrated by the populace with undisguised jubilation. The reputation and claims of Marxism-Leninism to possess the infallible guidelines for universal emancipation from wage slavery proved to be a fallacy of tragic dimensions when the entire system imploded at the end of 1989.[18] The focus now is on what resulted from the legacy of right-wing Hegelianism.

16. Rodden, *Repainting the Little Red School House*; Lewis, *Hammer and Tickle*; Schmidt, "Ulbricht klopft an die Himmespforte."

17. Interestingly, some old firms of distinction managed to survive in the GDR and to become relatively prosperous, such as the piano manufacturer of the Blüthner family in Leipzig. Their superb instruments have the reputation of belonging to the world's four best brands. In a personal encounter with Herr Blüthner, a man of culture who spoke fluently in several European languages, we agreed that even in a country of real existing socialism pianos were indispensable. Their exports earned much-needed foreign currencies for the otherwise economically mismanaged GDR.

18. Weitz, *Creating German Communism*.

4

The Fascist Lure of Limitless Power

THE MOST OMINOUS IDEOLOGICAL consequence of the conclusion of the Great War of 1914–1918 was the emergence of fascism in many European countries. It arose as a challenge to the apparent triumph of parliamentary democracy, albeit very brief in many countries, especially in Eastern Europe. The first and most spectacular example was the fascist party led by Benito Mussolini (1883–1945) in Italy, who rose rapidly to political power after the famous March on Rome in October 1922. This had made an indelible impression on Adolf Hitler, who began his political career with the Beer Hall Putsch in Munich, November 8–9, 1923, which, despite failing to take over the government of Bavaria, gained for Hitler subsequently considerable political notoriety.[1]

The movement that Adolf Hitler came to lead after its tentative beginnings in the early 1920s was finally during the Great Depression of 1929–1933 able to seize power over the German national parliament. On January 30, 1933 Adolf Hitler was summoned by Reich president Paul von Hindenburg to form a government. Under the predominance of the Nazi Party a process had begun that eroded all the civil rights enshrined in the democratic Weimar constitution of 1919. The once obscure "Bohemian corporal" had become the diabolical *Führer* (leader) of a remilitarized republic that cast its ominous shadow over Western, Central, and Eastern Europe from 1933 until its destruction in 1945.

1. Nolte, *Three Faces of Fascism*; Kershaw, *Hitler*, 1:16–29, 180–86.

Hitler by virtue of his histrionic rhetoric and skillful use of the radio and newsreels had reaped unprecedented public support. In vain did
convinced Social Democratic and Communist Reichstag deputies supported by remnants of the Catholic Centre Party oppose the conferring
of dictatorial powers on Hitler. Further, Hitler had three straightforward
objectives that enjoyed overwhelming public endorsement. These were
firstly to unburden Germany from the shackles and alleged deprivations
imposed on Germany by the Treaty of Versailles of 1919, secondly to
rearm the nation, and thirdly to solve the "Jewish problem." Behind all
this was the aim not only to stamp out the alleged Jewish influence on
world politics but also to free the world from the scourge of Communism
that was championed by Soviet Russia, and this could only be achieved
by means of all-out war against the Communist East as well as the democratic West. Nazi Germany was out to change the world.[2]

Hitler's long-term priority was to rid the international community of
Jewish and Communist influences. These twin aims led to the Holocaust
and the campaign to destroy the Soviet Union. To accomplish this, however, the Nazi leadership first needed to eliminate any military threat from
the Western European parliamentary democracies, chiefly France and
Great Britain. A clue to Hitler's intention was revealed in the Hossbach
Memorandum of November 5, 1937, which consisted of notes taken by
colonel Friedrich Hossbach (the *Führer*'s adjutant) at a meeting convened
by Hitler of his chiefs of staff at which he outlined his foreign policy aims.
These were based on the alleged need for the expanding German nation to
have more living space (*Lebensraum*). In concrete terms Hitler wanted to
annex both Austria and Czechoslovakia (*Sudetenland*) as soon as practically possible. That meant that when Germany had sufficiently rearmed to
take on the potential opponents of this policy, such as France and Great
Britain, war could confidently be declared.

By the mid-1930s Hitler had certainly become the most provocative
and dynamic political figure in Europe. That was signaled by his bold
move to reoccupy the Rhineland on March 7, 1936. The *Führer* had ordered this in contravention of the Versailles Treaty, having sent in three
battalions of troops who were intentionally not given ammunition and
ordered to retreat should the French and Belgians march against them.

2. The number of studies purporting to explain the origins and purpose of Nazi
policy is so great and driven by all manner of ideological conviction that it makes a list
of them here impractical. However, for a useful start one may consult Smith, *Ideological
Origins of Nazi Imperialism*, 231–58.

Hitler had taken a risk that surprisingly paid off because not only were the populations of the main cities of Aachen, Trier, and Saarbrucken jubilant, but the Western powers failed to respond, thus signaling the ineffectuality of the conditions laid down at Versailles in 1919. Hitler after forty-eight hours of sweating out the bluff was greatly relieved and his popularity magnified. In short, the successful outcome of the Rhineland crisis was a significant milestone in the *Führer*'s march to almost universal approval.

More was to come with the *Anschluss*, the unopposed march into Austria on March 13, 1938, where allegedly 99 percent of the population[3] were also jubilant: "*Heim ins Reich!*" ("Back home to the Reich") was the basis of Nazi foreign policy since it was Hitler's aim to unify all people of Teutonic blood and culture into one empire as the most recent research confirms. Hence the existence of German communities outside the 1919 German borders in other countries such as Poland or Luxembourg was a justification for the Nazi invasions.

With the lapse of time since the demise of the Third Reich many historians and other social scientists have furnished explanations for Hitler's career both as a dictator and a military commander. The most recent stems from the pen of German anthropologist Stefan Heep, whose insights throw a light upon the psychological-spiritual motivations of the *Führer*'s war aims. The value of Heep's research lies in its explanation of why Hitler acted as he did, rather than simply what he did.

ADOLF HITLER: CHARISMATIC *FÜHRER* AND PROPHET OF A NEW WORLD RELIGION OF RACE OVER HUMANITY

If somebody tried to persuade you that the greatest religious leader of the twentieth century was an ex-corporal of the German army of the First World War, who was before that a failed art student from Vienna, you would be forgiven for questioning their sanity. Adolf Hitler a great religious leader?[4] How would one arrive at such a conclusion? The *Führer*'s

3. This figure is almost certainly fictitious. Nevertheless, a significant section of the Austrian community endorsed the *Anschluss* while it was certainly opposed by Social Democrats and Communist sympathizers, many of whom fled the country.

4. See the recent study by Heep, "Hitler—das "Heilige in Erscheinung?" Stefan Heep's work must be regarded as a breakthrough in comprehending Hitler's inner motivation, namely that he perceived himself as the prophet of a new world religion. Dr. Heep has exhaustively evaluated of all major scholarship on Hitler, his rise to power,

career raises many questions. For example, in a nation where the professionalism of the officer corps was the highest in the world, indeed, a class of men who were traditionally very status conscious, aristocratic, and inordinately proud (vain) regarding their expertise in the art of war, how does one explain that a lower-class outsider, a virtual nobody, could rise to be their unquestioned supreme commander? Hitler constitutes a still unexplained mystery, the real enigma of German history. That is doubtless why there are so many books about him, and why some Germans at the present time want him posthumously stripped of his citizenship and given back to Austria, where he was born.

The purpose here is first to flag the role of the military in Prussian German history up to the end of the First World War and then to focus on the phenomenon of Hitler as the charismatic leader, and finally to explains why Hitler was successful even though it was only for twelve years of German history.

When one looks back over the history of the rise of Prussia-Germany to great power in the nineteenth century, one sees that the achievement of unification of Germany under Prussia was the consequence of three well-planned and swiftly executed so-called *Kabinettskriege*, that is, wars planned and executed for very specific and limited aims; certainly not wars of conquest for the sake of conquest, but rather for discreet political objectives planned by the political leadership, the cabinet, and executed by highly professional generals. Behind these nineteenth-century achievements was the remarkable history of the rise of Prussia to European power status under the Hohenzollern electors (*Kurfürsten*) and kings in the seventeenth and eighteenth centuries. It was they, particularly the king of Prussia from 1740 to 1786, namely Frederick the Great, who established the tradition of Prusso-German statecraft that rested on the *correct* relationship between the political leadership and the generals who served it. That means that the king was responsible for all policy planning, and if he decided that a war was necessary for reasons of state, he commissioned the generals to plan and execute it. In this way it was understood that maximum security for the country could be achieved.[5]

---

and his military campaigns. Most thorough and authoritative still is Ian Kershaw's *Hitler* in two volumes.

5. The studies of the nature of Prusso-German militarism are legion and it is by no means possible to find total agreement among the many authors, but the most persuasive in this writer's view is Schnabel, *Deutsche Geschichte*; see especially vols. 1–2. As well, see Borgstedt and Steinbach, eds., *Franz Schnabel*.

Obviously it must be kept in mind that in a land-locked country like Prussia-Germany with potential enemies on all sides, particularly Russia in the East and France in the West, statesmen had always to reckon with the possibility of war at any time and this permanent threat of attack, if not tomorrow, then certainly at some time in the future. In that situation the army always had be in readiness. Consequently, the technical proficiency of the soldiers was given the highest priority. Indeed, in Prussia-Germany after the unification in 1871 a process evolved in which the foreign policy priorities were established by the army. In short, the real policy makers were the generals. This was to prove disastrous, especially for Germany during the Great War of 1914–1918.

The Fateful Permanence of Franco-German Enmity

When Bismarck founded the Reich in 1871, it was at the expense mainly of France in the third war of unification. France had been brutally humiliated, the emperor, Napoleon III, having been captured and forced into exile. The country was then obliged to pay a massive indemnity while having to endure a partial occupation. In addition, a major province, Alsace-Lorraine, was ceded to Germany, which became a so-called *Reichsland* until the French reclaimed it after the First World War. Such humiliation meant that France had been turned into a permanent enemy of the new German empire and consequently one had to expect that sooner or later it would demand *revanche*, that is, to attack Germany to regain Alsace Lorraine. Otto von Bismarck, the German chancellor, was acutely aware of this and designed his foreign policy from that time on the assumption that France would always seek to join with another major European power to keep Prussia-Germany at bay and at the right moment to attack.[6]

This apparent necessity automatically prioritized the military, which had to be ready at moment's notice to counter any coalition willing to venture an onslaught on Germany. Consequently, the General Staff became preoccupied with war plans thereafter. Diplomatically, Bismarck had to head off what he called the *cauchmar des coaltions*, the nightmare coalition against Germany, that is, the one between the *Flügelmächte*, that is, the powers to the West and East, France and Russia. For Prussia-Germany at that time the entire point of diplomacy was to maintain alliances

6. Numerous biographies of Bismarck exist. Among the latest is the monumental work by Jonathan Steinberg, *Bismarck—A Life*.

as long as possible to delay the inevitable next war. Bismarck's concept was always to be *á trios*, that is, aligned within a group of three powers to checkmate any revanchist designs the French might wish to implement. It was in this situation that Bismarck in 1873 negotiated a pact among the three emperors of East/Central Europe, that is, Prussia-Germany, Austria-Hungary, and czarist Russia. In short, he always had to have two reliable friendly powers to sustain his alliance system. This, however, was going to prove extraordinarily difficult in the long term. Russia especially was not fully at ease with the arrangement, so Bismarck sought closer ties with Austria-Hungary in the Dual Alliance of 1879, which was really directed against Russia.

As European politics developed until the 1890s it was becoming increasingly clear that Bismarck's objective to sustain a reliable alignment of three powers was in practice not attainable simply because the vital interests of Russia and Austria-Hungary could not be reconciled for long enough, particularly in the Balkans, which was perennially a source of friction between them. Bismarck then tried to stitch up a separate deal with Russia to keep Russia in line with an arrangement called the Reinsurance Treaty from 1887. Eventually this also proved unworkable and the treaty lapsed formally after Bismarck was forced to retire in 1890 by the young *Kaiser*, Wilhelm II, who wanted to direct both foreign and domestic policy on his own.[7] In any case the Reinsurance Treaty had become a dead letter well before that. Curiously, though, German admirers of Bismarck have often tried to portray the Reinsurance Treaty as Bismarck's most brilliant concept. It was argued that had it been kept alive Russia and France could not have formed the military alliance they did in 1893. This meant that the nightmare coalition that Bismarck had wanted to prevent had finally arrived, and in retrospect the path to the First World War had ominously opened.[8]

The disastrous Legacy of Field Marshall Alfred von Schlieffen

In the post-Bismarck era of diplomacy, which proved so manifestly unworkable, the Prusso-German General Staff felt obliged from then on to

---

7. Still of key historiographical importance is the work of an outsider in the German historical profession, namely Erich Eych, *Das persönliche Regiment Wilhelms II*. As well, see his *Bismarck and the German Empire*.

8. For an analysis of this crucial phase of German diplomatic history, see Röhl, *Germany without Bismarck* and *Wilhelm II*.

prioritize the military solution to their diplomatic dilemma. They had already foreseen the eventuality of having to fight a two-front war against France in the West and Russia in the East and had placed the emphasis on strong defences especially in the East. However, now under the new chief of the General Staff, Count Alfred von Schlieffen (in office 1891–1905) a revolutionary new concept was envisaged, and it is important to evaluate what it reveals about the relationship between the military and the civilian government in the German empire.[9]

The first thing to keep in mind is that the German leadership, as has been seen, believed in the inevitability of another war with France and whoever her allies might be. The fact that this was the only solution that presented itself to Prusso-German foreign policy planners is matter of deep concern for any historical assessment. The worldview of these men was entirely limited to the most violent solution of all, namely *Blitzkrieg*. And according to von Schlieffen's assessment such a war would have to be fought on two fronts, namely against both France and Russia simultaneously. This posed a problem of logistics, but von Schlieffen had conceived a solution. It was based on a new concept—that is, new for modern times—called the "war of annihilation" (*der Vernichtungskrieg*), which was supposed to work as follows:

Because Russia was so geographically extensive and would take a considerable time to achieve full mobilization, it provided an opportunity first to destroy the French army in a "lightning war," a *Blitzkrieg*, that would be completed in a few weeks, as had been the case in 1870; and then, having annihilated the French, the bulk of the German army could be turned eastward to bring their smaller holding army against Russia up to full strength in that sector. Superior German armament, rail networks, and planning would take care of the slower-mobilizing Russians in time for all German soldiers to be home for Christmas. That was the concept bequeathed by von Schlieffen. Commentators have pointed out that it *militarized* German diplomacy even more.[10]

9. The studies of the famous plan called in German *Aufmarschplan gegen Frankreich* range from the apologeticm, such as Ritter, *Schlieffen Plan*, to the increasingly critical: Bucholz, *Moltke, Schlieffen*; Ehlert, ed., *Schlieffen Plan*; Wallach, *Dogma of the War of Annihilation*.

10. Fischer, *Krieg der Illusionen*, ch. 18, in English as *War of Illusions*. The remarkable thing about the German leadership's adherence to the Schlieffen Plan was that Schlieffen disregarded the political implications of the consequences of the violation of Belgian neutrality, which would automatically trigger British intervention. But as Fritz Fischer has pointed out (pp. 567–68), the possibility of a British expeditionary force appearing

What seems incredible from today's standpoint is that the civilian leadership, namely the Chancellor and cabinet, were not informed of crucial details. The most important one was that the plan in the West required the Germany army to march through neutral Belgium to be able as quickly as possible to get into position north of Paris to lay siege again to the city. Another German army was intended simultaneously to drive across the Rhine in the south and envelope Paris from that direction. As stressed, it was meant to be over in weeks, a "super-Cannae," as von Schlieffen called it in an allusion to the famous Punic Wars of antiquity. And it nearly worked. So, what frustrated it? To begin with, Belgium would not remain supine and permit foreign forces to march in unopposed without offering stubborn resistance. Secondly, the plan took no account of the intervention of the British on behalf of Belgium, with whom they had a treaty dating from 1839 (the London Protocol). Von Schlieffen may have considered a British intervention, but he regarded it as a mere irritation in the conviction that the British reputedly could not fight a land war, as witnessed by their dismal performance in the South African war against the Boers.

With hindsight one would have to say that von Schlieffen was at the very least basing his assessments on prejudice, because what really frustrated his finely tuned timetable from working was the intervention of the British Expeditionary Force in support of the French. The British infantry's ability to shoot rapid fire, a lesson learned from the humiliating experience in South Africa, played an essential role in holding up the German army, poised as it was in September 1914 to encircle Paris. It was stopped at the Battle of the Marne, September 6–12, just fifty kilometers from Paris by combined Anglo-French resistance.

The conclusion to be drawn was that the decision to march through Belgium automatically involved the British in the war on the side of the French and this fact contributed spectacularly to the inevitable collapse of the putatively infallible Schlieffen Plan. The point, however, is that it was both *politically* and *militarily* flawed to start with. After the war in his memoirs Chancellor Bethmann Hollweg admitted as much. In fact, when he had finally learned that the plan would automatically provoke the British, his nerve was effectively broken. The real government of Germany

---

in the West was not taken seriously. Further, it was decisive in German thinking that the plan could with relative ease complete the annihilation of any Western forces.

devolved into the hands of a politically incompetent, indeed brainwashed cadre of military zealots driven by fantastic dreams and delusions.[11]

The Continuation of the War of Annihilation: The Triumph of Irrationality

The failure of the Schlieffen Plan resulted in the appointment of a new commanding officer, namely Erich von Falkenhayn. He replaced the younger von Moltke on September 14, 1914. Falkenhayn believed, or rather affected to believe, he might still be able to achieve the original war aims in the West and the East, though he knew that the resources in both men and material were simply not adequate to the gigantic task. Indeed, the new commander-in-chief was never really himself totally sure that the military obstacles confronting Germany could be overcome. Already on August 4, 1914, at the very beginning of hostilities, Falkenhayn is reported as saying, "If in this undertaking we should be defeated, it was still a wonderful thing." In the original: "*Wenn wir auch darüber untergehen, schön war's doch.*" Expressed alternatively: "We feel obliged to go through with this even though it could, in all probability, end in disaster."[12]

Certainly, the situation simply became worse with the passage of time. Falkenhayn told the chancellor on November 18, 1914, "So long as Russia, France and England hold together it will be impossible for us to bring off a victory." Indeed Falkenhayn would have preferred to make a separate peace with each of them, but he appreciated that it was ruled out by the Allied negotiations in London on September 4–5, 1914, which obliged the three Allies to maintain a united front against Germany.[13] It is indeed not easy to explain the mentality of the German leadership in this dilemma; on the one hand they could grasp that pressing on could lead to a pointless catastrophe, but on the other hand they did not have the will or nerve to admit it openly. Consequently, they inflicted on the world four years of

11. Bethmann Hollweg, *Reflections on the World War*. See also Röhl and Roth , *Aus dem grossen Hauptquatier*, 116. Riezler, who was personal assistant to Chancellor Bethmann Hollweg, was present at the most high-level war-planning discussions and confided to his fiancé on August 24, 1914 from the army headquarters in Coblenz that the military were raving mad and wanted to annex half the world. (*Die Militärs sind ganz rabiat und wollen die halbe Welt annektieren*). For a perceptive analysis of Chancellor Bethmann Hollweg's marginalized role in war planning, see Jarausch, *Enigmatic Chancellor.*

12. Afflerbach, *Falkenhayn.*

13. Fischer, *Griff*, 218–19.

unprecedented mayhem in the illusion that a German-dominated *Mittel-europa* could be established in the long term, meaning permanent German control of the east of France, all of Belgium in the West, and all eastern Central Europe up to the Urals in Siberia. As well it was expected to gain control of all the African and Asian colonies of the conquered powers, including the British dominions in the Pacific. In short, the so-called pan-German illusion had captured the hearts and minds of even the most responsible of German statesmen. Only the Social Democrats and a few convinced pacifists consistently wanted peace based on the pre-1914 borders.

By failing to draw the logical conclusions from the collapse of the Schlieffen Plan, the German leadership both civil and military presided over the end of the old-world order of empires and laid the ground for the Second World War and ultimately the Cold War. In a word, the Great War of 1914–18 was the seedbed of all the world's subsequent crises, not least because one Austrian corporal came out of it with a determination to complete what the German General Staff had failed to accomplish for Germany at that time. But he wanted even more as the latest research divulges.

THE HITLER PHENOMENON

It is necessary first to know what the war aims of imperial Germany were and how the leadership tried to achieve them to comprehend what the "new Germany" after 1933 had set out to do.[14] In the beginning of this section, it was postulated that Adolf Hitler was the most successful religious leader of the twentieth century. For many that would be a problematic statement, except when it is realized that there were/are not a few religious fanatics in the world such as the late Osama Bin Laden who were/are quite happy to plunge the world into flames to accomplish their objectives. When these aims are supposedly derived from Allah himself (or providence), then it is perhaps not quite so bizarre as it might initially sound.

One needs to ask: what is a political-religious leader supposed to do? His aim is to unify the nation by convincing the people that he is called by almighty God (or some higher force) to accomplish great things in his/its name. Bear in mind that Germany lost the Great War in the most humiliating circumstances; the *Kaiser* was forced to abdicate and all the princely ruling houses in the Reich were deposed, homeland territory

---

14. Moses with Overlack, *First Know Your Enemy*.

was slashed, colonies ceded to the victorious powers, a huge reparations bill imposed, and the Rhineland occupied by French, Belgian, British, and American troops.[15] There was understandably a massive feeling of resentment, especially toward France and Britain. Further, the unprecedented postwar inflation compounded the degradation being felt, especially by the middle classes, who lost all their savings to boot.

On top of all that the new republican constitution of the Weimar Republic did not engender universal pride, many people seeing it as a kind of imposition by the victorious Allies. The US president, Woodrow Wilson, had stipulated earlier that any peace negotiations could only be undertaken with a popularly elected German government. So, conservative Germans harbored a grievance that they were pressured into constitutional change against their will. As well there was much debate over the "stab in the back," meaning that the Germans could still have won better peace conditions had there not been so many strikes and anti-war propaganda instigated by Social Democrats, Communists, and Jews, that were allegedly detrimental to the army's morale and fighting power.

The Nazi Party having become the diagonal within this parallelogram of forces was the product of these circumstances. This party had grown from very modest beginnings to become the most destructive force in world history up to that time. It had developed out of a small group of disgruntled unemployed ex-servicemen in Munich who called themselves the German Workers' Party. Adolf Hitler joined in September 1919 as the fifty-fifth member. After the war he had been hospitalized from wounds sustained gallantly doing his duty, and for that he had been awarded two Iron Crosses. It was in hospital that he abandoned his original ambition to become an artist and instead decided to work on becoming a politician. Soon afterward Hitler, still in the army, was employed as a so-called *Schulungsredner*, a lecturer whose job it was to instruct recruits in anti-Communist propaganda. This was deemed important because there had been a short-lived Soviet-style revolution in Bavaria and Munich was a city in political turmoil. The army was in any case at odds with the new republican federal constitution, so the political situation was extremely unstable. It was under these conditions that Hitler's rhetorical talents came to the fore.[16]

---

15. The occupation lasted from December 1918 until June 1930, although the American contingent was withdrawn in 1924.

16. Fully recounted in Kershaw, *Hitler*, 1:221–428.

How Hitler Became the Savior (*Heiland*)

The point has often been made that nothing Hitler believed in or said was original. Regarding his anti-Semitism, his hostility to the Treaty of Versailles, and his hatred of Social Democracy and Communism, he was simply a normal German.[17] In fact, he just expressed in a more vigorous way what the resentments and prejudices of most people were. No doubt also he was uniquely able to train himself to become a professional agitator, brilliant for the circumstances of the time because his appeal was like that of a revivalist preacher, a religious rabble-rouser. One may account for Hitler's rapport with the German population as follows:

First, there must be an audience of dispirited, downtrodden people who are yearning for a savior figure (*Heiland*) to deliver them from their despair. After the defeat of 1918 and the severe peace treaty of 1919, most Germans were in that category.

Second, this misery and degradation is not their fault. The agitator in the case of post-Versailles Germany could easily point to the "stab in the back." If it had not been for the Socialists and the Jews, the defeat would not have occurred, so the latter groups were blamed. Bear in mind that for an agitator to be successful s/he needs to have easily identifiable scapegoats.

Third, the savior must be able to convince the population that s/he has the answers to their problems and has the ability and determination that will lead them out of their misery to glorious times ahead if only they believe. And this is where the religious element is most obvious. Hitler repeatedly used the word "providence" (*die Vorsehung*) in his speeches. It was his euphemism for God, and in the official Nazi Party program it says they believe in a "positive Christianity" (*ein positives Christentum*), although Hitler had long since abandoned the Roman Catholicism of his birth and most of the party leadership would have had less than orthodox views about the church. Nevertheless, the rhetoric was sufficient to convince normal churchgoers that there was nothing in the Nazi Party program that the churches could not endorse.

Fourth—and this is the key to the demagogue's success—he addresses a downtrodden people but persuades the multitude that he cou-can deliver the nation out of its despair and lead it to its true destiny,

17. This assessment of Hitler was advanced in 1963 by the English historian A. J. P. Taylor, *Origins of the Second World War*. See the 1972 summary of the controversy on it by W. R. Louis, ed., *Origins of the Second World War*.

an objective that the nation had been cheated out of by the "November criminals."[18] So, the demagogue establishes a *vertical* link between the despondent masses with what they think is the will of God. It is a way of lifting the spirits of the humiliated, to tell them that by following the demagogue or prophet they will renew their identity as proud, successful, and ambitious Germans. Indeed, with their restored dignity they will take back what the internal enemy, the Jews and socialists, as well as the external enemy, the French and the British, had so wrongfully deprived them. That is the *vertical* function of the demagoguery. And there is a *horizontal* one, and that means telling the masses that they are all in this together. "We are all brothers and sisters in a common struggle against both the internal and external enemy. We are united against all those who would deny us out rightful place in history." The universal sense of grievance unites everybody across the classes from aristocracy, the bourgeoisie to even to sections of the non-socialist working class.

So, when Hitler began his demagoguery in Munich during the *Kampfzeit der Bewegung,* meaning the struggle period of the movement, this is what he did, and the pattern never changed. He was able to transform a minority party into the most remarkable mass movement in history to that point. And there was no doubt that it was a religious movement. Why? Because religion functions to give people a sense of solidarity. And this solidarity engenders self-worth and a transcendental goal. Hitler said in effect, "Follow me and I will make you into somebody again, a nation whom the world not only respects but also fears." And that appeals to the bully psychology in people: "We will avenge that which was wrongfully taken from us in the defeat of 1918–19."

This formula had remarkable success. The trouble is that it had to lead to another war for it to be sustained. One cannot promise "I will lead you to glorious times" without being ready with military force to smash all putative enemies. This is the warlord dimension that the famous German sociologist Max Weber wrote about even before Hitler came to power. Indeed, he pointed out that the phenomenon of the charismatic politician, the demagogue, was one of the greatest revolutionary forces in history. However, the charismatic authority derives not from the

---

18. "November criminals" refers to all those groups within the German empire, such as Social Democrats, trade unionists, Communists, liberals, and other democrats, and of course, Jews, who endorsed the German surrender in November 1918. They were those Germans who saw the utter pointlessness of trying to prolong the war. See Kautsky, *Diktatur des Proletariats.*

recognition of the masses; rather it comes from the ability of the demagogue to fulfill the goals he has set for the nation by the convincing power of his demagoguery. The people unanimously place their faith in him as a duty but only for as long as the leader can deliver on his promises. Once he fails to deliver, then he has lost legitimacy. On leadership theory there is a vast literature, but Max Weber is the classic authority and there is still a lot of warlord-ism virulent in the world today.[19]

Weber makes here a key observation. In categorizing warlords as religious leaders he was making an entirely value-free judgment. This means that the main characteristic is the capacity to articulate goals that resonate with the masses. Weber listed, for example, prophets and demagogues alongside figures like Pericles, Jesus, and Napoleon. The decisive thing is whether the charisma of the leader had validity and efficacy. But once these aspects have been shown to be empty of meaning, then the demagogue had no further legitimacy. The point is that rulers of this type must keep urging the attainment of ever more ambitious goals to sustain and justify the loyalty of their people and the continuity of the movement. That becomes very dangerous because the leader will be forced sooner or later to undertake projects for which the resources are just not available. Hitler's career illustrates all these characteristics. He could never settle down and simply name a successor like a traditional king; Hitler's kind of rule had to end in his destruction together with that of his supporters. The fact that Admiral Dönitz (1891–1980) tried ineffectually to take over after Hitler's suicide proves the point. The situation was beyond retrieval.[20]

Was Hitler Another "Enigmatic Chancellor"?

The enigma of Hitler is really the enigma of the German people. They celebrated him as a savior, except for major groups such as the Social Democrats, Communists, and some genuine liberals and pacifists. Most bourgeois elements succumbed to his demagoguery. Even those who were decent middle-class people who thought that Hitler was a dangerous clown mostly endorsed his anti-Jewish policies and his foreign policy against both the communist East and the liberal West. In short, there was a deeply engrained fear of Communism and an intense

---

19. Weber, *Soziologie, Universalgeschichtliche Analysen, Politik,* 159–85 *passim.* Here the themes of charismatic leadership and politics as vocation are developed.

20. On Grand Admiral Dönitz, see Dönitz, *Memoirs.*

resentment of France and Britain. Hitler had indeed something for everybody, except Jews, Gypsies, Slavs, and socialists of all shades. So, individuals did not have to buy the complete Nazi package to approve of Hitler and his system; any one of the aforementioned goals could suffice to attract a German subject to support Hitler. On the other hand if one had something to criticize, one learned to keep it to oneself. It was, after all, a terrorist regime.

Hitler and the Continuity of German History

There was an argument that without Hitler there would have been no National Socialism and no Second World War.[21] That is like putting the blame for everything that went wrong on the one individual, and that is manifestly untenable. Nevertheless, Hitler, the "Bohemian corporal," managed to pull all German racial prejudices and military aspirations together with enormous success, at least initially. There are political fanatics in all countries. At the time of Hitler there was a fascist party in England led by Sir Oswald Mosley. Even in Australia there was a fascist party called the New Guard.[22] Essentially they were regarded as a lunatic fringe, but not in Germany. Why? Because the wire-pullers within the German social structure, especially the financial and industrial elite and the army, helped the demagogue Hitler into power. The chief blame, however, must rest with the German officer corps, aided and abetted by German industrialists.[23]

It was the officer corps, though, that could have prevented Hitler and the Nazi Party from gaining power if they had chosen. If one traces the behavior of the German Officer Corps in the final stages of the Weimar Republic (1919–1933), it will be seen that they had seized the opportunity to get rid of the constitution and to free Germany from the restrictive conditions of the Treaty of Versailles. Consequently, they did not lift a finger to ensure during the great economic crisis that the successive governments could weather the storm; on the contrary, they wanted to be rid of the Weimar system, repudiate Versailles, rebuild the German army, and pursue those goals of territorial expansion that had

---

21. Orlow, *History of the Nazi Party.* Still of some value is the collection of essays edited by Gerhard Hirschfeld and Lothar Kettenacker, *"Führerstaat."*

22. Amos, *New Guard 1931–1935*; Moore, *Secret Army and the Premier.*

23. Of relevance here is Orlow, *History of the Nazi Party.*

been frustrated in 1919. All they needed was a government that would underwrite these aims. The army needed Hitler and Hitler needed the army.[24] So, that means there were deep-seated imperialist ambitions within the officer caste, but not only them, of course. The realization of these ambitions was understood as Prussia-Germany's very purpose for existence. If they could not be realized, then there was no point to Germany. And Hitler had imbibed the same ideology, namely that if a state was not expanding, it was declining.[25]

How Hitler Became a God

This is crucial to understand, and what helps here is Hitler's attitude to the Nazi private army, the *Sturmabteilung* (or "Brown Shirts"; this English term is from the German nickname, *Braunhemden*, not the formal name, *Sturmabteilung*). which under the leadership of Ernst Röhm (1887–1934) reached the impressive size of well over one million men, compared to only one hundred thousand in the regular army. It was Röhm's ambition after Hitler had seized power at the end of January 1933 to absorb the regular army into the SA, and that would have made him the most powerful man in the Reich. Hitler was faced with an internal threat to his leadership. Consequently, he could not tolerate any rival and, what is of key significance, he needed the military expertise of the old imperial Officer Corps for his long-term goals. The ragtag mob of Brownshirts was of no use here. So, he had two compelling reasons to eliminate Ernst Röhm.

How Hitler did this should have been an indication to the Officer Corps of Hitler's opportunism and lack of principles if they had not already drawn that conclusion. Hitler simply used his own private bodyguard, the SS (*Schutzstaffel*—the Blackshirts), to arrest Röhm and his lieutenants at the hotel in Bavaria, where they had been celebrating in a homosexual party on June 30, 1934. They were all then summarily shot in the prison where they were being held. Hitler then three days later had the Reichstag pass a law legitimizing the atrocity by alleging it was

24. Fischer, *From Kaiserreich to Third Reich* and *Hitler war kein Betriebsunfall.*

25. Srbik, *Geist und Geschichte*, 1:385–95. Here the Austrian historian designates Treitschke as the priest and prophet of the German Reich as a power state—"*des deutschen national Machtstaates*" (386), and goes on to affirm that the essence of the state was first power, secondly power and again thirdly power: "*Das Wesen des Staates ist zum ersten Macht, zum zweiten Macht und zum dritten wieder Macht*" (394). For Treitschke, weakness in a state was a sin against the Holy Ghost (398). See also Dorpalen, *Heinrich von Treitschke*, 149–53.

in defense of the state. The SA was then greatly reduced and rendered politically ineffectual.[26]

Hitler's next step was to conciliate the army, and this he did by requiring the officers and men to swear an oath of personal allegiance to him as *Führer* and supreme army commander at a ceremony in Berlin. The timing of this is of key significance. The elderly President Hindenburg had died in office on August 2, 1934. Within an hour Hitler announced that he wanted to merge in his person the office of chancellor with that of president, namely to become head of state as well as supreme commander of the army. To do this he had a law passed that was signed by leading personages of the conservative and military elite. By doing so they unwittingly signed away any further political influence they might have had. Few people had grasped what the so-called *Führerprinzip* really implied. In short, Hitler's self-perception had not been internalized by many people, even those close to him.[27]

The leadership principle of the Nazi party postulated that all political will in the nation emanated from the will of the leader. Everybody—man, woman, and child—regardless of rank, to be loyal Germans had to submit their individual will to him in a way not dissimilar to that required from people living under Communism; political will is determined by the party and in practice by the chief secretary.

Consequently, Hitler introduced a new revolutionary political concept that was an affront to all thinking people—conservatives, liberals, socialists, and in particular Christians. Obviously, the Western Enlightenment heritage celebrated the autonomy of the individual to be free to adopt or reject the storehouse of ideas in the Western tradition. And of course Christians are meant to conform their will to that of Jesus of Nazareth. Here it needs to be kept in mind that 95 percent of Germans were baptized Christians of all denominations and that included army personnel. Hitler was now going to apply the leadership principle to the army, requiring all soldiers to swear the following oath of loyalty, not to the constitution as before, but to the person of Adolf Hitler:

> I swear by God this sacred oath: I will render unconditional obedience to the *Führer* of the German Reich and People, Adolf Hitler, the supreme commander of the Armed Forces, and will

26. Hancock, *Ernst Röhm.*
27. Pangritz, "Dietrich Bonhoeffers Begründung."

be ready, as a brave soldier, to stake my life at any time for this
oath.[28]

This was indeed a revolutionary move; it placed the person of Hitler on
the plane of almighty God. Even the past German princes and emperors
saw themselves merely as servants of God, the ultimate authority, but
not Hitler; he was the savior, the *Heiland*, god of an entirely new religion. And his chief acolytes were to be the Officer Corps, the generals,
many of whom had already sworn an oath to the *Kaiser* and had pangs of
conscience about the oath that Hitler demanded of them. But this is the
key point: the vast majority bludgeoned their conscience into submission
and uttered the oath of loyalty to Hitler, a monumental error of judgment, and one needs to enquire why. The answer is because they wanted
to realize the old war aims of the *Kaiser's* time that had been frustrated
by Versailles. In short, these men sold their birthright to the devil for a
"mess of pottage" and thereby made Hitler's war aims seem achievable.

To be sure, a few of senior officers later resigned in the belief that
Hitler's war aims would only lead to yet another catastrophic outcome.
As well, a few concluded that the oath was not binding since Hitler was
an imprudent, reckless leader whose policies were simply far too dangerous. This was the basis of the officers' revolt, but it came very late, after the
disaster of Stalingrad (autumn–winter 1942), for example, when it was
obvious to at least some high-ranking officers that Germany's defeat was
inevitable.[29] But the point is that most officers were seduced into supporting Hitler, giving their oath in the belief that the "Bohemian corporal"
could accomplish what the *Kaiser's* generals in 1914–1918 could not.

Further, Hitler had the same effect on the senior public servants as
well as the educated middle classes. Although he was not a traditional
Christian German prince and had declared war on loyal German subjects
on racial grounds, he seemed capable of leading Germany to world domination, which the majority believed was to be the nation's destiny under
almighty God. In short, the German officer corps and the educated middle classes, despite possible reservations about Hitler's methods, willingly

28. Bullock, *Hitler*, 309. See also Erdmann, *Zeit der Wetkriege*, 382; Kershaw, *Hitler*,
1:524–26.

29. Ulrich, *Stalingrad*. On October 6, 1842, Hitler ordered the occupation of Stalingrad. He had not taken account of the material and morale recovery of the Soviet
army, which enabled their encirclement and siege of the key city that ended in the massive defeat of the *Wehrmacht* whose leaders believed their initial success in occupying
Stalingrad had guaranteed them virtual victory in the East. Instead it ended with the
greatest German military disaster hitherto (Ulrich, 56–57).

followed him by placing their undoubted expertise at his disposal and thus made the initial military successes possible.

After the war, in a spirit of self-recrimination many Germans used to say that the disaster was all attributable to a deception, *ein Betrug*, or the *Konzeptionslosigkeit* of the nation's elite, meaning the poverty of alternative ideas as to how to deal with political problems. That was no doubt true, but it was combined also with a peculiar *Charakterlosigkeit*, namely a lack of character and an absence of sound judgment and determination on the part of those officers and bureaucrats who should have known better. One needed to stand up against the foolhardy extravagances that the *Führer* insisted on and that predictably led to his downfall in May 1945. The big question is why intelligent people allowed themselves to be deceived by someone so manifestly fraudulent as Hitler. One possible answer was the tradition in German education and politics to give unquestioning obedience to those in office.

So, finally, it would be a mistake to underestimate the values of Western systems of education system, based as they are on liberal constitutional principles. They stand in stark contrast to those of the Germans at the time of the Second and Third Reichs. Most of Hitler's countrymen and women, who had for centuries been brainwashed to render unconditional obedience to the powers-that-be, opted for the prophet of a grotesquely false religion based on the myth of racial superiority of the so-called Aryan race and that the Jews and Slavs were not people but vermin to be enslaved and worked to death. Political culture is clearly not an insignificant factor in the history of the world. It challenges historians always to look over fence into the backyards of neighboring states to identify nuances of cultural differences out of which peculiar ideas and values emerge that could lead to frictions and then to violent confrontations.

Adolf Hitler as Prophet of the New World Religion: The Apotheosis of Race over Humanity

On May 10, 1941 a sensational announcement came over radios around the world. Anxious citizens were daily listening for news of the war: Rudolf Hess, Hitler's Deputy *Führer* was reported to have commandeered a fighter plane, which had been equipped with two extra fuel tanks to enable him to fly directly from Augsburg in southern Bavaria to Scotland. His intention, unbeknownst to Hitler, was to try to persuade the British government through the mediation of the Duke of Hamilton to change sides and join the German campaign against the Soviet Union to combat the threat of world Bolshevism. Rudolf Hess was clearly a desperate man, then aged forty-seven, to have undertaken the escapade, which ended when his plane finally ran out of fuel, causing him bail out and parachute into a crofter's field just south of Glasgow. On hitting the ground Hess severely injured an ankle. A startled farmer, totally baffled by this unexpected visitation from the sky, rushed out to investigate and to render first aid to the mysterious aviator.

Hess, who spoke fluent English, explained why he had come, and the farmer notified the local home guard, who took Hess to see the duke. Once it was clear why he had so unexpectedly dropped in, Hess was taken to London to see Prime Minister Winston Churchill. At this point the reportage of the incident becomes apocryphal. It was rumored that when Hess was shown into Churchill's office, the PM allegedly greeted him with words, "Ah, you are the lunatic [*Wahnsinniger*] from Berlin." But Hess hastened to correct him, saying, "No, not at all. I am only his deputy."

Regardless of the literal veracity of this story, it was indeed a bizarre situation because when Hitler heard of it, he declared Hess to be insane and ordered him to be shot on sight should he be returned to Germany. And according to the Geneva Conventions Hess could have been repatriated as a wounded and mentally disturbed POW but instead he was securely detained in various places including the historic Tower of London for the duration of the war and in October 1945 was sent to Nuremberg for trial. Far from being criminally insane, Hess had made a judgment about the war situation and genuinely believed that Germany should combine with the Western powers to stop the advance of the Soviet Union across Europe.

Obviously, this was an unworkable plan given the firm arrangements already in place among the British, American, and Russian governments. It was Hitler who was regarded as being criminally insane. But whether he was or just fanatically deluded is a question that still challenges both psychiatrists and historians. And this makes finding a convincing explanation for Nazi racial and foreign policy an unusually complex exercise that continues to attract investigators internationally.

There is now an attempt that goes beyond relating what Hitler planned and perpetrated as such eminent biographers as Joachim Fest and more recently Ian Kershaw and several others have done. First, one notes that while it is relatively straightforward to establish what Hitler planned and how he went about it, the present concern is with what was going on in Hitler's mind, from where he got his ideas; in short what really motivated him and why so many Germans followed their *Führer's* exhortations. The most recent scholarly contribution to unraveling this problem is by the aforementioned Dr. Stefan Heep of Cologne, in his extensive research report published in the journal *Zeitschrift für Religionswissenschaften*.[30]

Previously, the major authority for identifying a religious motivation in determining Hitler's appeal to the German masses was the article by the famous Swiss psychiatrist Carl Gustav Jung entitled "Wotan," published in *Neue Schweizer Rundschau*, March 11, 1936. Therein Jung apostrophized Hitler as a figure resembling the mythical Teutonic god Wotan or Odin. An incendiary troublemaker with restless explosive energy, Wotan went around startling humanity with his ferocious outbursts. This underlying restlessness had surged up at times of political crisis in Germany when the population needed a leader or savior figure who would rescue them from perdition.

Professor Jung's reportage was made after he had attended the Nuremberg Nazi Party rally September 8–14, 1936. Since then, via Jung, the explanation for Hitler's public appeal has challenged both historians and psychiatrists. History is full of examples of warlords in various civilizations who have arisen in times of despair to proclaim a message of salvation to their people. Such manifestations have even arisen in politically stable countries like the United Kingdom or Australia, where the would-be leaders of National Socialist movements such as Sir Oswald Mosely in the UK and Eric Campbell in Australia enjoyed short periods of notoriety. Perhaps the closest example of expressions of mass enthusiasm in British Commonwealth countries, however, occurred from early 1959 when the American evangelist Billy Graham toured both Australia and New Zealand for almost four months. It is estimated that during that period he attracted audiences totalling more than three million people. They came to hear his message of salvation and conversion. Remarkably, these normally hard-nosed and sceptical citizens[31] flocked in their tens of thousands into the Melbourne Cricket Ground, Sydney's Randwick Racecourse, and the Brisbane Exhibition Ground and other venues to hear the liberating message of the gospel according to Billy. That message

30. Heep, "Heilige in Erscheinung," 323–78.

31. Billy Graham toured Australia and New Zealand four times starting in 1959 and following up in 1968–1969.

was disarmingly straightforward. All one needed to do was to accept Jesus Christ as one's personal savior. In the process Dr. Graham had given a textbook illustration that values are culturally conditioned and his were the product of the American fundamentalist evangelical tradition, which had clearly resonated among like-minded Australian and New Zealand cousins. There is a remarkable religious naivety evident with the broader *petit bourgeois* Anglo-Saxon community.

In the case of twentieth-century Germany, Jung's explanation for the Hitler phenomenon had gained considerable currency. The renowned Swiss psychiatrist had traveled from Zürich to Nuremberg for that 1936 Nazi Party rally, listened to Hitler's speeches, and imbibed the febrile militaristic atmosphere that had been spectacularly contrived by Hitler's chief architect, Albert Speer. Jung then returned home and published his remarkable essay. Through his impassioned oratory Hitler was able to arouse the German masses out of their post-Versailles humiliation and despair to recover their identity as the "master race" and from there go on to revive and realize the frustrated war aims of 1914–1918, to which many educated Germans believed that the nation was being called by providence.

It was widely accepted in those patriotic circles in Germany that those great aims had been frustrated not by superior Allied forces but by the *stab in the back* from treacherous socialists and from profiteering Jewish business tycoons, both of which were elements totally alien to people of pure Aryan blood. In short, Hitler mobilized the stab-in-the-back legend to dramatic effect. In this way Jung explained Hitler's electoral successes during the Great Depression and the subsequent enthusiastic endorsement that he had witnessed in 1936 at the Nazi Party rally. Indeed, it must be kept in mind, even if one is sceptical about Jung's speculations about the reawakened spirit of *Wotan*, that his explanation of Hitler's appeal to the masses certainly makes sense. Germans had suffered not only the bitter humiliation of defeat and the impositions of the punitive Treaty of Versailles in 1919, but they had also been victims of the subsequent great inflation that had pauperized especially the once prosperous middle classes. Hitler's oratory was able to restore confidence in the nation and mobilize a will to rise phoenix-like from the ashes of despair.

Jung's portrayal of Hitler as a quasi-resurrected Wotan, that is, a religious figure, had earlier been noticed by a Russian-born political scientist in Germany who ventured to explain Hitler's appeal as a religious prophet. He was Professor Waldemar Gurian (1902–1954), who had in the meantime migrated to the USA and taught at Notre Dame. There he published *Hitler and the Christians* in 1936, explaining that Hitler perceived himself as the authentic champion of the history of salvation, namely that Germany was called through him by providence to eradicate Judaism, Christianity, as well as Marxism-Leninism, all of which propagated their separate salvation stories and in doing so were sources of inner discord. They were responsible for the widespread sectarian hostility on the one hand and for the pointless class struggle on the other. Hitler by virtue of his persuasive oratorical gifts propagated a revised version of a national, secular, non-party political faith, that is, a faith in the *Volk* to a highly receptive national audience. This proved to be an infallible formula for German resurgence. There would be no more quarrelling political parties but a stoutly united nation of people of the one blood.

Professor Gurian noted that already in 1874 one publicist named Paul de Lagarde had predicted that Bismarck's Second Reich was destined to become the truly racially unified nation in which Roman Catholicism on the one hand and Protestantism on the other would be eventually cast upon the dung heap of history, having been displaced by the national German religion, a religion based exclusively on the notion of racial purity. And prominent among the numerous authors who inspired Hitler was, first, the quirkish Englishman Huston Stewart Chamberlain (1855– 1927), Richard Wagner's son-in-law, who had published *The Foundations of the Nineteenth Century* in 1899, and then Alfred Rosenberg, author of *The Myth of the Twentieth Century* (1933). In the latter case this qualified Rosenberg to be made Hitler's minister for education and culture. All this prompts the question: just how much of the Nazi ideology did Hitler himself contribute?

One answer is provided by the German American historian Dietrich Orlow, who taught that National Socialism would never have had such influence over the German people were it not for the unique personality of Hitler driving it. The "Bohemian corporal" himself was the very embodiment of National Socialism. There is indeed a school of historians who say in effect that National Socialism was impossible without the peculiar personality of the *Führer* figure Adolf Hitler. This is strenuously maintained even though there is a long archaeology of anti-Semitism, anti-parliamentarism, and Prusso-German militarism and imperialism, all of which provided the necessary matrix out of which National Socialism obviously took root and flourished. As the Hamburg professor Fritz Fischer after the Second World War never tired of emphasizing, there was an undeniable continuity between the *Kaiserreich* and the Third Reich. None of that, of course, denied that Hitler possessed certain unique messianic qualities that enabled him to proclaim what the mass of the German population, and more particularly the Officer Corps, wanted to hear.

With all that in mind it needs to be recalled that 95 percent of Germans were baptized Christians, either Protestant or Roman Catholic, and a considerable number of these had joined in the so-called *Kirchenkampf* or "church struggle" to maintain independence from being forced into a pro-Hitler *Reichkirche*. This meant that Hitler could not frontally attack Christianity but had to present his message of salvation in a way not overtly in conflict with what most Germans believed. He was convinced that he had discovered from his reading of the above-mentioned authors, as well as influential German historians such as Heinrich von Treitschke and Leopold von Ranke, as the Stuttgart professor Eberhard Jäckel has shown, that he had discovered a better substitute for Christianity that was based on insights derived from his understanding of the superiority of the Teutonic race over all others. This was a typical Hitlerian doctrine that people were meant to believe but not necessarily understand. It became a new ethic based on a doctrine of social Darwinism and eugenics but was presented to appear reconcilable with Christianity. But it was precisely here, that is, with such policies as euthanasia and the persecution of the Jews, that Hitler encountered feisty opponents among certain church leaders such as Cardinal von Galen, and from Protestants, most notably the theologians Karl Barth and Dietrich Bonhoeffer.

That said, the idea of a *Volksgemeinschaft*, the "national community" to which the individual should selflessly sacrifice herself for the well-being of the whole, could easily be accepted as deriving from Christianity since it prioritized self-abnegation in the service of others. In short, Hitler's ideas, as now emphasized by Stefan Heep, followed formally the pattern of the Christian apocalypse, but his goal was not the beatific vision in an afterlife but an earthly kingdom, namely the permanent domination of the world by the Teutonic race. This explanation conflicts, of course, with the view that Hitler never wanted a final goal of eternal peace or victory over Germany's enemies and that he insisted on the need to keep fighting to preserve the National Socialist movement alive while the identity of the enemy remained essentially undefined on purpose. That the Jews as such were targeted was purely incidental. They were just a convenient scapegoat. Hitler's priority was allegedly permanent warfare. Could that have been his true objective?

Stefan Heep observes that obviously Hitler needed first to establish the *Ostimperium*, an empire in the East as the firm basis from which to expand and assert worldwide Teutonic racial superiority. And the optimum means of achieving this was because only in war could the best human material be forged, and so in order that this winnowing process could proceed undisturbed all Jews had to be eliminated from the Reich, and at the same time the chief ideological opponent, namely Bolshevism, had to be crushed and this required the ruthless campaign against the Soviet Union. This was a goal that could take decades, even centuries, to reach before the "new species being," namely the completely racially pure German Aryan, could be evolved and in a position finally to eradicate all Jews. When that was accomplished, world domination would be secured.

Heep's explanation continues by observing that because the course of the war was not proceeding smoothly according to the original plan Hitler had to recalibrate, so the objective to eradicate all Jews had to be ramped up together with the plans for much increased territorial expansion. Then there had to be a decisive battle that would mark the final achievement of the Third Reich. The revolutionary system of government that Hitler had initiated in January 1933 with the Nazi seizure of power provided the impetus for the movement. The idea cultivated by some of his lieutenants, namely that Nazism was all about eternal war, a war religion without resolution, meaning permanent war as the history of salvation, was certainly not what Hitler intended. What then did he really have in mind?

Essentially, Hitler wanted to create a Germandom (*Deutschtum*) that corresponded to his understanding of Judaism (*Judentum*), namely a prescription for life that followed the law of God. This expunged all foreign influences so that the identity of the new people of God might be preserved unadulterated. Indeed, the will of God, namely the commandment to love God and neighbor, was perceived now as a social Darwinist law of nature; the right of the strongest. Interestingly, Hitler acquired this from the Jewish Bible, that is, from the Ten Commandments, which, surprising as it may seem, are pre-eminently racist because they are meant to apply only to people of Jewish blood and sexist because women are designated mere chattels alongside cattle and worldly goods. As a Jew one was required to love one's neighbor and hate one's enemies. *Neighbor*, however, is exclusively someone of one's own tribe, not anyone of the surrounding tribes. One should note here parenthetically that Jesus of Nazareth, in his

Sermon on the Mount, revolutionized this commandment when he said, as recorded in Matthew 5:43–44:

> Ye have heard that it hath been said, Thou shalt love thy neighbor and hate thine enemy. But I say unto you, Love your enemies, bless them that curse you, do good to them that hate you, and pray for them who despitefully use you and persecute you.

In one sense it could be argued then that National Socialism was nothing more than Judaism turned on its head. Indeed, for the orthodox Jew the will of God was/is unequivocally racial legislation. Other races/peoples were excluded from the history of salvation. The Nazi worldview parallels this schema. By their compliance with the will of God the Germans in Hitler's view would be rewarded with the entire world as their fiefdom to enable them to establish a paradise on earth. Then the Aryan human being, who was both physically and intellectually superior, would stand as a model for all humanity. Indeed, Dr. Heep's schema is a challenging one. However, before being tempted to regard it as purveying fantasy, it is pointed out that this scenario was well understood by the German people: Israel inherits the promised land as a fiefdom in which the Jewish *Volk* would through its unique relationship with God sanctify itself and become the ethical model, leading all humanity to the Creator. Although the *Führer* may not have spoken exactly in these terms, it was perfectly clear what he meant, namely that the Germans were to assume the role of the new chosen people. The original chosen people had disqualified themselves as their history had shown. It was an unrelieved message of tribal decline into a materialistic decadence in the Nazi schema. In short, the Jews had lost the plot; in their place the purified Teutonic peoples had arisen to assume the mantle frivolously discarded by the Jews.

Modern Germany and ancient Israel were mirror images; one embodying the good, the other evil, respectively. That is why the Jews had of necessity to be eliminated. They were the existential enemy because wherever they went they created discord, division, and rancor. It is noted that in the late apocalyptic literature of the Old Testament the opponents of God had to be annihilated so that he could establish unlimited domination unchallenged. And now the existential question posed by Hitler was: it must be either Germandom or Judaism. There was absolutely no possibility for the coexistence of these two mutually exclusive entities.

To underpin his thesis Heep recalls that Hitler's apocalypse can be located in the long history of apocalyptic interpretations of historic crises that reaches back from twentieth century into the early-nineteenth-century Napoleonic Wars of liberation and then further back to the Middle Ages, and finally back to the imperial apocalypse of Emperor Constantine in the fourth century. Heep argues that without the apocalypse of the First Reich, namely that of the Holy Roman Empire established by Charlemagne in 800 and ended by Napoleon in 1806, Hitler's ultimate success would have been inconceivable. The historical precursors were well known to educated Germans and in the post-1919 phase of the largely unloved Weimar Republic circumstances favored the emergence of a savior in a brown military uniform.[32]

The *Führer*, who was hailed by the Nazi "German Christians," was able to arouse slumbering religious forces because his national leadership role had been psychologically preformed by events that had unfolded deep in the nation's past. Carl Gustav Jung would not have quarreled with that. It should be remembered that the references to Christ in the messianic expectancy movements of the 1920s can be traced back to the sagas of the medieval emperors and then the papacy of the Middle Ages. At that time the Ottones and Salarier legitimized the power of the Holy Roman Emperor, which under the *Hohenstaufen*, especially Frederick II (1194–1250), had reached its peak, a historical fact that Hitler used to draw a parallel to himself. And this impressed the German conservative elite greatly because they were anticipating that under Hitler the longed-for unification of Europe, which they called *Romanitas*, would eventuate.[33] They were of course deluded in believing that when Hitler invoked providence, he was referring to the same God as theirs.

The Nazi Party rode on the crest of this historical-emotional wave. The illusion that the Germans were the new chosen people appeared quite plausible to such conservative opinion. German idealism could unify the Christian idea of the history of salvation and the apocalypse of the Reich into a law of historical evolution, especially by appealing to such philosophers as Fichte and Hegel. So, as undeniably the new chosen people called to replace a corrupted Judaism, the Germans could realize the kingdom of God on earth. But remarkably in this schema, as Heep

32. Bergen, *Twisted Cross*; Barnett, *For the Soul of the People*. The literature on this topic in both German and English is extensive.

33. Munro, *Hitler's Bavarian Antagonist*, 209–64, *passim*. See therein the exposition of the concept of *Romanitas*, which meant an idea for the re-creation of a Europe under one religion as it allegedly was in the Middle Ages. However, the new religion in the twentieth century was not Catholicism but National Socialism.

points out, the old concepts of morality and love of neighbor were subordinated to the fulfillment of the laws of history by extreme violence. Hegel again!

Nationalism was thus infused with the pathos of religion and so the apotheosis of Germandom was accomplished in the popular mind. This became the true Christianity while via anti-Semitism Jews became the embodiment of the Antichrist. Hitler had now projected himself as the rallying figure who had successfully woven the laws of historical development into a social Darwinist racial ideology. In this way both strata of German society, the elite and the *Volk*, were predisposed and enabled to comprehend Hitler as a manifestation of the holy. And here Stefan Heep invokes the earlier teaching of Rudolf Otto. Hitler's outbursts of hate and rage were received as the *mysterium tremendum*. The *Führer*'s promises of a glorious messianic future were astonishingly successful, enabling the recovery of unprecedented national solidarity. Accompanying all that was a most remarkable upsurge of German industrial-military power that occurred within a mere six years of Nazi rule. And German rearmament encountered minimal resistance either from within or without the Reich. In short, the Nazi movement transformed the hopelessly humiliated victim of Versailles into the greater Germany in which the symbols of the First Reich were returned, and all this was perceived as a miracle wrought by Adolf Hitler, who was hailed literally as the "redeemer" (*Erlöser*).

Very plausible is Heep's thesis that Hitler's worldview derived from a cluster of ideas that he forged into an idiosyncratic but persuasive explanation of the historical position in which the Germans found themselves post-Versailles. Hitler was able to replace their despair with a revival of transcendental values, which became the foundational pillars of their reality and the final points of orientation for thinking, believing, and acting. And finally, the Germans experienced the numinous and the holy, which communicated to them the feeling of redemption. It fulfilled the definition of religion that Rudolf Otto had formulated. Without doubt we have to do with a religious faith in a deity from which all norms of truth are derived. As Stefan Heep argues, we ought to think about National Socialism and its high priest as essentially a diabolical mutation of popery (read: dictatorial Catholicism).

As indicated, not everyone understood this or agreed with it. But the fullest reception of Hitler's belief system was to be found in his schooled praetorian guard, namely the SS, and among the higher echelons of the officer class. The dominant personalities in the Third Reich such as Rudolf

Hess, Josef Göbbels, Heinrich Himmler, and Alfred Rosenberg shared the core of Hitler's convictions but each cultivated their own variations that were not necessarily shared by their *Führer*. That, of course, was characteristic of the chaotic emotional-mental syncretism of National Socialism. Many of the party functionaries certainly shared Hitler's core beliefs while the ideas among the wider *Volk* remained diffuse. What they appeared to hold in common, however, was a veneration of Hitler as savior of Germany as well as the idea that the man Adolf Hitler personified true Christianity. This fact may not be underestimated because of its power to validate the alleged mental-spiritual integrity of National Socialism.

TO RECAPITULATE

Hitler propagated a *völkisch* apocalypse that defined the Germans as the new chosen people, the Jews as the Antichrist, and the German Reich as the kingdom of God. This, however, was given a new twist because its basis was not love for all humankind, as in the Sermon on the Mount, but a version of social Darwinism. The notion of a purified Aryan race as God's order and basis for morality was prioritized. In the process the image of God as *Abba*, the loving father, was replaced by the apotheosis of an imaginary pure Aryan *Volk* the triumph of which providence would ensure. This end goal presumed the exercise of unprecedented violence. Significantly, as well, National Socialism did not need to impose a totalitarian regime by means of terror because the German people largely submitted to it voluntarily, though many begrudged it. The legacy of Christian *salvation history* and apocalypse was perverted by National Socialism so that these ancient Christian beliefs were distorted into a diabolical history of salvation. Many of Hitler's associates cultivated their own peculiar versions of it and condoned its essential violence. Certainly, with few exceptions, they placed their individual talents, whether military or administrative, at the disposal of the *Führer* in the pursuit and consolidation of his aims in the Second World War. This process only terminated with the unconditional surrender of all German forces in May 1945.[34]

---

34. The literature on individual Nazi service personnel and bureaucrats is legion. For a prominent German pacifist's critique of the mental state of Hitler's henchmen, and in particular the betrayal of high-ranking scholars who since the nineteenth century had laid the groundwork for a perversion of German *Kultur* and indoctrinated generations of students and future officers with a toxic nationalism, see Foerster, *Erlebete Weltgeschichte*, 78–88, *passim*.

Finally, the explanatory power of Stefan Heep's research is convincing because it comprehends such concepts as *Volk*, that is, a tribe with a memory of the shaping forces of the past. This national memory endows the people with their unique cultural characteristics and shapes their *Sendungsbewusstsein*, that is, their national "sense of mission." *Kultur* certainly enshrined violence on an unprecedented scale, coupled with the yearning for a savior figure who would lead the *Volk* to their historic destiny. So, to show, as von Ranke memorably enunciated, "how it actually was," the historian must acknowledge the mystical and irrational features in all nations. And since we are dealing with features of the human psyche, the explanations will be as numerous as the number of scholars who venture to crystalize their reflections for the edification of their contemporaries.

5

The Choices Have Run Out.

History has shown for all with eyes to see and ears to hear that humanity is confronted with an existential threat, not just from illiberal ideologies such as atheistic Communism. One could argue that the even greater threat to world peace is the careless indifference of people and nations who are more concerned with "bread and circuses" or on fulfilling nationalistic dreams and delusions than with the long-term survival of species. It is certainly apparently impossible for the nations to get on the same page, as was tried with the 1919 League of Nations and the post-1945 United Nations. The latter organization still exists and valiantly seeks to reconcile international rivalries in several practical ways.[1]

In this chapter the aim is to draw attention to the major Christian authorities who have lived through the totalitarian experience of the contemporary world and proffered solutions to the problem. An analysis of their perceptions should prove instructive to political decision-makers by advocating more humane ways of resolving the political differences between rival nations and power blocs. In short, these thinkers are valuable sources of ideas for paradigm change (Thomas Kuhn). This means in practice the recommendation and adoption of a universal set of values that ensure peace among otherwise belligerent states and religions.

---

1. Kennedy, *Preparing for War in the 21st Century* and *Parliament of Man*.

DIETRICH BONHOEFFER'S PARADIGM CHANGE

Arguably the most perceptive champion of paradigm change in politics and religion in the twentieth century was the German Protestant theologian Dietrich Bonhoeffer (1908–1945). He has been designated the most significant religious thinker in the West since Martin Luther (1483–1546). As the world was under threat from the scourge of National Socialism, Bonhoeffer emerged as the foremost perceptive, energetic, and courageous leader of resistance to the knout of Nazi totalitarianism.[2] The *Kirchenkampf* or "church struggle" in Nazi Germany became the most dramatic test for Christians, both Roman Catholic and Protestant, to decide where their true allegiance lay, that is, either to the nation state as defined by Adolf Hitler (*der Führerstaat*) or to the gospel of Jesus Christ. The situation brought about by Hitler's seizure of power in Germany in January 1933 posed for Christians the so-called *status confessionis*. As Dietrich Bonhoeffer formulated it, the state had to be called to account for its violation of the principles of Christian-based humanity. Thus, the Nazi regime was guilty as charged because it persecuted of its own subjects: the Jews on racial and religious grounds and Communists and Social Democrats on political grounds.

In the Christian understanding of the state since St. Paul's time and the implementation of his principles of government by Emperor Constantine beginning in 312 AD, the state under God was there to protect life and well-being for all its subjects regardless of their racial identity or religious persuasion. Hence a state that discriminated against a section of its subjects/citizens or declared war upon them was not a true state; it was a godless regime that had forfeited all right to demand loyalty and obedience from its subjects. In addition, under Hitler the Reich pursued a foreign and war policy that was so reckless that it placed in jeopardy the very existence of the nation by provoking a world of enemies. Such a regime had lost all legitimacy and needed to be overthrown.[3]

The foregoing outlines the principles upon which Christian resistance to Nazi totalitarianism was based. In that German situation it required a rethinking of Martin Luther's doctrine of the state, which, unsurprisingly, was based on the Reformer's comprehension of St. Paul's evaluation of

2. Oppen, *Unerhörte Schrei*; note especially the final section, "Ausblick: Bonhoeffer's Erbe als Theologie nach der Schoa," 109–21.

3 Oppen, *Unerhörte Schrei*, 109–21. For an elaboration of this subject see Moses, *Reluctant Revolutionary*, ch. 6, "The Ethics of Conspiracy," 131–47.

the Roman Empire as adumbrated above. If the Christian emperor now perceived himself as the protector of all subjects, who were free to practice their various religions, then obedience to the state could be rationally conceded. One could be confident that justice would be meted out to all subjects without fear or favor. The Christian recognized the institutions of the state as necessary for the general good. For human civilization to flourish there had to be law and order, and the Roman Empire provided that.

THE PRIMROSE PATH TO SUBSERVIENCE

By the time of the sixteenth-century Reformation, however, the concept of the prince as ruler of the state to whom unconditional obedience had to be rendered had become sacrosanct. The principle of obedience to the powers-that-be within German principalities at that time engendered in the population a spirit of subservience or *Untertanengeist*. As many commentators have pointed out, this was the long-lasting downside of Luther's Reformation in Central Europe because it hindered the growth of an independent democratic spirit among the subjects.[4] This, as has been shown above, played a significant role in the broad acceptance of the dictator Adolf Hitler as the power ordained by God to rule Germany and to lead the nation to glorious times. Bonhoeffer, however, recognized that Hitler was certainly not the kind *Obrigkeit* that Luther had envisaged because of both his racial and church policies. Hitler was an anti-*Obrigkeit* who had demanded from all Germans the supreme blasphemy, namely that they had to pay their personal allegiance to the leader—in short to abandon their will to a mere mortal instead of to almighty God.[5]

Bonhoeffer's life and witness both before and during the Third Reich stamp him as one of the leading political-theological luminaries of the twentieth and indeed twenty-first centuries, since his legacy still inspires people both in Germany and in the wider world. The young German martyr has arguably bequeathed the most convincing rationale for church-state relations in what he called "a world come of age," meaning a pluralistic society characterized by different competing ideologies and in which Christianity is only one among many.[6] Nevertheless, the church

4. More recently, Huber, *Von der Freiheit*, 15.

5. Pangritz, "Dietrich Bonhoeffers Begründung."

6. Bonhoeffer wrote about "a world come of age" in his *Letters and Papers from Prison* (*Widersand und Ergebung*), published posthumously by his close friend Eberhard Bethge in 1959. On July 16, 1944 Bonhoeffer wrote to Bethge saying, "And we

remains the "body of Christ," the element in society that points to a better way for all humanity. Obviously, Christianity is crippled from fulfilling this role because of the many divisions within it and this is why the ecumenical movement that Bonhoeffer came so earnestly to advocate was/is so important to the mission of Christ to the world.

THE HEALING POTENTIAL OF ECUMENISM: UNITY IN DIVERSITY

Ecumenism recognizes that humanity is comprised of a multitude of races and religious traditions but that despite these divisions all are united in Christ. So, there is "unity in diversity." Peoples who claim to follow Christ are obliged to show the utmost tolerance of each other based on the insight that everyone is unique, endowed with a variety of gifts to be used in the service of the other. There is thus an organic uniformity to humanity precisely because it exhibits such a variety of personalities (John 17). That insight is, however, not shared by fundamentalists of either Roman or Protestant obedience. They insist that to be Christian one must conform oneself to the precepts of an exclusivist church. This is a form of authoritarianism that stifles all creativity and surely denies the reality of the world and the essential message of the gospel. There cannot be an exclusivist church. Such a concept is a contradiction in terms. So, to be truly universal (catholic) the church must be inclusive of "all sorts and conditions of humanity."

Dietrich Bonhoeffer's biography shows how he came to see the world beyond the confines of his native Germany via his experiences in Italy, Spain, the United States, and England. He was greatly impressed by the people he met outside Germany, and these included such personalities as the Swiss theologian Karl Barth, the English bishop George Bell, the Frenchman Jean Lasserre, the Afro-American Frank Fisher, and lastly another Swiss, Erwin Sutz. Each of these theologians out of their different life experiences taught Bonhoeffer the true meaning of being Christian in "a world come of age." No one nation had a mandate from God to impose its peculiar culture on the world, and this equipped him to critique the

---

cannot be honest unless we recognize that we have to live in the world *etsi deus non daretur* ["as though God did not exist"] And this is just what we do recognize—before God! God himself compels us to recognize it. So, our coming of age leads us to a true recognition of our situation before God. God would have us know that we must live as men who manage our lives without him" (translation by present writer).

absurdities and decry the abominations of the Nazi movement. All this Bonhoeffer did in fragments of writing toward the end of his short life of thirty-eight years, chiefly in his 1943 circular entitled "After Ten Years" and in the posthumously gathered fragments published by Eberhard Bethge in 1949 as *Ethik* and in English as *Ethics* in 1995.

Both texts are key criticisms of the behavior of the German middle and upper classes in their reaction to the Third Reich. Their importance in German intellectual history cannot be overestimated. After the war the Council of the Protestant church of Germany convened at St. Mark's Church in Stuttgart on October 19, 1945 and produced a "Declaration of Guilt." This could only have occurred because of the critique of Bonhoeffer alongside that of his loyal supporters such as Hans Joachim Iwand and Karl Barth. Many other Germans had clearly found the experience of the Third Reich totally irreconcilable with their understanding of the ethics of the New Testament and that was the precondition for the founding of the Confessing Church and the *Kirchenkampf*. Hitler's church policy was never going to work.

Understandably, Christians of all denominations in postwar Germany were engaged in a protracted discussion about how and why they had become derailed by the Nazi movement. The legacy of Prusso-Germany political culture had to be interrogated and that meant the question of unconditional obedience to the powers-that-be. The issue really revolved around the inviolability of basic human rights versus abandoning individual autonomy to an irresponsible warlord. The latter position had resulted in the virtual devastation of the Reich. It was the hardest lesson an otherwise civilized nation had to learn. 1945 has gone down as the zero hour (*das Jahr null*) in German history. A fresh start had to be made, and none other than Dietrich Bonhoeffer had foreseen this. Both the Roman and Protestant churches found themselves confronting their past behavior. Many clergy had been confused about how to discern their duty to maintain loyalty to the gospel on the one hand and their patriotism on the other.[7] The lesson of the Third Reich for all churches and nations is that there can be no prioritization of "fatherland" or national uniqueness over the comity of "all sorts and conditions of men." The recovery of unity in diversity became the precondition for the rescue of life

---

7. The classic case is the biography of Pastor Martin Niemöller, who perceived himself as a patriotic German willing to serve his fatherland in time of national danger, but who finally came to see that service to Hitler was a violation of his Christian convictions. See Schmidt, *Martin Niemöller im Kirchenkampf*; and Bentley, *Martin Niemöller*.

on planet Earth. And this would not be achieved by the last remaining murderous utopia of Marxism-Leninism-Maoism.

THE CONTINUATION OF THE CHURCH STRUGGLE IN EAST GERMANY, 1945–1989

At the end of the Second World War the defeated Third Reich became the focus of the power struggle between the Soviet Union in the East and the victorious Western powers led by the USA. Due to the Soviet policy of promoting world revolution, meaning the establishment of Communism as the prevailing ideology for all nations, the Cold War resulted. This lasted effectively from 1945 until the implosion of the Soviet bloc at the end of 1989. It was a time of permanent international tension between the capitalist West and the communist East characterized by the doctrine of brinkmanship, which had morphed into a poker game in which the rival players were politicians and their military advisers, who disposed over the potential to bring about a "nuclear winter." This meant that each of the ideologically driven rival alliances, NATO in the West and the Warsaw Pact countries in the East, engaged in a nuclear arms race with the intention of staring each other down.[8] World peace appeared to be guaranteed by a "balance of terror." The well-known outcome was the final implosion of the Soviet empire. Certainly, it may have appeared to some commentators at the time to have been the case, but the real reason was Gorbachev's aim to implement much needed domestic economic reforms with his policies of *Glastnost* (openness) and *Perestroika* (restructuring the Communist economy).[9]

MIKHAIL GORBACHEV, THE GAME CHANGER

When Gorbachev and his popular wife, Raisa, toured both parts of Germany in April 1986, they were very warmly received. The couple projected a totally new image of a system that had hitherto terrorised the world. As far as the East German regime was concerned, however, the legacies of Walter Ulbricht, who was in power 1945 to 1971, and his successor Erich Honecker, from 1971 to 1989, when the wall finally came down,

---

8. Siracusa, *Reagan, Bush, Gorbachev*; Siracusa with Warren, *US Presidents and the Cold War.*

9. Gorbachev, *What Is at Stake Now.*

was arguably the most egregious example of real existing socialism in the Soviet bloc. It not only disregarded any concept of human rights; its economy was both inefficient and corrupt while the entire country was dominated by the ruthless secret state police known as the *Stasi*.[10] East Germany 1945–1989 was thus a terror state that kept its subjects permanently oppressed and was so corrupt that it could not deliver the goods and services to its people to enable "civil society to reproduce itself."[11] In short, the German Democratic Republic was an anti-state dominated by a clique of atheist officials who were essentially robbers and liars.[12] They notoriously feathered their own nests, wielded power arbitrarily to crush all elements of opposition, and were particularly concerned to delimit the influence of the Christian churches within the population.[13]

The determination of the Protestant church in East Germany to remain proactive within socialism turned out in retrospect to have been crucial in influencing the implosion of the Communist regime at the end of 1989. This factor seems to have escaped the notice of many secular-minded historians and political scientists. It seems to have been largely forgotten that the Communist bureaucracy could not afford to eliminate the church-run charities such as hospitals, asylums, and other such agencies operating in East Germany as the maintenance of these would have fallen to the responsibility of the state. In short, as reported above, the Communist state was financially and administratively incapable of maintaining such charities, which ironically were kept afloat not least by injections of financial aid from the West German churches.[14]

LUTHERAN BISHOP ALBRECHT SCHÖNHERR'S RESISTANCE TO COMMUNISM

Further, the posthumous influence of Dietrich Bonhoeffer had become strikingly evident during the leadership of Albrecht Schönherr

10. The *Stasi* was the agency of state control (Ministry for State Security) whose ruthless *modus operandi* was unveiled in the study by Funder, *Stasiland*.

11. Mason, "Primacy of Politics."

12. Dibelius, *Obrigkeit*, 121–37. Dibelius was the Lutheran bishop in East Germany from 1948 until 1960, when he was declared *persona non grata* by the East German regime. He was a doughty opponent of the Communist regime, steadfastly refusing to acknowledge it as a legitimate authority in the sense that St. Paul had defined in Romans 13.

13. Moses, "Collapse of the GDR"; "Church Policy of the SED Regime."

14. Bahr, *Was Nun?*

(1911–2009) when he was bishop of the Federation of Evangelical Churches in the GDR from 1972 to 1981. In those years Schönherr, who was a
very tall and imposing man with a visage radiating strength of character
and conviction of faith, stood up to the Communist regime with great
confidence. Drawing upon his unshakable faith inspired through his earlier close personal association with Dietrich Bonhoeffer, whose student he
had been, and his unshakable Lutheranism, Albrecht Schönherr was the
personification of Christian resistance to atheistic Communism.

As such the outspoken bishop constituted a massive challenge to
the church policy of the East German regime. No Communist party
in power can openly concede that Christianity can have any influence
on its subjects because it projects a worldview based on myth whereas
Communism is demonstrably scientific. But is it not really the other way
around? Here it is recalled that the Christian view of human nature is
frankly realistic. It acknowledges that human beings are flawed creatures,
prone to moral derailment (sin) at any time as St. Paul had stressed so
long ago. Human beings left to their own devices repeatedly fall victim to
any of the seven deadly sins. As Martin Luther, echoing St. Paul, had reiterated, the world is the "devil's beer house," meaning that it is a place in
which there are many thieves, cutthroats, murderers, scoundrels, pimps,
and prostitutes, all preying upon the law-abiding subjects who are pursuing their various vocations within the economy of God. So, to prevent
the descent into *chaos* (the opposite of *cosmos*),\ there must be a strong
state bureaucracy to maintain civil society. In short, the state bureaucracy
functions alongside a church, which is there to proclaim the good news of
salvation to all who repent; hence the doctrine of the two kingdoms, the
spiritual and the secular. The Christian view of humanity is based on the
recognition that every person comes into the world flawed and therefore
prone to all manner of temptations ranging from petty infringements to
the most heinous of crimes.

THE FALSE IMAGE OF HUMANITY IN MARXISM-LENINISM

The Marxist-Leninist image of humanity is, however, very different. Marx
began by assuming that once the toiling masses were liberated from wage
slavery they would develop into "new species beings." This was a delusion
on a massive scale as the dismal record of Communist regimes in various countries has documented. As stressed above, real existing socialism

(RES) was a system devised to ensure the continued dominance of the *Nomenklatura* over the labor power of the proletariat. Far from liberating the toiling masses from wage slavery, the system guaranteed their continued enslavement to the capricious whims of the party bosses. This was based on the self-serving doctrine that "party is always right," meaning there was never any redress from the arbitrary decisions made by the party officials. It was a system based on institutionalized caprice. For Germany, a cluster of tribes whose culture had been nurtured from time immemorial in the ethics of the New Testament, this situation had to create a condition of massive *cognitive dissonance* among the subjects.

Put simply, this meant that the Christian educated populations of Central and Eastern European countries were forced after 1945 to live under Soviet-style dictatorships, which meant they were confronted with a totally novel situation. Whereas formerly there had been a so-called *Rechtsstaat*, that is, a system of government based on moral precepts inherited from centuries of Judeo-Christian-Graeco-Roman values (read: Law of Moses, Sermon on the Mount, Graeco-Roman law), now a completely secular and materialistic philosophy of man was substituted as the *raison d'être* for the world. In short, a new "image of man" (*Menschenbild*) was projected. Man was no longer a spiritual being or creature of mystical origins, but simply the putatively rational, autonomous creature destined to produce consumer goods necessary for sustaining life. The idea of a creator God who is the source of all life was abandoned by governmental decree and those who still insisted upon it ere deemed to be enemies of the people because they allegedly based their philosophy of existence in a manifest absurdity.

This is why an examination of the countries forced to live under a system of real existing socialism is highly instructive. The distinguishing feature of RES is that it is no longer necessary for the economy to be subject to the laws of supply and demand for goods but by the goals arbitrarily set by the party in power, the so-called command economy. The results are mostly mind-bendingly irrational, resulting in oversupply of commodities in some areas and an undersupply in others. Political decision-making is prioritized over economic realities. The party in power determines what the public needs.

One cannot escape the observation that command economies set up an unresolvable tension between what the people really need and what their rulers think they need. This is because of the assertion that the command economy will produce the new species being. This new kind of person will be distinguished from those who grew up under capitalism because they will be no longer driven by the desire to amass wealth in the form of capital and consumer goods. That desire will be eliminated because the need to produce surplus value for further investment will have evaporated. But this situation has nowhere ever been achieved. Meanwhile a bridging system has been developed known as "real existing socialism," which means that the *Nomenklatura* will determine when that situation has arrived. Of course, it never comes because the *Nomenklatura*, the officials of the ruling Communist party, are just like all the other government officials in history have been, namely fallible human beings prone, as reiterated above, to fall prey to any or indeed all the seven deadly sins.

As Lord Acton memorably wrote, "All power corrupts, and absolute power corrupts absolutely." St. Paul had got it right as did Martin Luther and all other notable theologians down to Karl Barth, Dietrich Bonhoeffer, Hans Küng, John Spong, and John Polkinghorne. But foremost among the East German church leaders was Albrecht Schönherr because he had to mount a case for the church's continued role even under the command economy of RES. Here the point has been labored that the champions of the command economy did not allow for the existence of alternative worldviews such as religion of any kind for an explanation of life. In fact, religion as Marx insisted was simply the "opiate of the people," and as such a matter of total irrelevance to the real world.

UNDERSTANDING THE CHURCH'S ROLE UNDER COMMUNISM

As we have seen, however, the historic situation of the church in the former German principalities left the church with considerably property and control over various *caritative Einrichtungen* (charitable institutions). This constituted a problem for the Communist state and its command economy. As bishop in charge, Albrecht Schönherr possessed considerable political leverage over these institutions and was not shy of making the regime aware of it. This emerged in all his publications for his clergy, and he could also lecture the state that it could do well by listening to the voice of Lutheranism, which he did at the synod of the Evangelical Church in the GDR in 1971. On that occasion Schönherr memorably announced that the church did not want to continue existence beside the state or against the state but rather it wanted to be "the church in social-ism." What prompted that formulation was the criticism the GDR's Sec-retary of State for Church Affairs, Hans Seigewasser, had made after the revised GDR constitution of 1968. At that time Seigewasser had warned the church against criticising or denigrating socialism and its humanistic policies, especially its foreign policy.[15]

Schönherr seized the opportunity to respond with his slogan "the church in socialism." It was a feisty declaration of resistance to the pres-sures of the atheistic regime to marginalize the church. The bishop had instructed the powers-that-be that the church was not planning to wind down its operations under Communist rule, and neither was it going into hibernation like the Roman Church but it was determined to remain an active element in society, upholding the ethics of the gospel.[16] Under-standably, this stand was a challenge to the party ideologues of the GDR. Two ideologically mutually exclusive mindsets were locked together in a standoff situation. The history of the peculiar persecution of Protestant clergy in East Germany makes for chilling reading. As related above, the *Stasi* had developed its own techniques for intimidating outspoken pastors, thereby providing a supreme example of the violation of human rights in the GDR.[17]

The Protestant church in the GDR had indeed to cope with the ca-price of a regime whose objective was to marginalize it in the long term and by whatever means it took. So, the maintenance of a regular church life was a challenge every pastor had to face, each in his or her differ-ent ways. Those who were old enough to have experienced the church struggle under the Nazi regime such as Albrecht Schönherr were intent on upholding their Christian witness come what may. They followed the guiding principles derived from by Dietrich Bonhoeffer. Others, how-ever, sought to re-evaluate Bonhoeffer's legacy to enable a compromise to be reached with the regime by producing a theological schema that

15. See, "Zum Gebrauch des Begriffes, Kirche im Sozialismus," in *Information und Texte der theologischen Studienabteilung beim BEK.*

16. For a comprehensive history of the Protestant churches struggle in East Ger-many, see Neubert, *Geschichte der Opposition in der DDR*. More recently, see Childs, *Fall of the GDR*; Kettenacker, *Germany 1989 in the Aftermath of the Cold War*; Tyndale, *Protestants in Communist East Germany*.

17. For an insight into the methods of the *Stasi* in intimidating and silencing church people in the GDR, see Braw, *God's Spies*.

brought Communism in line with the gospel. A champion of this this remarkable venture was Pastor Hanfried Müller (1925–2009).[18]

THE BIFURCATION OF BONHOEFFER'S LEGACY IN EAST GERMANY

Hanfried Müller had begun his theological training in the West at the Universities of Bonn and Göttingen, at which time his mentors were Karl Barth, Hans-Joachim Iwand, and Karl Wolf. He had become an adherent of what is known as "dialectical theology." However, by 1952 Müller elected to transfer to East Berlin, where he completed his doctorate on Bonhoeffer at Humboldt University. But in contrast to Schönherr he theologically reassessed Marxism-Leninism and argued that Bonhoeffer's life and witness as a martyr to the evil of fascism could be interpreted as pointing to the fusion of Christianity and real existing socialism. In short, protestant Christianity and real existing socialism were not mutual exclusive worldviews but totally compatible and capable of working together to produce a social order consonant with the gospel of Jesus of Nazareth.[19]

Müller advanced to become the Protestant apologist for the state of real existing socialism, having been appointed first *Dozent* (lecturer) and then full professor of systematic theology at Humboldt University in 1958. Together with Gerhard Bassarek (1918–2008) Müller founded a group of pastors calling themselves the Weissensee Circle. His ideas had obviously found some resonance among his fellow clergy. Understandably, the prospect of life under a regime of Marxism-Leninism was numbing as no one could predict how long it would last. Consequently, traditional Lutherans were thrown back to Luther's application of St. Paul's notion of the obedience to the powers-that-be. That was the precondition for all civilized society regardless of whether those in power were observant Christians. So, the East German pastorate was split on the question whether the Communist regime constituted a legitimate *Obrigkeit* (the powers-that-be) in the Pauline sense. This was a problem because many pastors like Schönherr considered the regime of Marxism-Leninism to be as incompatible with Christianity as was Hitler's National Socialism. And the figure of Dietrich

18. See Neubert, "Müller, Hanfried."

19. Hanfried Müller's pro-Communist ideological interpretation of Bonhoeffer was published as *Von der Kirche zur Welt*.

Bonhoeffer, who so valiantly resisted Nazism, presented itself paradoxically as one that could satisfy both the advocates of liberal democracy on
the one hand and Marxism-Leninism on the other.

The official Communist attitude toward Bonhoeffer was initially determined by the fact that he was remembered as a heroic fighter against
fascism.[20] He had courageously given up his life for the cause of freedom
as he understood it. As an individual of such prominence, he was difficult
to ignore; the other conspirators of July 20, 1944 had been consigned to
historical oblivion because they were aristocratic or bourgeois in origin
and hence had clearly not been inspired to act on behalf of the working class. Precisely why it was legitimate to single out Bonhoeffer, whose
bourgeois credentials could not have been more apparent, is only expli-
cable within the framework of Marxist-Leninist casuistry.

A prime example is supplied by the communist writer Gerhard
Winter who took the occasion of Bonhoeffer's 75th birthday (4th February 1981) to spell out why such a bourgeois and Christian was worthy of
remembrance in a society destined to become entirely atheistic.[21] This
example of communist preoccupation with Bonhoeffer, one suspects, is
rooted in a fear that he could become the focus of an ideological opposition to the regime. This would explain why a communist apologist like
Gerhard Winter would try on the one hand, to dignify Bonhoeffer's memory while, on the other, emphasizing the inadequacy of his motivation for
resistance because it was, after all, Christian rather than "scientific" and,
as such had only limited efficacy. Nevertheless, since Bonhoeffer's views
could be said to point in the direction which led to Marxism-Leninism,
communists and Christians in the GDR could find common cause. As
Winter argued:

> This awareness of responsibility, this preparedness to sacrifi-
> cial action, this determination to struggle against a society in
> which human rights are being trampled underfoot binds the
> communists with the faithful Christian. However, in contrast
> to Bonhoeffer we identify the spiritual/intellectual means for
> the establishment of a society commensurate with human dig-
> nity in Marxism-Leninism, the scientific *Weltanschauung* of

20. The following excursus is taken from Moses, "Bonhoeffer Reception in East
Germany," being his contribution to *Bonhoeffer for a New Day*. What follows is a revised
and an updated revision: *also eine neu durchgesehene und leicht überarbeitete Fassung
des Originals*.

21. Winter, "Dietrich Bonhoeffer."

the working class. So, while we do not ignore this contrast, we remain aware of that which binds us.[22]

Winter and other party strategists investigated Bonhoeffer's writings such as *The Cost of Discipleship* and *Letters and Papers from Prison* and gleaned ideas and values they felt coincided sufficiently to be of use in Communist propaganda. Obviously, the faithful Christian and the Communist strove for world peace. This and other elements such as the demand for social justice enabled a Christian-Communist dialogue, and Bonhoeffer's witness and martyrdom, despite his obvious limitations from the Communist point of view, were valuable sources for collaboration. One thing in particular commended Bonhoeffer as a role model for the times. While he would never be able to locate the root cause of imperialism, he did wage a consistent struggle against bourgeois nationalism; this was important because of the way nationalism had always been used to manipulate people into becoming willing cannon fodder so that capitalists could reap the profits of war.[23] So, by emphasizing Bonhoeffer's commitment to world peace and in particular his efforts to mobilize the ecumenical movement to that purpose, the Communists invoked Bonhoeffer's memory to persuade the contemporary international ecumenical movement to make common cause with them against the warmongering West.

A second field of Bonhoeffer activity from 1933 that the Communists tried to exploit was his critical role within the Confessing Church and his uncompromising repudiation of "German Christians." The racial ideology that much of the latter group justified as a component of the Christian faith, its identification of the Nazi Reich with the kingdom of God, its adulation of the *Führer* as a virtual savior, and finally its transformation of the Evangelical Church into a fascist state church were consistently and energetically opposed by Bonhoeffer. Indeed, his critique of the Third Reich from his radical Christian standpoint made Bonhoeffer a most attractive bourgeoise for the Communists, and his doctrine of passive resistance developed in *The Cost of Discipleship* stamped him as a foremost non-Communist opponent of fascism.

Further, if that were not sufficient justification for Communist recognition of bourgeois anti-fascism, there were elements in Bonhoeffer's political theology that led him to endorse certain goals of the politicized working class. This pronounced prolabor direction in Bonhoeffer's

22. Winter, "Dietrich Bonhoeffer," 15.
23. Winter, "Dietrich Bonhoeffer," 18.

thinking is adumbrated in sections of his *Ethics*, which indicate that the experience of fascism led Bonhoeffer through the barriers that under ordinary circumstances would have hindered him from collaboration with Communists. Consequently, Gerhard Winter argued that the lesson to be drawn from an investigation of Bonhoeffer's thought is that Christians could work in good conscience together with Communists in building up a new and genuinely humane society.

Gerhard Winter's interpretation of Bonhoeffer was clearly designed to convince the thoughtful Christian layperson in the GDR of both the legitimacy and importance of collaboration with the SED state. Hanfried Müller, as a regime-friendly professional theologian with a particular Bonhoeffer expertise on the other hand, directed his analysis of Bonhoeffer's career to convincing the pastorate in general to accept the rule of the RES as perfectly consistent with the essence of the gospel. He did this by seeing Bonhoeffer's church struggle as a repudiation of the nationalist tendencies within German Protestantism, which had led in a linear progression from Luther to Hitler.[24] So, for Hanfried Müller the path of German Protestantism, allied as it was in the past to the military monarchies and capitalism, and currently to NATO in the Federal Republic, had been historically disastrous.

By the time of Hitler's seizure of power two rival elements competed for the control of the church: one of these Müller termed the "clerical fascists"; the other the "German Christians." The clerical fascists wished to monopolise the social influence of the church, that is, to use its position to keep the *petit bourgeoisie* and peasant masses loyal to the ruling classes so that they would continue to vote for the conservative forces in peacetime, and in wartime volunteer to serve in the armed forces. By this means the clerical fascists hoped to avoid ceding their religious authority to the Nazis. They wanted to be partners with the state and to participate in the exercise of power. Indeed, they supported the anti-Versailles foreign policy and the anti-Communist domestic policy of the Nazis but wished to preserve the social prestige of the church and to construct a dam against the rising tide of secularization. They admired the successes of Mussolini in Italy and of Franco in Spain.

> In contrast to the "clerical fascists" the "German Christians" accepted the Nazi Party's church policy and wanted less to use fascism in the service of the church than to place the church

24. Müller, "Dietrich Bonhoeffer," 33.

totally in the service of fascism. In this rivalry, argued Müller, the German Evangelical Church disintegrated. Out of this situation arose the Confessing Church, which owed much to Bonhoeffer's rigorous biblical commitment. Nevertheless, this new association was unable to extricate itself entirely from the legacy of past clericalism. As Müller commented:

> The church struggle was carried out *in* the Church *for* the Church and *against* the Church, that is against the Church which as a secularised Church wanted to sacralise the world, and out of fear of the emancipation of society from ecclesiastical tutelage it repeatedly aligned itself with reactionary forces until it even resorted to collaboration with the Nazis for fear of Communism.[25]

Only gradually could the Confessing Church free itself from the clericalism that defined it, and one of its most radical and self-critical champions was Dietrich Bonhoeffer. In his *Letters and Papers from Prison*, according to Hanfried Müller, Bonhoeffer enabled pastors to free themselves inwardly from the clerical tradition in Lutheranism and the religious illusions of its *Weltanschauung*. Indeed, those letters pointed the way to a new orientation toward Marxism-Leninism as the revolutionary world movement.[26]

Just how many people were taken in by this highly propagandistic interpretation cannot, of course, be quantified, but it was probably a negligible number. However, as Wolf Krötke has pointed out, the Communists believed it was necessary to lay exclusive claim to Bonhoeffer and project him as a champion of proletarian liberation so that residual counterrevolutionary elements in the GDR could not enlist him in the service of anti-Communist propaganda.[27]

Of central relevance here is Wolf Krötke's essay "Der zenzierte Bonhoeffer,"[28] in which he reports how official state censorship in the GDR, which monitored all publications, affected the reception of Bonhoeffer's publications. Krötke had spent some time going through the files of *Gutachten*, that is, "expert opinions" on the publication of

---

25. Müller, "Dietrich Bonhoeffer," 37.

26. Müller, "Dietrich Bonhoeffer," 37.

27. Krötke, "Bonhoeffer als Theologe der DDR." This was among the goals of the Communist-oriented Bund evangelischer Pfarrer in der DDR, founded in Leipzig in July 1958. It had sent invitations to six thousand pastors to attend the foundation meeting. Only sixty appeared. It never achieved popularity and was dissolved in 1971. See Besier, *SED-Staat und die Kirche*, 294, 301.

28. Krötke, "Zenzierte Bonhoeffer."

Bonhoeffer's work and on literature about Bonhoeffer. Some of the more important of these "opinions" were prepared by theologians Christoph Haufe (1932–2011) and Kurt Meier (*1927), who allegedly belonged to the "most progressive" younger faction to come out of the seminar of the regime-friendly Emil Fuchs (1874–1971) at the University of Leipzig.

It is worth noting that their negative opinions were sometimes overturned by the literature board of the Ministry of Culture (*Amt für Literatur des Kultusministeriums*, later called *Hauptverwaltung Verlage*). Consequently, *Letters and Papers from Prison* was finally published in 1957 as the third of Bonhoeffer's publications in the GDR, the others being *Life Together* (1954) and *The Cost of Discipleship* (2nd ed., 1956).[29] The generally negative opinions by the "expert readers" clearly resulted from their anxiety that Bonhoeffer's readers might draw parallels between the situation under National Socialism and that under the RES. The literature board on the other hand clearly decided that in these cases the public would understand that Bonhoeffer's critique was against the Nazi system, which, as every well-schooled Communist was aware, was the antithesis of socialism.[30]

It was, from the point of view of ideological class struggle in the GDR, a not unimportant ploy on the part of the regime to promote Bonhoeffer's thought as eminently compatible with Marxism-Leninism. The common humanism of the two belief systems was a feature worth exploiting to bring the remaining Christian element in the GDR population into alignment with the goals of the regime. This gave rise to a curious theological enterprise based chiefly at Humboldt University and directed by Professor Hanfried Müller, who promoted an intensive Bonhoeffer industry. In addition Müller, supported by his wife, Rosemarie Müller-Streisand, and like-minded colleagues formed the above-mentioned Weissensee Circle, which was designed to persuade the wider Protestant pastorate to accept a pro-Communist version of a refunctioned Bonhoeffer theology of church and state. According to their argument the cause of the gospel would be best served by advancing the realization of Communism and abandoning the traditional role of the church in society. Here is where Bonhoeffer's concept of "religion-less Christianity" was advanced, unsuccessfully as it turned out.[31] Pastors were generally unimpressed by such

29. *Die Zeitschrift für Theologie und Kirche* 92 (1995) 3, 320–56.

30 *Die Zeitschrift für Theologie und Kirche* 92 (95) 3, 320–56.

31. When in March 1963 church leaders in the GDR began seriously to appreciate that the Communist system was no mere passing phase, they drew consciously on the

efforts to reinterpret Bonhoeffer, and so the enterprise of the Weissensee Circle achieved only modest resonance.

Meanwhile, alongside the ideological undermining of traditional Christianity by means of the less-than-subtle promotion of what surely amounted to heresy, the RES state set about intimidating the church and individual Christians by means of the elaborate and wide-ranging activities of the secret state police. Indeed, the *Stasi* perceived itself as the "sword and shield" of the ruling party. This policy of targeted oppression, as Professor Richard Schroeder[32] has pointed out, indicates that the state perceived the church as a source of ideological opposition that needed to be rendered as ineffectual as possible. The entire policy of the regime toward the church was attributable to the anxiety of the party leadership that Christianity could delay the socialisation of the population, particularly the children and youth, into "new species beings" in accordance with Marxist-Leninist ideology. Certainly, the aim was to create conditions in which the continuance of traditional Christian consciousness would be very difficult. But since the churches had a constitutional right to exist, every available method of frustrating the appeal and growth of church membership was called into service. For this reason, the state maintained six theological faculties at the universities of the GDR, which fostered a form of religion based on the premise that socialism and Christianity were mutually reenforcing. But regardless of whether the staff were responsible for or committed to teaching "Bonhoeffer," they had to subscribe to the allegedly sole validity of Marxism-Leninism, that is, its claim to absolute truth. This meant, officially at least, that they all had to bring the gospel into alignment with that ideology.[33] For the conscientious Christian this situation was fraught with difficulties. The system was in

---

Barmen Declaration of 1934 to state their position vis-á-vis the new form of totalitarianism and atheistic state. They did so in "Ten Articles on the Freedom and Service of the Church." The regime, however, saw in this a hostile act, and the regime-friendly Pastor Hanfried Müller drafted a rebuttal formulated as the "Seven Articles of the Weissensee Circle." This made much of the "religion-less" interpretation of Bonhoeffer's theology. These impact on the wider pastorate was, however, negligible. See the account of this episode in Besier, *SED-Staat und die Kirche*, 540–53. The respective texts are reproduced in *Kirchliches Jahrbuch der EKD* (1963) 181–98. For the theological discussion of Bonhoeffer's concept of religionless Xhristianity, see Neumann, ed., *Religionloses Christentum*.

32. Schroeder, *Deutschland schwierig Vaterland*, 43.

33. For information concerning the SED attitude toward the teaching theology in the GDR at universities, see Linke, *Theologiestudenten der Humboldt-Universität*, 10–75.

every sense ideologically oppressive and openly designed to ultimately marginalize the church out of existence.

Wolf Krötke confirms that the investigation/reception of such theologians as Karl Barth and Dietrich Bonhoeffer among pastors in the GDR was only limited. Neither was the teaching of their theology at any of the six theological faculties in the GDR or the three separate church-run theological colleges particularly significant because traditional Lutherans had alleged reservations about both men.[34] Having noted that, Krötke goes on to observe that it is nothing to be proud of that the first complete analysis of Bonhoeffer's theology was that produced by Hanfried Müller in 1961.[35] Müller justified his *work, Von der Kirche zur Welt,* by alleging that in Bonhoeffer's work there was irrefutable evidence that he, Bonhoeffer, had come to believe in laws of historical progress, and indeed he had cultivated a *Fortschrittsgläubigkeit* as Marx had allegely scientifically discovered. In short, one could interpret Bonhoeffer's theological refutation of National Socialism as an indication of his conviction that genuine Christianity operated against all factors in history that retarded human emancipation. Hanfried Müller had imaginitively set out to show that Bonhoeffer's life and work could be assessed as a progressive mental edifice that in collaboration with Marxism-Leninism could lead the world to peace. Bonhoeffer's anti-fascism indeed was grasped by Müller as opening new prospects for the future.[36] It was, however, at best an interesting attempt made at a time when it seemed that Marxism-Leninism would succeed in taking over the world.

As Krötke observed, for Bonhoeffer to be of any use to the Communists it was necessary to locate in his writings an arguable openness to the idea of regularity of laws of history that conformed to those allegedly discovered by Marx. According to Hanfried Müller, perceiving this connection would liberate Christians to adopt an atheistic, non-religious *Weltanschauung.*[37]

Müller's justification for his study must have been persuasive because, after the censors' demands for some rewriting had been met, the work was published. This in turn qualified Müller for an appointment to the theological faculty of Humboldt University in Berlin. From this position Müller came to exert great influence on the censorship process,

34. Krötke, "K. Barth," 282.

35. Müller, *Von der Kirche zur Welt.*

36. Müller, *Von der Kirche zur Welt,* 13–14.

37. Krötke, "Der zensierte Bonhoeffer," 335–36.

usurping the former dominance of the Leipzig faculty. From the early 1960s, then, all Bonhoeffer literature, to the extent it was theologically censored, had to satisfy the so-called Berlin interpretation.[38] This, however, did not presage a sudden increase in the publication of Bonhoeffer's works in the GDR. *Creation and Fall* had appeared already in 1960; *The Prayer Book of the Bible* had to wait until 1967. Then a selection Bonhoeffer's writings in one volume, *Christus für uns Heute: Eine Bonhoeffer Auswahl*, finally appeared in 1970 after much wrangling with the censors. It was reissued a year later, edited by Walter Schultz. A new edition of *Letters and Papers from Prison* then came out in 1977. All titles quickly sold out.

The problem for the SED was that Bonhoeffer's thought had to be persuasively exploited to conform to the party line. For example, it was deemed necessary in the view of the Müller-Streisand group that there had been a hiatus in Bonhoeffer's thinking that enabled a plausible change in a Marxist-Leninist direction. This, however, was staunchly opposed by such authorities as Albrecht Schönherr. He maintained there was no such hiatus and insisted that there was a demonstrable continuity in Bonhoeffer's convictions and actions. Certainly, there were serious points of disagreement between the rival camps of pastors in the GDR. Remarkably, though, a publication was sanctioned that allowed both sides to ventilate their views side by side.[39] That was the result of a party political decision to overrule the censors. SED church policy was undoubtedly capricious, sometimes ruthless, and sometimes conciliatory. For example, there were times when it was considered prudent to make concessions toward the church if these could be seen to serve the interests of the regime.[40] Nevertheless, theology had to be written in such a way as to conform to the

38. Krötke, "Zensierte Bonhoeffer," 335–39.

39. Krötke, "Zensierte Bonhoeffer," 335–39, 340. See Schönherr and Krötke, eds., *Bonhoeffer Studien.*

40. See Moses, "Church Policy of the SED-Regime." For example, in the 1980s the regime was particularly concerned to build bridges to the Church and portray Martin Luther as national hero, indeed a forerunner of proletarian revolution. It therefore comes as no surprise that permission was granted for the complete works of Bonhoeffer to be published. Between 1986 and 1988 volumes 1, 2, 5, and 9 appeared. See Krötke, "Zensierte Bonhoefer," 339 and note 38, as well as page 351 and note 91. There it is suggested that the positive personal response of then then Secretary of State for Church Affairs, Klaus Gysi, to Albrecht Schönherr helped to dampen the party fanaticism of the Berlin censors. This resulted in the appearance of not only the said volumes but also of Eberhard Bethge's renowned biography of Bonhoeffer in 1986. See Gysi, "Meine Begegnung mit Albrecht Schönherr."

situation in the GDR as judged ultimately by the Central Committee of the SED. This had the effect of causing scholars to write in vague or impenetrable language when it was deemed unavoidable to make references to political situations.[41]

Publishing theologians in the GDR were in the same situation as all creative writers. They all had to submit their work to the political censors before it was allowed to be printed. It was, however, not possible to seal off the entire GDR from outside influences completely; it was even less possible to isolate the church and to obstruct the publication of at least some of Bonhoeffer's works as noted. That also applied to works about Bonhoeffer as in the case of Hanfried Müller. This was particularly so starting in the late 1970s and early 1980s, when the church was becoming more and more the *de facto* public sphere, meaning the only place where critical public discourse could take place.[42] And a benchmark in the church's "public sphere" activity was the fourth International Bonhoeffer Congress, held in the church's retreat center outside Berlin in Hirschluch, June 12–17, 1984. Bonhoeffer scholars from both the Eastern bloc and the capitalist West attended. That this took place with the official sanction of the Central Committee of the SED indicates that the church policy of the regime was still driven by the notion that Bonhoeffer's legacy could be instrumentalised to persuade evangelical Christians to endorse GDR-style socialism. The regime had even sanctioned the participation of Bonhoeffer aficionados from capitalist countries.[43]

It was in this context that the collection *Bonhoeffer Studien* appeared in 1986. The volume encompassed seventeen contributions in an ideologically pluralistic manner. Clearly, it had to satisfy the authorities and so it contained essays by regime-friendly theologians such as Hanfried Müller alongside theologians who maintained a considerable distance from them.[44] Remarkably, this political-theological pluralism in the midst

41. Krötke, "Zensierte Bonhoeffer," 344.

42. Krötke, "Dietrich Bonhoeffer als Theologe der DDR," 308, where he speaks positively of the role of the church in the disintegrating GDR, out of which a better kind of state should emerge. For a more critical view of the role of the church in the GDR, see Pollack, *Kirche in der Organisationssesellschaft*. See also Moses and Munro, "Assessing the Role of the German Churches."

43. See *Newsletter of the International Bonhoeffer Society* (English language section) 28 (November 1984). The SED's Secretary for Church Affairs, Klaus Gysi, even dignified the event by inviting some delegates to a special reception. The conference papers were edited by Pastor Martin Kuske, *Weltliches Christentum*.

44. The volume in question was coedited by Albrecht Schönherr and Wolf Krötke

of RES bears witness to the fact that the church had successfully resisted the *absoluter Wahrheitsanspruch* of the SED. Thereby a *de facto* separation between state and party was revealed, making the situation in the GDR unique among all Eastern bloc Soviet-ruled countries. In this process the investigation of Bonhoeffer's theological-political legacy proved to be of central significance because once a situation of intellectual-ideological pluralism was recognized as a functioning reality and tolerated by the SED, the Communist claim to sole and indisputable authority to legislate what transpired in the world of ideas was overthrown. This is why the vagaries of the church policy of the SED merit close attention in any explanation for the ultimate failure of the regime to win the hearts and minds of the population. No regime, however authoritarian, can legislate what people think. As the old German folk song proclaimed, *"Die Gedanken sind frei"* (one's thoughts are free).[45]

THEOLOGIAN OF "THE CHURCH IN SOCIALISM"

Wolf Krötke's statement that the influence of Karl Barth and Dietrich Bonhoeffer on theologians in the GDR was only slight because their thought was alien to the traditional Lutheran mind must be balanced by the observations of those who identified Bonhoeffer as the theologian of "the church in socialism."[46] Krötke would count himself among their number. Indeed, he observed that when the church in the GDR struggled with its independent identity and wherever individual pastors and Christians encountered Barth and Bonhoeffer, they discovered hitherto hidden possibilities for freedom of the church and its fundamental ability to meet the challenges imposed by the system of RES. Clearly some BEK

---

and entitled *Bonhoeffer Studien—Beiträge zur Theologie und Wirkungsgeschichte Dietrich Bonhoeffers*. Even Australia was represented by the church historian Professor John Tonkin from Perth, Western Australia (personal communication).

45. *"Die Gedanken sind frei"* is an anonymous traditional German folksong still frequently heard at student Christian gatherings. Its origins go back to the end of the eighteenth century and was revived by Hoffman von Fallersleben in 1842. Its content emphasizes that no matter how one might be tortured into conforming to a tyrant's will, one retains one's inalienable autonomy as a human being.

46. Krötke, "Karl Barth und Dietrich Bonhoeffers," 282. Here the author addresses the question whether there was a widespread investigation of Barth and/or Bonhoeffer in the GDR and he concluded that it was "fairly thin." Even in the theological sections within the universities the concern with Barth or Bonhoeffer was not particularly strong. Despite the comparative paucity of information on Bonhoeffer, however, the idea held that the church should, come what may, stay fixed on gospel teaching.

and other high-profile churchmen drew inspiration from these theologians in their struggle to maintain loyal witness to the gospel against the
surreptitious efforts of the regime to marginalize the church. Further,
a significant number of parishes engaged in serious reflection on the
question of what it meant to be the church in an atheistic state and were
similarly affected.[47] It was then a case of the church actively reinvoking a
specific tradition, namely that of the Confessing Church during the Third
Reich. In the GDR changes were made in synods that unequivocally appealed to Bonhoeffer.[48]

When church leaders founded committees dedicated to Bonhoeffer
studies, such as that founded in 1977 by the BEK, there was undeniable
evidence of a groundswell of interest. This fifty-member strong committee, which included members from Hungary and Czechoslovakia,
coordinated the work of previously existing groups, thus indicating that
there were significant Bonhoeffer cells scattered throughout the entire
GDR.[49] Church historians in the Federal Republic (West Germany) made
the point that that a full comprehension of the behavior of the church in
the GDR with regard to the state is only possible if Bonhoeffer's legacy is
taken into account.[50]

Quantification here is a less-than-helpful tool of inquiry. Ideas,
faith, and conviction are categories that do not lend themselves readily
to statistical analysis. What the historian can, however, observe is the
effect of these mental-spiritual entities. It cannot be overstressed that
that political circumstances in the GDR were particularly oppressive for
the church. The atmosphere was drenched with the ideological rivalry
between two agencies, each of which was seeking to advance their version of truth, indeed of salvation. Theologian Edelbert Richter observed
that in a real sense there were two rival denominations opposed to each
other in the GDR: Christianity and Marxism-Leninism.[51] Certainly, the
spokespersons of the regime perceived themselves as virtual heralds of

47. Krötke, "Karl Barth," 296.

48. Schönherr, "Bedeutung Dietrich Bonhoeffers," 42.

49. Schönherr and Krötke, *Bonhoeffer Studien*, 10. This committee was responsible
for the production of the collection in 1986. In the foreword the editors drew attention
to the fact that the "numerous parishes and churches" in the GDR bear the name of
Bonhoeffer and that books about him were usually quite quickly sold out.

50. Personal communications with such leading experts in field as the late Leonore
Siegele-Wenschkewitz (Arnoldshain, Schmitten) and Christoph Klessmann (Potsdam).

51. Richter, *Christentum und Demokratie*, 275.

salvation (*Heilsbringer*).[52] The pastorate and the various dissident groups that some of them fostered, directly or indirectly, however, formed an obstruction that became increasingly more determined the more the legacy of Dietrich Bonhoeffer was appropriated.

The peculiar situation of the church in the GDR is summed up in the above-mentioned ambiguous title it acquired, namely "the church in socialism." And so, the church wore this designation cheerfully because it allowed its people stoutly to maintain that they were not by any means disloyal to the state. In short, an autonomous church in the GDR enabled it to behave in the all-important public sphere. This could by no means please the regime. In line with Marxist-Leninist doctrine, it was expected that the church should become an obscure niche in society lacking any social or political relevance, eventually disappearing. On the contrary, the church produced the leadership required to denounce the repeated instances of abuse of human rights by the regime, including discrimination against children and students of church families. In a defiant address, "Christ Liberates, Therefore Church for Others," delivered at the synod of the BEK, June 1972, in Dresden, the Erfurt prior (*Domprobst*), Heino Falcke, stressed that the church was not going to assume the supine role assigned to it by the SED regime. In this milestone proclamation Falcke demanded freedom and social emancipation, drawing heavily on Bonhoeffer's *Ethics*.[53] The doughty *Domprobst* characterized the role of the church as one of "critical loyalty" toward the political system, strongly implying that RES required the critical input of Christians. In short, the regime stood in great need of improvement. This critique did not go unnoticed by the authorities, which had to accept the permanent political-ideological opposition of a broad section of its subjects toward the "leading *Weltanschauung* of the working class."[54]

It is noted that not all evangelical churchmen agreed with this stance derived from Bonhoeffer's memorable example, but it was a statement of opposition from an indisputable champion of the traditional Lutheran church from which there was now no turning back. A proactive element was aroused in the church that belatedly, so it seemed, endorsed the views formulated by Otto Dibelius in the decade 1949–1959.[55] Undoubt-

52. Krötke, "Kirche und die friedliche Revolution in der DDR," 539.

53. Cf. Neubert, "'Obwohl der scheinbar tiefe Frieden.'"

54. SED und Kirche, *Eine Documentation ihrer Beziehungen*, 2:211–12.

55. Krötke, "Karl Barths und Dietrich Bonhoeffers," 294. Krötke implies strongly that the church was guilty of a grave error of judgment in declining to accept the

edly this change was enabled by the spreading awareness of Bonhoeffer's thought. That it made a difference is evidenced by the spirited statements of bishops and parish pastors such as Albrecht Schönheer, Wolf Krötke, Heino Falcke, Erhart Neubert, Edelbert Richter, and many others.[56] There can be no doubt that Bonhoeffer's ideas contributed significantly to a radical relearning process within the leadership of the German Evangelical Church in both parts of Germany. In the East, however, it was particularly crucial because, paradoxically, the regime wanted to instrumentalise aspects of Bonhoeffer's thought to legitimize RES. It is now with hindsight apparent that the East German evangelical leaders just named steadfastly refused to identify RES with the "world come of age"; they successfully challenged the notion that militant atheism equated with "hopeful godlessness" or that the building up of socialism could be understood as "immanent righteousness."

Wolf Krötke summed up in four key points where the challenge of RES to the church had to be confronted, employing Bonhoeffer's categories:

1. The state of RES with its claim to absolute power in all spheres of life and society came to be assessed as an opportunity for the church to abandon its own claim to power and social privileges and finally to rely completely on God through Jesus of Nazareth to rule.

2. Historical and dialectical materialism, as the official ideology, was projected as a militant declaration of "coming of age of the world" and could thereby be interpreted as "hopeful Godlessness." It was "hopeful" because fundamentally it rested on the concept of building up a more just society. And precisely because of that Christians were called to collaborate as autonomous individuals. Indeed, this was not a privilege, but a duty imposed by Christ by virtue of his propitiatory sacrifice on the cross.

3. The church was not a haven or retreat from society. It was the "church for others" living in solidarity with "the others," who, as the religionless, were pledged to build up socialism "with a human face" which

---

challenges in Dibelius's agenda during the 1950s. Partially responsible for this was Karl Barth's encouragement to the pastorate to adopt an attitude of "loyal opposition" to the regime. See the detailed discussion in Besier, *Der SED-Staat und die Kirche*, 301–26.

56. For a collection of the key synod statements of all these churchmen and their resolutions in the BEK, see Bodenstein et al., *Gemeinsam Unterwegs-Dokumente*; and Demke et al., *Zwischen Anpassung und Verweigerung*.

RES was not. In this sense, as Albrecht Schönherr formulated it, the church was not a church *beside*, not *against*, but *in* socialism.

4. The church should witness in this society without fear for its own existence by concentrating on its crucified Lord who is and continues to be the real ruler of the world.[57]

This appeal to Bonhoeffer enabled the church to see in its oppressed situation in the GDR the opportunity and promise to be the church, purified and unencumbered. What indeed appeared to be designed to marginalize and enslave the church was in fact liberating and empowering it. This was not an encouragement, to those who adhered to an extreme form of the doctrine of the two kingdoms,[58] to withdraw into hibernation; on the contrary, it was the obligation to collaborate with the religionless in the construction of a more just society that required a proactive response from Christians. This was made most publicly apparent on April 30, 1989 at the Dresden synod, where a twelve-point manifesto was promulgated that addressed itself to all the problem areas in both domestic and foreign policy for the GDR.[59]

Erhart Neubert has designated the manifesto as the Magna Carta of all dissenting groups because it provided both the justification and the practical goals for what became the totally unexpected "Protestant revolution." Its publication and reception were arguably the key factors in spurring on the burgeoning conciliar process then taking place all over the GDR.[60] The undeniable line of continuity between the witness of the persecuted Bonhoeffer in the Third Reich and the opposition movement in the GDR contributed significantly to the overthrow of the Communist regime. Neubert, as the pre-eminent champion of the idea of the Protestant revolution among the East German pastors actively opposed to the regime, identified the elements of opposition as having been directly and indirectly influenced by Protestant thought. In other words, the dissidents, including those among the Marxists, drew upon ideas and example of Protestant critics, whose voices were being heard increasingly from 1972 onward.[61] These were the intellectual-spiritual precursors

---

57. Krötke, "Dietrich Bonhoeffer als Theologe der DDR," 302–3. See also Krötke, "Spectrum der Bonhoeffer Rezeption in der DDR," 103.

58. Richter, "Zweideutigkeit der lutherischen Tradition."

59. See translation in the appendix.

60. Neubert, "Sozialethische und charismatische-evangelikale Gruppen," 311–12.

61. Neubert, *Eine Protestantische Revolution*, 14–17.

(*Vordenker*) of the revolution in whose mental-spiritual formation the legacy of Bonhoeffer had played a key role. It was due to their existence that they were able by 1988 to bring the disparate voices of the opposition in the GDR increasingly into focus. They had been in fact the latent internal opposition within the system, that is, an element that in the face of the all-powerful instruments of repression at the disposal of the regime could still reproduce and assert itself.

The pastorate of the eight provincial churches in the GDR was heir, of course, to several theological traditions all of which affected their attitude to the regime. Among them were residual conservative elements that, as Edelbert Richter had pointed out, cultivated a radical form of the doctrine of the two kingdoms.[62] Their preferred mode of behavior was virtual hibernation to preserve the purity of the gospel as they understood it. Another group of conservatives was prepared to see in the SED regime a legitimate *Obrigkeit* to which the only opposition came from Otto Dibelius in the 1950s. Others, obviously conscious of the legacy of the Confessing Church, were ready to take advice proffered by the Swiss theologian Karl Barth in 1958 and for a time at least believed it might be possible to support the regime as a kind of "loyal opposition."[63]

Hanfried Müller and the Weissensee Circle tried to instrumentalise Bonhoeffer's theology into underpinning what would have amounted to the most extreme form of the doctrine of the two kingdoms, where the church would have been eventually merged into the state.[64] Finally, there were other heirs of the Confessing Church for whom Bonhoeffer became the pre-eminent prophet of emancipation. These came to prevail in the *Kirche im Sozialismus*, proving to be, in the words of Wolf Krötke, the representative for a vastly better form of government. He wrote that when we consider the final collapse of socialism, meaning RES, from today's standpoint it was no coincidence that in the end the church embodied and projected a far better concept of the state.[65]

62. Cf. "Zum Gebrauch des Begriffs 'Kirche im Sozialismus,'" in *Information und Texte der Theologischen Studienabteilung beim BEK* 15 (March 1988), 2.

63. Barth and Hamel, *How to Serve God,* with an introductory essay by Robert McAfee Brown for an explanation of Barth's position at that time and the response it provoked.

64. Zimmerling, "Ja zur Entfaltung der Kraft des Lebens."

65. Krötke, "Dietrich Bonhoeffer als Theologe der DDR," 308. I have paraphrased the German original, which is: "Es war—wenn wir das Ende des Sozialismus betrachten—auch aus heutiger Sicht kein Zufall, dass die Kirche am Ende in einer Stellvertreterfunktion für ein besseres Staatswesen dastand."

Finally, the stance adopted by the church, always insisting against the express demands of the regime, that Christians had a right and duty to collaborate in the realization of freedom withstood and discredited the regime's ideological terrorism. It was in the end the church that was prepared to follow Bonhoeffer's notion of collaboration with the religionless, to accept the state, but the ideologically ossified custodians of the state in the GDR refused to accept such a gracious offer.

Addendum
The Historiographical Debate

THE COLLAPSE OR IMPLOSION of the Communist regimes in Central and Eastern Europe that began at the end of 1989 challenged the international community of contemporary historians for a rational explanation.[1] Why did the walls suddenly and almost simultaneously come tumbling down? The explanation for each country was as expected different as the prevailing circumstances in each case. There were, however, elements held in common by all of them. Bad economic management was obviously the major problem that haunted all countries in the Soviet bloc. Real existing socialism had been weighed in the balance and found wanting. Civil societies could not reproduce themselves in situations of unpredictable commodity deficits. A pall of hopelessness hung over especially those countries close to the border of the capitalist Federal Republic of Germany. East Germany, Austria, Poland, and Hungary could receive West German television stations, which featured advertisements of consumer goods that showed what was on offer in the bountifully stocked department stores, the variety of foodstuffs, fashion goods, clothing, household appliances, and of course cars. What Communist countries could boast of such outstanding automobile quality as Mercedes-Benz, BMW, or Audi? But apart from all that there was also pressure on the enjoyment of cultural products such as literature in all forms, music, and opera. Entertainment and education were especially subjected to ideological control and people with a prewar university background were forced to put their mind on hold and swallow the party dogmas without dissent. Philosophy and theology were obviously both disciplines that regimes committed to the "absolute truth" of Marxism-Leninism had to marginalize. The

---

1. Maier, *Dissolution.*

churches were supposed to retreat into niche existences and play no part whatsoever in public life.

To be sure, the Christian religion constituted a major problem for all Communist regimes, especially in strongly Roman Catholic and Orthodox countries with long religious-cultural histories such as Poland, Hungary, and Russia itself. Here a case is made for religion, especially in its peculiarly German Lutheran form, which was arguably the major factor in preventing the regimes of RES from gaining total control over the mind and spirit of their respective peoples. Also, in predominantly protestant East Germany the Reformation heritage of Martin Luther and John Calvin has been indelible. Indeed, Protestant theology in each of these latter forms had worldwide impact, especially on Western democratic thought, in governing commercial behavior as well as in defining the nature of political authority and the rights and duties of the individual subject/citizen regarding the state and as well not least in defining the work ethic.

Luther's comprehension of St. Paul's teaching about the *Obrigkeit* had a complex, even contradictory reception in the land of his birth. On the one hand Luther was the celebrated liberator of the individual Christian from medieval priestcraft and popery. On the other hand his public statements about obedience to rulers justified the absolutist authority of monarchs, and as such the Reformer was appealed to as the advocate of rigid and certainly anti-democratic political structures. Nevertheless, first and foremost as a theologian in his self-perception Luther was primarily concerned about the spiritual health of individuals. His insistence on unquestioning obedience to the powers-that-be in the Holy Roman Empire of the German Nation, did, however, have dire long-term consequences for the political culture of the Reich. Luther's legacy is at the very least ambiguous, and his writings have been the court of appeal for advocates of Wilhelmine militarism prior to the First World War, down to the ideologues of RES as was manifested in the GDR under Walter Ulbricht and Erich Honecker some eighty years later. As has been shown, those Communist demagogues certainly did try to instrumentalise a version of Luther's doctrine of the two kingdoms to persuade subjects in the GDR to accept the rule of Marxism-Leninism without demur. Paradoxically, however, there were those Lutheran scholars trained in the GDR who attributed to Lutheranism the culture of dissent that took firm root and became efficacious in the final decade of the Communist regime.

When one focuses attention on the fate of Communism in the GDR, one is inevitably confronted with the issue of Protestantism, especially in its ambiguous Lutheran form. The GDR is therefore a special case and its peculiarity accounts for the plethora of serious scholarly studies dealing with the relationship between church and state from 1945 until 1989. Among the variety of authors there are memoirs from within the church, the bureaucracy, and the security services alongside the accounts from secular scholars. All evince a greater or lesser degree of personal involvement in the events leading up to the *Wende*, the German term applied to the implosion of the SED regime at the end of 1989. Consequently, there is a wide scope for conflicting interpretation of church-state relations.

The reason for this situation is that the church virtually took center stage in the momentous events in the GDR between October and December 1989. In fact, ever since the church's active participation in the peace movement from the early 1980s onward, there had been an increasing perception of the church as a venue for expression of discontent with and opposition to the regime's Marxism-Leninism. The church constituted the only relatively free space either physically or ideologically in which criticism of the regime, its foreign as well as its oppressive domestic policies, could be mounted. Simply through its very existence the church became a focal point for dissident groups of all political shades. That said, however, it was by no means the case that from within the church itself there was a coordinated plot to overthrow the existing political order. Rather the church's problem was how to arrive at a *modus vivendi* with an avowedly atheistic government, the key aim of which was to eliminate all sources of ideological opposition, especially from the church.

The situation is best characterized by postulating a confrontation between two separate, totally incompatible belief systems each claiming to be in possession of the truth. In essence the problem was that the continued operation of the church within a system that denied its legitimacy on "scientific" grounds signified the failure of the "truth" of Marxism-Leninism. In short, the stubborn refusal of the church to retreat into a niche and as well to demand from the state the right to proclaim constructive criticism of RES could be represented as the triumph of the gospel and the ethics derived from it over the ideology and ethics of Marxism-Leninism. It is not surprising that this problem has attracted a range of studies seeking to establish the precise role of the church in the ultimate collapse of the regime of RES in the former GDR. A survey of representative works from that era will provide a framework of understanding of the various issues involved and at the same time account for the specific line taken in this present book.[2]

❖ ❖ ❖

The *Wende* at the end of 1989 signaled the beginning of a historiographical debate among German historians and theologians about the role of the church in the forty-year history in the GDR. The main reason for this was because of the prominent role that the church appeared to have taken in the unprecedented mass movements that led ultimately to the breaking down of the infamous Berlin Wall and the integration of the GDR into the Federal Republic of Germany. "Was this a Protestant revolution?" asked some commentators. The problem with this question is twofold.

First, how does one understand "Protestant"? Are we talking about the official church (*Amtskirche*) that could have conceivably plotted the subversion of an atheistic state? No compelling evidence of this having been the case has ever come to light. Nevertheless, the designation "Protestant revolution" has stuck and that can be explained by the concept "Protestant," which encompasses not only bishops and pastors with their worshipping congregations but also the wider German community that derived its distinguishing characteristics from a distinctly German Protestant culture. But that too may be drawing too long a bow because it assumes that Protestantism constituted the essential core of German culture. That, of course, was the position taken by many members of the *Bildungsbürgertum* who still were influenced by such prominent writers as Thomas Mann.[3] In addition, there were the entire Prussian and neo-Rankean schools of history that dominated the profession up to the First World War. These men were overwhelmingly stamped by the Protestant milieu even if they personally had long since abandoned what they had learned during their confirmation training.[4] Nevertheless, despite the very high profile of these advocates of Prusso-German expansionism,

---

2. All the studies consulted for the present study derive from the period post-1945 until the early 1990s, when there was intense feeling among many writers including secular historians, pastors, and theologians who were themselves divided on how to interpret the events leading up to and during the collapse of real existing socialism.

3. Mann, *Betrachtungen eines Unpolitischen*, 39–40. One should also note that Thomas Mann's brother, Heinrich, took issue with the views of Thomas in his various writings such as *Der Untertan* (1918; English: *The Man of Straw*) and *Zola* (1920).

4. Iggers, *German Conception of History*.

which they undoubtedly possessed, there were other significant intellectual and religious streams within Prusso-German history.[5]

The second reservation concerns the concept of revolution itself. If it presumes a conspiratorial movement over a long period that was driven by an ideology propagating the urgent destruction of the prevailing order, that is, power relationships, to be replaced by a superior one, then what happened in the GDR does not qualify as a revolution. Participants in the unprecedented mass demonstrations in Berlin, Leipzig, and Dresden in December 1989 may certainly have perceived these events as revolutionary but there is sometimes sharp disagreement among historians, political scientists, and sociologists on that score.[6] Various theologians have been ready to employ the designation "peaceful revolution" and affirm that there can be a reversal of power relationships with minimum violence.[7]

Since the inauguration of the GDR with its ideology of real existing socialism policed via the Ministry for State Security, each of the Christian churches knew they were forced into opposition. It of course took some time for the opposition to become concentrated, and then it only enveloped sections of the Protestant church because, as has been shown, there were high-profile Protestant bishops and theologians who opposed the idea of any kind of revolution. The Roman Church adhered to its policy of hibernation. The point is that there is no evidence to suggest that opposition from within the Protestant churches ever became conspiratorial. That is, none of the eight territorial churches of the BEK, the *Amtskirche*, ever adopted an anti-regime policy. Nevertheless, there had to be a sufficiently widespread basis of resentment at the grass roots in the parishes toward the regime to enable it to bring about the implosion of the system of RES. Obviously, the regime never enjoyed the endorsement of the entire population; most DDR burghers had no sympathy for the system because it could never allow civil society to reproduce itself. There were very few to mourn its passing. And since RES had failed to win the hearts and minds of the population, it was certainly manifest that the reason for this at least to a considerable degree was due to the opposition of church people.

5. Srbik, *Geist und Geschichte vom deutschen Humanismus*; see vol. 1, ch. 12 on the Prussian (Protestant) school, and vol. 2, ch. 14 for Catholic German historiography.

6. Zwahr, *Ende der Selbstzerstörung*.

7. For example see Krötke, "Die Kirche und die friedliche Revolution"; and Fulbrook, "Limits of Totalitarianism."

That organized or traditional Christianity was never going to be the motor of revolution has been spelled out by the sociologist of religion Detlef Pollack. On the other hand Pollack affirmed that the church became the "advocate of modernization" (*Anwalt der Modernisierung*), and the distinguishing characteristic of modern societies is pre-eminently their pluralism, which assumes the existence of at least several political parties functioning in a parliamentary system. In addition, there must be an independent judiciary and law enforcement agency (police), a free-trade union organization, as well as an education system insulated from ideological interference. All these elements constitute an open society in which free communication is the touchstone. Together they make up the so-called public sphere. Dictatorships on the other hand are the antithesis of pluralism. In East Germany the only element in society that was practically not under the control of the regime was the Christian church.

No doubt in the constitutional theory of the GDR freedom of religion was assured on paper, so the churches continued to exist and by that very fact they constituted a *de facto* public sphere.[8] Into this space there eventually streamed the dissident groups who otherwise would have had nowhere else to convene to criticise the regime, that is, communicate. To this extent the church was a structure in which opposition could be expressed. This movement took place under the nose of the official church, which of course never planned social upheaval; rather it had always sought to come to an accommodation with a hostile regime so that it could carry out its *Evangeliumauftrag*, that is, its commission to preach the gospel of Christ. There was, however among certain evangelical bishops and theologians divided opinion about how this should be managed.

Pollack went even further to downplay any supposed revolutionary ardor among dissident groups that met "under the roof of the church." All of them acknowledged the leadership role of the party in power "and sought nothing more than dialogue with it, the creation of a public sphere, more information and more participation in the social process, in short, a democratisation of an otherwise unchallenged, dictatorial and capricious socialism."[9]

Pollack recognized the growing oppositional and provocative activity of the various groups but neither the dissident groups nor the church believed it would have been possible to stage a revolution, nor did they

---

8. Habermas, *Theory of Communicative Action*.

9. Pollack, "Religion und gesellschaftlicher Wandel," 255–56. See also Pollack's *Kirche in der Organisationsgesellschaft*.

even wanted one. He pointed out that the priority of the official church was to mediate and avoid conflict. At best it became the conscience of the nation, especially in blatant instance of fraudulent behavior by the regime such as had occurred in the communal elections in May 1989, when the polling was closely monitored by the church. On that occasion the church was able to show how the actual results differed from the doctored and exaggeratedly favorable results published by the regime. But even at that late stage neither the dissident groups nor the church believed it would have been possible to stage a revolution.[10]

Indeed, as stressed above, it is very unlikely that the church ever perceived self as a revolutionary force in the GDR and yet it became a major factor contributing to the collapse of the regime. This occurred because the church constituted an informal public sphere where communication without obvious state interference could take place. Citizens who wanted to discuss politics sought out the free space of the church.

To this extent the church was a democratic Trojan horse in an otherwise rigid dictatorship. But a Trojan horse is ineffective unless it contains soldiers. As such it never could have out of its own resources brought about a revolution. And that applies also to the dissident groups who met "under the roof of the church." They were far too remote from the center of real power in the regime and were in any case numerically far too small to have been effective on their own. In this light the events during December 1989 in the GDR must be better described as the collapse of a fragile social structure sealed off from the outside world and having only been sustained artificially by repressive measures domestically and supported from the outside by the stationing within its borders of some twenty divisions of Soviet troops. When the Moscow regime was no longer capable of sustaining itself, let alone the other states within the Soviet bloc, the GDR proved to be no longer viable.[11]

While Pollack's contribution to the debate confined itself to the examination of political and sociological categories, that of Gerhard Besier investigates in detail the personal interaction between representatives of the *Stasi* and the clergy. Besier and his assistants have demonstrated that over a long period of time a range of church personnel had been collaborating with the secret state police in providing data on the mentality and attitudes of other church people. These documents, published prior

10. Pollack, *Kirche in er Organisationsgesellschaft*.
11. Pollack, "Umbruch in der DDR," 71.

to the passing of a law to archive the files of the Ministry for State Security, have purportedly unmasked many church officials, both clerical and lay, as informal collaborators.[12] Certainly, it was a highly embarrassing situation for the church, unleashing a debate concerning to what extent such apparently compromising files had any real significance in those abnormal circumstances. Further discussion of this issue will be necessary below. Besier sees the files as evidence of the church's very questionable dual strategy of on the one hand attempting to arrive at a *modus vivendi* with a hostile atheist regime and on the other hand seeking to preserve the integrity of the church itself. This tension, he claims, led to a damaging confusion among ordinary parishioners. The church was sending conflicting messages to its people and had thereby betrayed its essential duty to proclaim the gospel. Indeed, it had virtually entered a pact with the forces of the ungodly and thereby become a pliant tool in the hands of a cynical regime to manipulate the population.

That was a harsh judgement that drew an indignant response from many church people. Besier stood accused not only of having failed to take into account the peculiar circumstances of the official church, which was forced to deal with the Communist power brokers, but also of a lack of sympathy for the circumstances of ordinary pastors and parishioners at the grass roots who were the subjects of secret police surveillance and various levels of intimidation.[13] It is argued that compromises were inevitable, that church people had no alternative but to respond when approached by individuals who could only have been agents of the Ministry for State Security. A dossier that was created on such discussions did not necessarily mean that the individuals involved had betrayed the cause of the church. While Besier had succeeded in his multivolume project in minutely documenting the course of church-state relations in the GDR, his work must be regarded as essentially an indictment rather than a balanced historical evaluation. What can be said, however, is that by throwing a light on the weaknesses in the church's response to the regime's policy of marginalization over forty years, Besier exploded of the myth that the church was the undisputed heroine of resistance against an oppressive regime.

Conservative pastors have also indicted the behavior of the church in the former GDR mainly because of their traditional understanding of

---

12. Besier and Wolf, *Pfarrer, Christien und Katholiken*, 71.

13. Mau, *Eingebunden in dem Realsozialismus?*, 178–86 *passim*.

the doctrine of the two kingdoms, *die Zwei Reiche Lehre*. According to this view the official church in the GDR had betrayed its heritage. This it had done by adopting the attitude by 1970 at the latest of being willing to accept the status quo, the commitment to being "the church in socialism." This stance allegedly compromised the church to such a degree that it would never have been able to stage a revolution. Indeed, its stance amounted to an endorsement of the atheistic regime and thereby compromised the genuine witness of the true church. Confronted with Marxism-Leninism and its flawed image of humanity, there was no possibility of creating a true state, that is, one acceptable to Protestant Christians. Collaboration at any level was thus reprehensible. When the revolution came, it did so "in spite of the Christians and in spite of the church."[14]

This is, of course, the assessment of totally apolitical churchmen. For them it was impossible for the godless regime to create an ordered society on Earth such as envisaged by St. Paul and Martin Luther. The GDR was destined to fail and in the meantime one simply had to go into hibernation until that point was reached. This is the way people acculturated in the "old Lutheran spirit" were accustomed to think. In politics the church was supposed to be strictly neutral, neither submitting to nor openly resisting the state. In the GDR the church had failed to live up to this precept. Socialism was a false teaching of the most insidious kind, and pastors who imagined that they could come to terms with it, or indeed reform it, were either hopelessly naïve or cynically opportunist. Conservative pastors within both the GDR and the Federal Republic considered the efforts of reformist pastors in the GDR such as Heinrich Schorlemmer in Wittenberg or Heino Falcke in Erfurt as at best misguided. The idea that one could collaborate with secular, let alone Marxist, reformers and allow them into the confines of the church was unthinkable for a truly conscientious German pastor.[15]

This diversity of understanding about what constituted the correct role for the church in RES had clearly a lot to do with the theological position adopted by each individual pastor. And precisely here there was a great range of theological opinion stretching from the conservative Lutheran view to one advocated by a group of regime-friendly pastors under the influence of the theology professor in Leipzig Emil Fuchs (1874–1971), who advanced the idea that the gospel came closest to its social realization

14. Matthias Hartmann, "SED-Staat, die Kirchen und die Gruppen," 538.

15. Kandler, *Kirchen und das Ende des Sozialismus*.

in RES. And this enterprise was advanced by Hanfried Müller from his vantage point at Humboldt University in Berlin. Some colleagues were indeed persuaded to promote the idea that Dietrich Bonhoeffer's concept of "a world come of age" (*die mündige Welt*) would be realized if the church were to allow itself to become absorbed by the state.[16] There was indeed a journal dedicated to this idea entitled *Die Weissenseer Blätter*, though it achieved little resonance among the wider pastorates. It was another aspect of Bonhoeffer's theology that won more hearts and minds in the GDR, namely "the church for others," the church that derived its inner strength precisely from its impoverished and oppressed status.[17]

To this extent Bonhoeffer's theology experienced a renaissance because his reputation as a martyr to the gospel in Nazi Germany recommended him in the eyes of not a few pastors as the champion of "the church in socialism." Having so manfully struggled against racism, oppression, and war, Bonhoeffer appeared to be seriously relevant for Christians in the GDR, located as they were on the very fault line of the Cold War between East and West. But even here Bonhoeffer's theology was hardly conspiratorial. Rather it was appropriated by groups of Christians seeking theological re-enforcement in their struggle for survival against a regime intent on their marginalization.

Judgements on the behavior of the church in the GDR vary depending on the theology and/or political standpoint of individual commentators. For example, some took exception to the activity of the church at the ecumenical level, that is, during international conferences abroad, and have accused the church in the GDR of allowing itself to be instrumentalised in the service of the GDR's Marxist-Leninist foreign policy. It was true that ecumenical delegates from the GDR had acted as spokespersons at international conferences to justify the "peace" and racial policies of the entire Eastern bloc. Such behavior has been condemned not only as reprehensible but also as based on ignorance of international economics. The GDR delegates, so it was argued, appeared to live in the illusion that the cause of the gospel was better represented by international Communism than by the social market economy.[18]

The critics of the church in the GDR, then, fall into two broad categories. The first, like Detlef Pollack, took a strictly non-theological

16. Krötke, "Bonhoeffer als Theologe der DDR." Instructive in this context is the essay by Wolfgang Huber, "Deutsche Bonhoeffer-Rezeption in ökumenischer Sicht."

17. Kraft, ed., *Kirche und Welt*.

18. Motschmann, *Pharisäer*, 239–46.

approach, analyzing the church as a special sociological category in a country where the state strove to occupy the entire public sphere. Certainly, it held a monopoly on education, culture, and communication, supported on the outside both in its defense arrangements with the Warsaw Pact and through its economic ties within the Soviet bloc. But this monopoly was challenged by the simple fact of the existence of the free space occupied by the church. When the population could no longer endure the tutelage of the system and the associated deficit of communication, the church became the location of opposition. And when the outside supports collapsed, the regime imploded.

Second, as in the case of conservative critics like Gerhard Besier, there was the added theological dimension that accused the church in the GDR of dereliction of its obligation to witness to the gospel. Such critics abhor Marxism-Leninism not only for being economically disastrous but also for its atheism and for its hubris in claiming to be able to reincarnate humanity with a socialist personality. It was the Christian image of humanity that was the true one, namely the fallen creature before God as inherently sinful and standing in need of redemption. Further, it was totally wrong to apply Luther's doctrine of the two kingdoms to the GDR because, given its atheistic ideology, it could never be a true *Obrigkeit* or powers-that-be in the sense taught by Luther. Therefore, service to the regime was inherently wrong. In these hostile judgements one perceives a combination of both faith positions and scholarly analysis.

❖ ❖ ❖

Turning to the work of pastor Erhart Neubert on the history of the church in the GDR, we have an example of a critique informed both by theology and history. Neubert was also a trained sociologist and had consistently advocated the thesis that without due attention to the Protestant heritage in Germany, no adequate understanding of life in the GDR and of its collapse is possible.[19] Consequently, Neubert championed the concept of a "Protestant revolution" while conceding that it was a revolution of a peculiar type. Quite empirically Neubert saw the events during the autumn of 1989 in the context of prevailing world-historical movements, especially international economics and the restructuring of other East-Central European countries. In the GDR itself, however, one had to be

---

19. Neubert, *Protestantische Revolution.* Since then Neubert has unpinned this thesis in a detailed study of the oppositional movements in the GDR, *Geschichte der Opposition in der DDR.*

aware of both individual actions and those of dissident groups within their regions. They all revealed characteristics in common that derived from the historic German Protestant political culture. In short, there was an observable program to promote reform within GDR socialism. No integration into the Federal Republic was intended. That later development constituted a frustrating second phase in the movement brought about by the attraction of imagined sudden Deutsche Mark prosperity and the desire of Germans for national unity. This program of reform socialism was developed and projected by the various groups that had sprung up sporadically over time in the GDR and formed together "under the roof of the church." And here Neubert advocated the view that even where these oppositional groups were led by individuals who had no formal links to the church, they were still inspired by an inherited German Protestant spirit. Indeed, they were the result of a deep-rooted Protestant political culture that in the crisis created by the corrupt misrule of RES developed an organically, that is, historically rooted, instinct for the injustice and corruption of the ruling party. And this made the regime inherently obnoxious.

Such a provocative view is not an isolated one. It is shared by several leading Protestant personalities including both theologians and church historians.[20] What is historiographical significant for these writers is their common emphasis on traditional ideas, inner conviction, and intellectual formation in explaining the actions of individuals. In short, they share the view that cultural heritage functions to co-determine the path that history takes. And Neubert is of the firm conviction that the dissident groups in East Germany functioned to bring the spiritual-intellectual achievements of the Reformation back into the spiritually eviscerated vacuum that the misrule and economic maladministration of the SED had created. The intention was to reform socialism and to restore a measure of spiritual purpose to the lives of its deprived citizens. Clearly, there was a widely felt need to address problems that the state, locked as it was in its ideological Procrustean bed, refused to recognize. With this aim the various dissident groups initiated the process of liberalization and democratisation to ignite a public debate. Out of these groups grew, according to Neubert, "the political subjects of the GDR revolution."[21]

---

20. The names Richard Schröder, Edelbert Richter, Heino Falcke, Wolf Krötke, and Wolfgang Bialas stand out.

21. Neubert, "Sozialethische und charismatisch-evangelische Gruppen," 280.

Neubert stressed that the "new social movement" formed by the various dissident groups, a feature of all Eastern bloc countries at the time, as well as in the Federal Republic, was in East Germany very specifically a religious movement or at least one with religious-historical roots. This was affirmed by Neubert even if by far not all participants had been socialised in the church. And to make this assertion Neubert employed a sociological concept of religion that extends beyond the formal definition limited by membership in the institutional church. It sufficed to satisfy the designation "religious" if the groups concerned had any affinity with Christian values. This was evident because, in contrast to the earlier dissident groups in the GDR, those that sprang up in the 1980s consciously or unconsciously sought out the free space of the church. They obviously were convinced that their objectives would be best advanced in that historic sphere. Neubert and his colleagues attributed to the church a historical dimension that through its "myths, symbols, knowledge, rituals and the like has mediative functions." And that happened despite the reservations within the official church.[22] The fact is that individual citizens had a cultural relationship to the church because the political tradition of Germany had been stamped undeniably by Protestantism. This Christian orientation and behavior had been absorbed into the DNA of secular life.[23]

The events of autumn 1989 were the proof of this historical development in Germany since the culture of religious resistance and its symbols of expression, such as regular prayers for peace, the slogan of non-violence, and demonstrations in the form of candlelight processions, made the link with secularised humanity. And here Neubert made a telling observation to strengthen his thesis. In the forty years of its domination, Marxism-Leninism had been totally unable via its social policy to consolidate a political culture that could have replaced the existing protestant culture. In short, attempts to establish a socialist society with its own culture, producing individuals with a corresponding behavior pattern, meaning socialist personalities, failed and left a yawning spiritual-intellectual gap that was then filled by age-old Protestant cultural values.

One does not have to live very long as a churchgoing foreigner in Germany to realize that what Neubert has argued explains the cultural differences between one's own cultural formation and that of one's hosts.

22. The fact is that individual citizens had a cultural relationship to the church because the political tradition of Germany had been stamped indelibly by Protestantism.

23. Neubert, "Protestantische Kultur und DDR-Revolution," 24.

At the risk of repetition, the Lutheran Reformation within the borders of the Holy Roman Empire produced a specific political culture of obedience to the powers-that-be. Henceforth the individual was justified, made righteous, and stood alone before God without any mediating ecclesiastical hierarchy. No longer was the individual merely the *object* of saving grace, but now the participating *subject* in possession of absolute certainty of salvation before the beneficent Creator. And precisely this was the theological basis for the argument for inalienable legal rights of the individual in the community and the basis upon which the doctrine of inalienable human rights could be established and sustained. The contrast in worldview between Lutheran Christianity and Marxism-Leninism could not be more graphically demonstrated.

The Protestants in the GDR stood in this tradition, and it was this that enabled the committed Christian there to become so involved in the contemporary debate about human rights and to assess their own oppressed situation in the light of it. And it was the human rights debate that was gradually taken up by the various dissident groups both outside and inside the church. This was a crucial historical development from the 1970s onward because the church was compelled to address the issue and become the advocate of victims both within and outside the GDR. But within the GDR the caprice and dysfunctionality of the system had to be confronted more and more. Pastors and church officials were overwhelmed by appeals for assistance from citizens who were for various reasons victimized by the state.[24]

From the mid-1970s GDR Christians were involved in the international ecumenical dialogue on justice, peace, and the preservation of the environment and this stimulated criticism of the very dubious policies of the SED regime. As Neubert stressed, this discussion culminated in the twelve-point resolution passed in the spring of 1972 by the ecumenical assembly of the Federation of Protestant Churches (*Bund der Evangelischen Kirchen*—BEK) at Dresden. It was this resolution that really constituted the Magna Carta of the *Wende* in the GDR. And this development had come from the long-standing efforts of the church to engage the various dissident groups concerned with social and ethical questions in the conciliar process for justice, peace, and preservation of creation. Thereby the intrachurch communication with the dissident groups was sustained and

---

24. Neubert, "Protestantische Kultur und DDR-Revolution." These appeals for assistance exceeded the church's capacity to deal with them or to influence the state bureaucracy. Nevertheless, people turned to the church.

the territorial churches (*Landeskirchen*) and the participating parishes gained via the dissident groups an undeniable social significance.[25]

The system of RES in the GDR had thus been exposed as part of a worldwide malaise induced by Marxism-Leninism, which eventually was rejected by all the Eastern bloc populations, who refused to be socialised by its fraudulence. As well, in the economy the famous "Protestant ethic" was alive and well, contradicting the labor ethics of Marxism-Leninism. Despite the widespread laziness in the work forces it may not be forgotten that the memory of the Protestant ethic still functioned as the model for proper economic behavior and thus frustrated all efforts to re-educate the populations to a socialist understanding of labor and prosperity.[26]

For Neubert and others such as Wolfgang Bialas and Edelbert Richter[27] the Protestant ethic as Max Weber described it was of central relevance for the "Protestant revolution." It lived on in the GDR despite the best efforts of the regime to marginalize religion. Indeed, its deeply rooted presence revealed the socialist work ethic imposed by the conditions of the so-called command economy of RES to be essentially a deception because it led to an alienation of the workforce and the general population. The system described by Rudolph Bahro as "organized irresponsibility" was incapable of generating a satisfactory work ethic. The spirit of socialism that the SED aimed to cultivate in the community collided with the Protestant spirit, which is expressed first in the inner obligation to do an honest day's work and second in the justified expectation of an appropriate recompense for one's efforts. And that, of course, is the spirit of capitalism. The SED may be said to have tried to harness the spirit of Protestantism in the service of socialism. If that objective turned out to be spectacularly hopeless, the values that crystalized out of the Protestant Reformation and were mediated over centuries by the church have survived and, as history documents, triumphed.[28]

Regarding the church's mediating function in the transmission of values through time, the work of Christoph Klessmann is instructive. He drew attention to the existence of the "Protestant milieu" in the GDR

25. Neubert, "Sozialethische und charismatisch-evangelikale Gruppen," 311–12. The full text of the twelve-point resolution passed in Dresden in the spring of 1989 is published in *Ökumenische Versammlung für Gerechtigkeit*, 3–108.

26. Neubert, "Politische Kultur und DDR-Revolution," 25.

27. See Bialas, "Protestantische Revolution"; and Richter, "Zweideutigkeit der lutherischen Tradition."

28. See the discussion on this in Bialas, "Protestantische Revolution," 420–25.

and showed how the values of Protestantism amid the godless environment of RES were sustained. This was the case not only in the churches at
service times but in the family life of pastors in their vicarages as well as
via the long-established social agencies of the church. In addition, however, Klessmann drew attention to the cultural-artistic impact of highly
professional church choirs with one of the richest musical traditions in
Christendom. How, indeed, could a godless regime ever completely eradicate the influence of such a cultural dynamo as Johann Sebastian Bach
on the population? To that the persistence of Bach festivals bore eloquent
witness.[29] Indeed, the best efforts of the regime to mould a socialist "new
species being" in the GDR had to overcome a cultural-spiritual heritage
of greater antiquity and efficacy than Marxism-Leninism. Jesus, St. Paul,
Martin Luther, and J. S. Bach proved to be irradicable.

❖ ❖ ❖

Sufficient has been said to indicate that in the historiography of the *Wende*
the Protestant heritage had to be evaluated. Indeed, Protestantism was
the virtual riverbed of modern German history that atheistic Communism found impossible to divert. There is a convincing case to be made
for this view as Edelbert Richter pointed out. He had analysed the church
policy of the SED and identified in it the deeper reasons for the collapse
of the GDR.[30] In contrast to Gerhard Besier, Richter posed the deeper
question as to why such a policy as the marginalization of the church
was considered essential by the ruling party. Research needs to show how
much opportunism and expediency influenced citizens' behavior vis-à-
vis the powers-that-be. One needs to know more precisely when, where,
and why church people collaborated with the *Stasi* and allegedly betrayed
the gospel, and as well to enquire why such a situation arose in the first
place. There were no doubt many examples of weakness among church
personnel under pressure from the regime on the one hand and also of a
heroic refusal to collaborate on the part of others. In between there was a
broad spectrum of attitudes.

Richter's point of departure was that it would have been pointless
for the church to have adopted an active oppositional stance to the SED
regime particularly since the Federal Republic and not a few Western

---

29. Klessmann, ed., *Kinder der Opposition*, 29–53; and "Opposition und Dissidenz
in der Geschichte der DDR."

30. Richter, "Zweideutigkeit der lutherischen Tradition," 409.

states, including Australia, had recognized the regime and negotiated with it during the Cold War. Secondly, the church was itself internally split on how to approach this new state, whose existence had been designated as the end of the "Constantinian Age." This was a consequence of the conservative Lutheran interpretation of the doctrine of the two kingdoms that some bishops in the GDR had adopted.

As Richter explained, Luther in the sixteenth century had been confronted by the separation of church and state. This needed to be theologically reappraised and so Luther reformulated the doctrine of the two regiments, the secular and the spiritual. Behind each sphere Luther recognized a revelation of the love of God in the eternal struggle between good and evil. Inevitably, however, the doctrine led to a rigid juxtaposition of the private life of the individual on the one hand and the public sphere on the other. Neither sphere was supposed to encroach on the other, and this led to the concept that the state operated in an autonomous space in which the moral precepts of the gospel did not a apply, while they certainly did for the individual Christian as a private person. So, it was a doctrine freighted with a high potential for misunderstanding and misuse. In the beginning it had been Luther's intention to contribute to the formation of a state restricted by law, the concept of the *Rechtsstaat*. With the passage of time, however, the doctrine of the two kingdoms in Germany led to the sanctioning of the Hegelian *Machtstaat* ("power state") and in its extreme form that was taken to empower the state with the right to employ any means deemed necessary to ensure the continued existence of the state. In short, the doctrine released the state from the obligation to observe any moral considerations in the pursuit of its policies. This development Richter designated as a "revelation dualism" (*Offenbarungsdualismus*) because the state became the executor of the divine will on earth.[31]

Richter accused some bishops in the GDR of having justified their opportunism in collaborating with the regime by applying this doctrine and cites the example of the bishop of Thuringa, Moritz Mitzenheim (1897–1977). In 1961 Mitzenheim had no difficulty in supporting the regime's new defense laws in opposition to others who believed the church should resist compulsory military service in order to bear witness for peace. The SED certainly endorsed such regime-friendly bishops and pastors as Mitzenheim. Thereby they made manifest the deep split among church leaders. On the one hand there were those who firmly

31. Richter, "Zweideitigkeit der lutherischen Tradition," 409.

opposed the regime. On the other there were those like Mitzenheim for whom subservience to the atheistic regime posed no problem; indeed such behavior was totally consistent with Lutheran teaching.

In the light of such polarisation Edelbert Richter judged that any assessment of the role of the church in the GDR had to take account of the way the doctrine of the two kingdoms was interpreted and applied in practice. Obviously, it hindered the church from comprehending the SED state as an implacable enemy, and Richter identified four stages through which the church had to work to finally recognize this.

First, Bishop Dibelius had published his booklet *Obrigkeit* in 1963, in which he roundly attacked the idea that the SED state could be regarded as a legitimate powers-that-be. Remarkably, most of his co-religionists distanced themselves from their bishop because they initially accepted that the new regime was indeed functioning according to the will of God. Therefore, they had no alternative but to submit to the judgment of history.

Second, this submissiveness to the new state was only questioned during the 1970s, when the human rights debate was raised internationally. However, the neo-Lutheran doctrine of the two kingdoms was so deeply entrenched in the mind of many pastors that they made their commitment to human rights conditional on the fulfillment of the subject's obligations to the state.

Third, partly because of the traditional Lutheran theology of the state, the GDR churches evinced an underdeveloped ability to critique the state in its social-ethical deficiencies. Not unsurprisingly, many pastors acknowledged that the SED state was what it claimed to be, namely a genuine socialist society. This occurred at the latest when the church in the GDR described itself as "the church in socialism," a development that appeared to some as voluntary submission to the tutelage of the state. And this tutelage remained virtually unchallenged until 1988.[32]

Fourth, during the entire period of the GDR there occurred no real confrontation by the church to the state's interference in religious affairs. That could be explained by the church's adherence to the doctrine of the two kingdoms. But there was never any attempt to engage in an

---

32. There was, however, one notable exception. That occurred at the 1972 Erfurt synod when *Domprobst* Heino Falcke made the bold statement that the socialism of the GDR could be improved by allowing open dialogue. For the Marxist-Leninist claim to possess the absolute truth, Falcke's hope for dialogue had to appear to those in power as delusionary.

intellectual-theological debate with Marxism-Leninism. The efforts of Hanfried Müller and his Weissensee Circle to identify the true gospel with socialism, according to Richter, were not energetically refuted.[33]

The image of the church as projected by Richter is one of an essentially supine body crippled in its ability, in part, at least to critique the system that oppressed it. Nevertheless, the church constituted a long-term problem for the SED and the irony is that the party itself had picked up the doctrine of the two kingdoms and even recommended it as a way of confining the church exclusively to the cultic sphere.[34] On the surface it appeared as though the state was granting virtual independence to the church but in reality the church was being maneuvered into a position in which any initiatives that the church might take in the public sphere could be obstructed by the regime.

Of key importance to note is that in its efforts to establish itself as the sole source of truth as well as power in the GDR, the SED party only succeeded in conjuring up a mass rejection of the system in the public mind. Whereas initially Communism was expected to realize human freedom, the opposite occurred. Freedom as normally understood was actual crushed. The regime's promises to relieve all want and inequity and thereby inaugurate the birth of the "new species being" succeeded only in producing massive disappointment and skepticism in every sector. The daily denial of the stated goals of the system simply robbed it of any credibility. Against this background, so argued Richter, the regime revised its church policy in the late 1970s to project Protestantism as a source of transcendental hope to replace the emptiness of Communist chiliasm.[35] This situation spawned a revision of the figure of Luther in previous Communist histories of Germany.

The SED had obviously been casting about for new ideas to make socialism acceptable to a people whose Protestant (read: Lutheran) acculturation had over centuries contributed so much to shaping the German mind. And so there occurred a state-initiated Luther renaissance in the GDR.[36] The key to this endeavor was the doctrine of the two kingdoms because it could serve as a way of sustaining a state system that was becoming increasingly bereft of new ideas. And just how bereft of ideas the

33. Richter, "Zweideutigkeit der lutherischen Tradition," 410–11.

34. Falcke, "Place of the Doctrine of the Two Kingdoms"; see the section "The Two Kingdoms Doctrine as an Opportunist Ideology for the Elimination of Conflict," 26–29.

35. Richter, "Zweideutigkeit der lutherischen Tradition," 411.

36. Moses, "Politicisation of Martin Luther."

system was is evidenced by the fact that despite the worldwide economic crisis in Marxist-Leninist countries, they were incapable of revising well-known doctrinaire domestic and foreign policies. Despite the deleterious impact on the ecology of the countryside as well as on relations with the capitalist West, these policies were sustained. However, as Richter points out, under both Ulbricht and Honecker there was an emphasis on strengthening the party's public esteem and trying to improve consumption and to take more account of the everyday day needs of citizens with the aim of winning over more hearts and minds.[37] It is in this context that the new church policy since 1978 is to be understood because it signified not only a more benign attitude to the church but actually a minimum of practical cooperation. This had unexpected implications.

According to Richter, this meant nothing short of the state abandoning its monopoly on truth as claimed in its official ideology and accepting the fact that there were two belief systems functioning side by side in the GDR.[38] It came down to a *de facto* concession by the state that there was indeed real freedom of religion, that in questions of worldview the state remained a neutral agency acknowledging the separation of the ruling party from the state. And the consequence of that new church policy from the end of 1970s and the early 1980s, when dissident groups began to form, was the evolution of nothing less than a pluralistic society. The *de facto* dualism of church and state served as the precondition for the demands for more freedom of opinion, of speech, of assembly and association.[39] All these demands erupted in the events of autumn 1989 and these were unambiguously connected in the meeting of increasingly vocal and articulate citizens taking place "under the roof of the church."

The foregoing assessment received subsequent affirmation from East German scholar Hans-Peter Krüger,[40] who subjected the mental structures of most of the GDR population to a systematic investigation. He saw their predominantly Protestant heritage as paradoxically at first assisting the regime in its socialist objectives but later having paralysed

---

37. Richter, *Christentum und Demokratie*, 275.

38. In a similar vein Wolf Krötke assessed the conflict between Christianity and Marxism-Leninism in the GDR, where the state purported to be the deliverer of a secular (godless) form of salvation in the here and now but had dramatically failed in the attempt. That left the church in the dying phase of the GDR to fulfill a virtual representative function for the state, indeed as a better kind of state.

39. Richter, *Christentum und Demokratie*, 276.

40. Krüger, *Demission der Helden*, chapter entitled "Das strukturelle Rätsel 'DDR' und die protestantische Mentalität der ostdeutschen Mehrheit," 29–63.

the system into inaction by becoming fertile ground for the growth of oppositional reform groups. The power brokers in the GDR then saw they had no alternative but to establish the *Stasi*, an extensive surveillance apparatus, to maintain stability in the Marxist-Leninist sense. But right from the beginning the project was flawed. Massive resources had been allocated just to maintain control over a few thousand dissidents. Apart from the 1953 uprising in East Germany, opposition there, in contrast to countries like Hungary, Czechoslovakia, and Poland, was characterized not by revolutionary but by reform attempts. And in this regard the predominantly Protestant mentality of the GDR population, in contrast to the Roman Catholic or Orthodox mentality of the other Eastern bloc countries, was responsible. The essential difference lay in the fact of the high degree of secularization and rationalization of Christianity in Germany consequent to the Reformation. This lent to Protestant Germans the capacity to interiorize social contradictions and stolidly to adopt a certain asceticism in their living standards.

Further, the regime sought to exploit or harness this mentality by means of "humanistic" modifications to the practice of Marxism-Leninism and projected the Protestant values of frugality and community spirit into RES. The reciprocal relationship between the Communist regime and the Protestant mentality resulted in an identifiably different kind of socialism, indeed a *Protestant socialism*, which during the 1960s and 1970s was significantly more successful than that which emerged in either Roman Catholic or Orthodox countries.

While that was indeed the case, since the mid-1970s a growing alienation between the population and the regime occurred that gained expression in the opposition of a socially and democratically oriented Protestantism. The regime was notoriously unable to keep its promises and this provoked the emergence of a series of informal communication networks of disgruntled citizens that formed themselves to subject the dysfunctional regime to increasingly trenchant criticism. When Soviet leader Mikhail Gorbachev in the second half of the 1980s on the fortieth anniversary of the GDR made clear that the 450,000 Soviet troops stationed in the GDR would no longer be available to support the SED regime, it was taken as a green light for the opposition movement.

Krüger makes some penetrating observations about the last two decades of the GDR. It was a country to escape from, so bad was the repression, abuse of human rights, and blatant hypocrisy. Around 30,000 of its citizens had literally been sold into freedom to the Federal Republic while thousands fled illegally. It only existed through the operations of the *Stasi.* The question is raised as to why the GDR was able to sustain itself for so long, especially after the Prague Spring of 1968, which demanded a democratic form of socialism with which clearly most East Germans could have lived contentedly. But the GDR held on until the last months of 1989. But then it collapsed like a house of cards, and why so peacefully?

None of the summaries canvased above have addressed this question, so some reflection on the sweep of church-state relations in the GDR is required. First, there was a degree of alignment between Christians and Communists in the Soviet zone of occupation attributable to their common opposition to National Socialism. After the zero hour in German history, that is, the year 1945, it appeared possible to lay the foundation for a mutually beneficial collaboration given that the 1949 constitution guaranteed freedom of conscience. In addition, both Christians and Communists shared a structural affinity insofar as both in their separate ways aimed to improve the human condition. Then, however, with the passage of time Communism, despite its humanistic facade, revealed itself as determined to realize its aims through the arbitrary decisions and actions of a brutal dictatorship. To this initially the church had no choice but to bend. However, by virtue of the Protestant heritage of community solidarity, commitment to honest work, and acceptance of an ascetic lifestyle under straited circumstances, the population buckled under to make GDR socialism the most efficient in the Eastern bloc. In brief, the German Protestant mentality rendered the population initially submissive to the new powers-that-be and by so doing served to stabilize the system. However, these same mental structures functioned during the last two decades of the GDR to frustrate the objective of the Marxist-Leninist regime to win hearts and minds among the population.

The chief reason for this, according to Krüger, in agreement with Richter, was the failure of Communism to deliver what it claimed it would, namely a more egalitarian and just society in which want would be eliminated. This led to a credibility deficit in the eyes of most of the population and so groups formed informal communication communities that eventually crippled the regime's ability to rule in accordance with the official ideology.[41] And here several points need to be noted. First, the *Stasi,* despite having expanded its staff from a full-time membership of

41. Krüger, *Demission der Helden,* 33.

around 100,000 to at times 200,000 using "informal collaborators," was still incapable of making the population conform. Many citizens went into the well-known "inner emigration" as in the Nazi era, that is, withdrawing into the private sphere while awaiting the advent of better times.

Secondly, as it became known after the *Wende*, approximately half the oppositional groups were unofficial *Stasi* collaborators. Indeed, in the highly articulate and critical groups, such as authors, artists, scientists, historians, sociologists, managers, lawyers, pastors, and catechists, it was possible that one in five had been a *Stasi* collaborator. Thirdly and finally, there had been a total of 2.3 million members of the SED but none of these was prepared to lift a finger to save the regime when it imploded. It was a totalitarian regime that was both dysfunctional and had no deep roots in the community.

Summing up, the facts are that since the second half of the 1980s the SED no longer functioned as a close-knit unit. Neither did the bureaucracy. Indeed, all three elements within the state that were supposed to exert a monopoly of power, namely the party, the state, and the security agencies, were internally divided. In all three sections there was a struggle, muted but occasionally louder, between those officials who insisted on the official rigorous conservative Marxist-Leninist line and those who favored reform. And this took place against a background of economic, political, and cultural backwardness in the GDR compared to the Federal Republic. From the mid-1980s the citizens of the GDR came to see this deficit as quite hopeless. This was not only attributable to the effects of West German television and visits of pensioners from the GDR to their relatives in the West. It is recalled that from 1984, when it was made legally possible to travel, hundreds of thousands of workers visited the Federal Republic annually. And then came Mikhail Gorbachev's encouragement to reform. All this led to an increasingly rapid decline of confidence in virtually all organizations and institutions, including the SED itself as well as the *Stasi*. But the reformers in the GDR at that time had come too late, in comparison to other countries in the Eastern bloc, to bring about a similar renewal in the GDR. Indeed, in the light of the overwhelming will for German reunification, the discredited *Nomenklatura* had no chance other than to play a transitional role leading up to reunification. What the reformers had done in those last weeks of 1989

was paralyse the SED regime and they did this by virtue of their peculiarly German Protestant mentality.[42]

THE IMPLOSION OF THE GDR: THE IDIOCY OF
IDEOLOGICAL RIGIDITY

The above interpretations of the church's role in the implosion of the
GDR within the late Soviet bloc are intended to serve as an indication of
the complexity of historical explanation. The way in which any country
copes with crisis, sudden social change, or extreme forms of revolution
is the result of the cumulative influences from its past. In the German
case the religious-political experience of the past was particularly potent
as the various authors considered above have illustrated. Above all, the
spiritual-mental formation of Germans over the centuries since the Reformation imposes the obligation on the historian to take due account
of the religious component in the formation of national cultures. It is
no longer a factor that can be ignored if anything close to a satisfactory
historical explanation is to be furnished.

As the different historians discussed above have demonstrated,
there is considerable difficulty in identifying the essential cause, although
the religious factor looms large in many of the explanations. Each author
had written persuasively from their individual religious-political perspective. The student is left to judge for herself which analysis is the most
convincing.

Instead of broaching that discussion, the question is posed here as
to what a society without religion would look like, say as in the case of
Germany, if there had been no organized Christianity. How would the
communal-political life of formerly Christian countries be decently and
humanely be conducted? In this post-Christian era, though it is not entirely religionless, the Christian churches have suffered a startlingly diminished influence on public life. They clearly have sustained a dramatic
marginalization compared to their status in all Western countries prior
to the catastrophes of the twentieth century. It could be argued, as did
the German theologian Dietrich Bonhoeffer in writing about Germany
during the Nazi period, that the world has "come of age" and no longer
regards the precepts of morality and civilized culture inherited from the
Bible and passed down to the twentieth century by the Christian church

---

42. Krüger, *Demission der Helden*, 38.

as any longer relevant. Human beings are autonomous, and the individual can and should make up her own mind without reference to Christian ethics as to how to behave in everyday circumstances. The Christian story is simply one myth among many and in any case has forfeited any right it might have had throughout history to exert any authority over nations or individual citizens. So much for the cynics and critics of Christianity.

Furthermore, the history of the church universal throughout millennia has not exactly demonstrated that its hierarchy could be trusted to carry out the mission they were obliged in theory to pursue. Instead, there were many instances of blatant betrayal of that mission and that occurred in all denominations within divided Christendom, and it still occurs in the present. Examples of hierarchical apostasy are legion, so why would intelligent human beings submit their will to the guidance of such a morally flawed and organizationally fractured institution or pay any attention to it at all?

In trying to answer that question one needs to keep in mind the following: the Christian faith is based on the recognition that all human beings are flawed as St. Paul had eloquently pointed out so long ago. He even accused himself of practicing evil when he well knew what was right (Rom 8:13–20). That means that everybody may subscribe to the ethics of the New Testament but at any time may become derailed into committing the most heinous of crimes. In a word, the potential to oscillate between altruism and criminality is just part of being human. One can never be certain how one will react under the pressure of temptation. As St. Augustine realized, echoing St. Paul, so long ago in his struggle to maintain purity, he inevitably found himself sinning repeatedly. So, what is the circuit breaker in this downward spiral? It is the teaching about forgiveness dealt with at length earlier in this book. If one knows one is forgiven via the merits of Christ on Calvary, then one can make a restart. The phenomenon of contrition enables the sinner to accept divine forgiveness. One needs to contemplate what the outlook for humanity would be if this possibility were not available. It would be most unimaginably dismal. This becomes especially poignant with the need emphasized by Jesus (in his Sermon on the Mount) to forgive one's enemies. It is the Christian teaching about forgiveness that enables civilized life on Earth to continue. Add to that the conviction that the essential content of life is "being there for others," as Dietrich Bonhoeffer summed it up. The true Christian perceives him/herself as a servant. Jesus made that clear when washing his disciples' feet (John 13:1–17).

Postscript

THE FOREGOING ESSAY, AS stressed in the prologue, is the result of a combined historical and theological training the author experienced in both St. Francis' Theological College and at the University of Queensland in Brisbane, Australia, and further as a postgraduate student at the universities of Munich and Erlangen in Germany through the years 1961–1966. The two years in Munich were stamped predominantly by the influence of Professor Franz Schnabel, a liberal Roman Catholic. While at the University of Erlangen for three years, my history training was directed by three professors all of whom were liberal Protestants of varying backgrounds, namely Waldemar Besson, Walter-Peter Fuchs, and Karl-Heinz Ruffmann. Common to all these mentors was their democratic conviction. All cultivated a great respect for the liberal-democratic heritage of the United Kingdom, France, and the United States. They were all very much transatlantic-oriented scholars. Both in their lectures and seminars one could readily discern their indebtedness to the ideas of 1688 from the UK, of 1776 from the USA, and 1789 from France.

As an Australian in their classes I was occasionally asked to comment on and give seminar papers on how the British heritage contributed to shaping Antipodean political culture, which included the growth of cabinet government, the idea of free elections, the sovereignty of parliament, basic human rights, and the right of association as in trade unionism.

It transpired that I was far ahead of my German contemporaries in my grasp of these things simply because of having been born and educated in a country that has had for the most part a radical democratic predisposition. And here I am not forgetting how long it has taken to begin earnestly to remove the racial stain on Australian democracy regarding settler treatment of the first inhabitants. Not insignificantly, this issue is still at the forefront of public discourse in the country.

What is noteworthy about this issue is the cleft in the viewpoints of the government and opposition about changing the constitution to allow a unique voice to the original inhabitants. They are already legally citizens with the same rights as all other Australians, whose ethnic ancestry is so manifestly diverse. This a situation replicated in many other countries of Europe and both North and South America.

The point in mentioning this here is to underline the motivating convictions of it advocates. Many citizens are clearly driven by their awareness of their Christian and/or their Enlightenment heritage. However, whether the idea of granting to a section of society separate privileged access to federal government via the constitution is wise or desirable has proved to be a divisive issue. It is nevertheless an issue that compels the citizenry in general to think about how to realize social justice for all in a color-blind environment. In a post-Christian society people are being made to reflect on the essential meaning of decency. This kind of public debate does not happen in totalitarian countries, where people of liberal and/or Christian conviction are marginalized. Divergency of opinion in democratic societies is, in contrast to totalitarian countries, to be expected and it is precisely that which distinguishes the one from the other. In a democracy one has a right to express one's opinion on any issue so long as it does not encourage violence of one party toward another. Everybody should have a right to an abundant life (John 10:10). Indeed, it is the duty of all democratically elected governments to ensure that this is possible.

Where governments discriminate against ethnic minorities, they are betraying a central principle of Western Christian heritage. This heritage has meant that all peoples regardless of race, culture or religion are of equal value and have a right not only to survival but respect from their neighbors. Indeed, the overwhelming lesson of history in the West at least is that we should live recognizing that all nations should prosper in justice and peace, united in a common purpose to preserve the environment from which all humanity derives sustenance. If this path is not chosen by the nations the outcome will not be pretty.

It has been shown that regimes based on totalitarian convictions can never fulfill this aim because they are inflexibly committed to an allegedly fixed "truth" formulated by a quasi-infallible authority, deviation from which constitutes an unpardonable crime against the regime. Sadly, it is not a forgone conclusion that all people in a democracy appreciate this. There is undeniably a deficit in the civic training of many citizens despite the best efforts of the education system to introduce new immigrants from many alien cultures to the essential meaning of democracy and the institutions that are necessary to preserve it.

I recall the visit to the University of Queensland of the notable American professor of history Vincent De Santis (1917–2011), who in a staff seminar about American identity told his Australian colleagues that all immigrants to the USA intending to become citizens had to attend classes in their neighborhood in which they were instructed in the workings of the federal constitution. Then they would be examined on this subject, which they were required to pass before being eligible for citizenship. In the ensuing discussion the question was raised whether this training was a form of indoctrination. The good-humored professor agreed that it was. It meant that to become a US citizen one had to endorse a list of principles enshrined in the constitution. These principles guarantee the continuity of civil society. If they are not consistently followed, the outcomes will inevitably be disastrous.

Appendix

HERE FOLLOWS THE TRANSLATION of the twelve points presented by *Domprobst* (provost) Heino Falcke as president of the Committee of Christian Churches in the German Democratic Republic at the synod held in Dresden on April 30, 1972.

THE TWELVE AGREED RESOLUTIONS OF THE ECUMENICAL GATHERING (*ERGEBNISTEXTE*)

1. Return to Justice, Peace and Preservation of Creation/ The Basic Theological Principles.

2. Life in Solidarity—A Response to the world-wide Structures of Injustice.

   Life in Solidarity with all Foreigners of both Genders.

3. More Justice in the GDR—Our Task and Expectations.

4. The Transition from a System of Intimidation to a System of assured political Peace.

5. Orientation and Guidelines for Decisions concerning National Military Service and pre-military Training.

6. Aspects of Peace Education.

7. Becoming the Church for Peace.

8. The Search for a new Way of Life in a threatened Creation.

9. Serving Humanity—the Preservation of Life.

10. Ecology and Economy

11. Energy for the Future.

12. The Importance of Information promoting Awareness of the Environment.

Source: The Ecumenical Gathering for Justice, Peace and Preservation of the Creation, held at Dresden and Magdeburg. *Evangelisches Zentralarchiv*, Berlin, 2002/178.

COMMENT

The above text, designated as the Magna Carta of the December revolution 1989 in the GDR by Erhart Neubert,[1] is the distillation of protest initiatives going back to 1972 led by provost Heino Falcke. At that time, consequent upon the changeover from Walter Ulbricht's leadership of the SED in 1971 to that of Erich Honecker, political conditions in the GDR became characterized by a greater flexibility in the former Stalinist hardline pursued by Ulbricht. There was now a greater readiness to compromise both externally with West and domestically with those elements that demanded what amounted to a "socialism with a human face," to borrow the famous phrase from the Prague Spring, formulated by the Czech anti-Communist reformist leadership and announced by the Alexander Dubcek. This, however, had been forcibly overturned by an invasion of the Moscow-led armies of the Warsaw Pact, including those of East Germany carried out by the end of August 1968. The crackdown was observed with great disappointment by the sympathetic West.

It was against this background that Heino Falcke addressed the Dresden synod (June 30 to July 4, 1972) of the recently formed Federation of Evangelical Churches (BEK). The churches in the GDR had in 1969 been forced to sever all ties with the German-wide EKD, that is, the all-German association of Protestant churches. In that very isolated situation German Protestants living under the SED regime had to reappraise their position. It fell to Heino Falcke as provost to deliver the keynote address at the opening session of the Dresden synod. It was called "*Christus befreit—darum Kirche für andere*," meaning "Christ liberates; therefore, we are the church for others."

At that time Falcke was also principal of a theological college (the *Gnadauer Predigerseminar*) and he reminded his colleagues that it was

1. Neubert, *Oppostion in der DDR*, 792.

high time that the church should perceive itself as a "critical public," meaning it should perceive itself as the space in which Christians as concerned intelligent burghers should without fear or favor express their constructive views to a regime that was clearly not listening to its people. Indeed, it was not right that people be cowed into submission by the repressive measures of the state. Instead, they should openly give vent to their misgivings about the regime. The bottled-up reservations about the system under which they were forced to live and complain about only in private was no way for convinced Christians to live. Under those conditions people developed split personalities, outwardly conforming but inwardly very disgruntled. It was time for church people to exercise the democratic right to expose the injustices and absurdities in the administration. It should be recalled that the policy of the SED regime had been to marginalize the church as a source of contrary opinion about human society. Obviously, a Marxist-Leninist regime that claimed to possess the *absolute truth* had to engender a kind of psychological dysfunctionality or cognitive dissonance among thoughtful church people who genuinely wanted to be good citizens, productive worker,s and faithful Protestants at the same time, but they were permanently frustrated.

Under these circumstances it should be remembered that the church was accused of being a NATO church, that is, one that received its directives from the West German government to manipulate co-religionists in the East into becoming a kind of capitalist, anti-socialist Trojan horse. Certainly, the power brokers within the SED located in Pankow, East Berlin, had to regard the church as an ideological obstacle to their aim of capturing the hearts and minds of all burghers of the GDR.

What the thoughtful circle of Protestant church leaders around Heino Falcke wanted was a creative transformation in the existing regime, namely to challenge it to tolerate a virtual loyal opposition. Falcke and his colleagues had read the published works of Marx and Lenin and concluded that the regime had marginalized the earlier writings of Karl Marx and prioritized those of Lenin. Applying the earlier Marx to the conditions prevailing in the GDR, they found a decidedly emancipatory element that real existing socialism with its deference to Lenin had neglected. It was this impulse in Marx that gave hope for a liberating movement within the existing SED state. Out of it came the "Twelve Agreed Resolutions" of the 1972 synod in Dresden, presented by Heino Falcke.

These resolutions stressed that the world could and must be improved, and for that a liberated church was essential. One needed to activate the principle that the discipleship of Christ liberates people from crippling submission to an oppressive system and calls them to energetic and constructive collaboration (*mündige Mitarbeit*) with the authorities. In authentic socialism one had to work toward the abolition of alienation and subordination and demand the right to freedom. The church was the voice of the liberating Christ calling for solidarity with suffering humanity, namely the toiling masses. In short, inhumane conditions had to be abolished and genuine justice and freedom realized. What had been happening in the GDR under real existing socialism was a total disappointment because the enunciated socialist goals remained chimerical and cynically distorted. Heino Falcke concluded his critique by saying, "In upholding the promises of Christ we will not tire of stressing our hope for an improved socialism."[2]

The historical significance of Heino Falcke's address with the twelve points lies in the fact that he had delivered the intellectual-theological framework for the ensuing oppositional inner-church movement. Although its publication at the time was forbidden, it served to recall among concerned colleagues such as Albrecht Schönherr the earlier protests mounted by Dietrich Bonhoeffer against the totalitarianism of National Socialism. The seeds of a freedom movement in the GDR had been sown and were slowly but surely growing within the church. Interestingly, however, the hierarchy of the church never publicly endorsed the movement; it remained undercover in the ideological diaspora of groups of pastors and laity within the existing territorial dioceses of the protestant churches in the GDR. Falcke's address with its twelve points for reform were a skilfully composed formulation of an alternative imagining of a truly liberated socialist oriented society that hoped to counteract the blatant misrule or real existing socialism. It was never allowed to be published during the entire time that the GDR existed. Nevertheless, numerous copies were secretly circulated, and the idea content form the basis of re-oriented East German protestantism as Erhart Neubert and others have made abundantly clear.[3]

2. In the original: "Unter der Verheissung Christi werden wir unsere Gesellschaft nicht loslassen mit der engagierten Hoffnung eines verbesserlichen Sozialismus." I am indebted to Frau Dr. Dana Rathmann-Sens of the Evangelisches Zentralarchiv in Berlin for her collaboration in forwarding to me the summary of Heino Falcke's famous synod address from 1972, prepared by journalist Karsten Krampitz, who interviewed Herr Falcke fifty years after the event.

3. See Neubert, *Opposition in der DDR*, 792. The archive copy bears the instruction: "Nur für den innerkirchlichen Gebrauch," meaning restricted for internal church use only.

Bibliography

Acton, H. B. "Hegelian Political and Religious Ideas." In *Dictionary of the History of Ideas*, vol. 2, edited by Philip E. Wiener. New York: Scribner, 1973.

Afflerbach, Holger. *Falkenhayn: Politisches Denken und Handeln im Kaiserreich*. Munich: Oldenbourg, 1994.

Amos, Keith. *The New Guard 1931–1935*. Melbourne: Melbourne University Press, 1976.

Anderson, Robert. ed. *Re-reading Paul: A fresh Look at His Attitude to Torah and to Judaism*. Melbourne : Council of Christians and Jews Victoria, 2001.

Apelt, Willibald. *Geschichte der Weimarer Verfassung*. Munich: Biederstein, 1948.

———. *Hegelscher Machtstaat oder Kantischer Weltbürgertum*. Munich: Leibniz, 1948.

Avineri, Shlomo. *Hegel's Theory of the Modern State*. Cambridge: Cambridge University Press, 1972.

Bagehot, Walter. *The English Constitution*. London: Kegan Paul, 1949.

Bahr, Egon. *Was Nun? Weg zur deutschen Einheit*. Berlin: Suhrkamp, 2019.

Bainton, Roland. *Early Christianity*. Princeton, NJ: Van Nostrand, 1960.

Barclay, William. *The Letter to The Romans*. Edinburgh: St. Andrew's, 1983.

———. *The Plain Man looks at the Beatitude*. London: Collins, 1965.

Barnett, Victoria. *For the Soul of the People: Protestant Protest against Hitler*. New York: Oxford University Press, 1992.

Barth, Karl. *The Epistle to the Romans*. Oxford: Oxford Universtity Press, 1968.

Barth, Karl, and Johannes Hamel. *How to Serve God in a Marxist Land*. New York: Association Press, 1959.

Bentley, James. *Martin Niemöller*. Oxford: Oxford Universtity Press, 1984.

Bergen, Doris L. *Twisted Cross: The German Christian Movement in the Third Reich*. Chapel Hill: University of North Carolina Press, 1966.

Berger, Michael. "Das Ende des konstantinischen Zeitalters." *Zeitschrift für Politik*, neue folge, 16.2 (1969) 261–72.

———. *Evangelisches Staatslexicon*. Stuttgart: Kreuz, 1975.

Berlau, A. Joseph. *German Social Democratic Party, 1914–1921*. New York: University of Columbia Press, 1949.

Bernstein, Edward. *Ferdinand Lassalle as Social Reformer*. London: Swann and Sonnenschein, 1893.

Besier, Gerhard. *Der SED-Staat und die Kirche—Der Weg in die Anpassung.* Munich: Bertelsmann, 1993.

Besier, Gerhard, and Stefan Wolff. *Pfarrer, Christen und Katholiken und das Ministerium für Staatssicherheit und die Kirche.* Neukirchen Vluyn: Neukirchner, 1992.

Bethmann Hollweg, Theobald. *Reflections on the World War.* London: Thornton Butterworth, 1920.

Bialas, Wolfgang. "Die protestantische Revolution und der Geist des Sozialismus." *Deutschland Archiv* 4 Jg. (April 26, 1993) 417–25.

Biggar, Nigel. *Colonialism: A Moral Reckoning.* London: William Collins, 2023.

Bodenstein, Roswitha, et al. *Gemeinsam Unterwegs—Dokumente aus der Arbeit des Bundes der Evangelischen Kirchen in der DDR 1980–1987.* Berlin: Evangelischer, 1989.

Bonhoeffer, Dietrich. *Ethics.* In *Dietrich Bonhoeffer Works*, English edition, vol. 6. Minneapolis: Fortress, 2014.

———. *Widerstand und Ergebung: Briefe und Aufzeichnungen aus der Haft.* Edited by Eberhard Bethge. Munich: Chr. Kaiser, 1959.

Braw, Elisabeth. *God's Spies: The Stasi Cold War Espionage Campaign inside the Church.* Grand Rapids: Eerdmans 2019.

Breckman, Warren. *Marx, the Young Hegelians, and the Origin of Radical Social Theory.* Cambridge: Cambridge University Press, 2001.

Bucholz, Arden. *Moltke, Schlieffen and Prussian War Planning.* New York: Berg, 1991.

Bullock, Alan. *Hitler—A Study in Tyranny.* New York: Harper & Row, 1963.

Bultmann, Rudolf. *Jesus and the Word.* New York: Scribner, 1980.

———. *Jesus Christ, and Mythology.* New York: Scribner, 1958.

Burgess, John P. "Church-State Relations in East Germany: The Church as a 'Religious' and 'Political' Force." *Journal of Church and State* 32.1 (Winter 1990) 17–35.

———. *The East German Church and the End of Communism.* Oxford: Oxford Universtity Press, 1977.

Byrne, Brendan. *Romans.* Collegeville, MN: Liturgical, 1966.

Carnley, Peter. *Arius on Carillion Avenue—More than a Memoir: A Trinitarian Saga.* Eugene, OR: Wipf & Stock, 2023.

———. *Reflections in Glass : Trends and Tensions in the Contemporary Anglican Church.* Sydney: HarperCollins, 2011.

———. *The Structure of Resurrection Belief.* Oxford: Clarendon, 1987.

———. *The Subordinate Substitute: Another Wrong Turn on Carillion Avenue.* Eugene, OR: Wipf & Stock, 2024.

Carver, Terry, ed. *The Cambridge Companion to Karl Marx.* Cambridge: Cambridge University Press, 1991.

Chandler, Andrew. *British Christians, and the Third Reich: Church, State and the Judgment of Nations.* Cambridge: Cambridge University Press, 2022.

———. "Catholicity, Anglicanism, History and the Universal Church in 1947." *International Journal for the Study of the Christian Church* 18 (2–3) 261–63.

Childs, David. *The Fall of the GDR.* London: Routledge, 2001.

Clark, George. *The Later Stuarts 1660–1714.* 2nd ed. Oxford: Oxford Universtity Press, 1953.

Collins, Paul. *The Birth of the West: Rome, Germany, France, and the Creation of Europe in the Tenth Century.* New York: Perseus, 2013

Cowdell, Scott. *René Girard, and Secular Modernity*. Notre Dame, IN: University of Notre Dame Press, 2013.

Dack, Mikkel. *Everyday Denazification in Post-War Germany*. Cambridge: Cambridge University Press 2023.

Dähn, Horst, and Joachim Heise. "Kirchen im geteilten Deutschland." In *Aufschwung oder Niedergang?* Frankfurt am Main: Peter Lang, 2003.

Davies, Paul. *The Mind of God: Science and the Search for Ultimate Meaning*. London: Penguin, 1992.

Dawson, William Harbutt. *German Socialism and Ferdinand Lassalle*. London: Sonnenschein, 1891.

Decker, Oliver, et al. *The Dynamics of Right-Wing Extremism within German Society: Escape into Authoritarianism*. London: Routledge, 2022.

Denzler, Georg. *Widerstand ist nicht das richige Wort: Katholische Priester, Bischöfe und Theologen im Dritten Reich*. Zürich: Pendo, 2003.

———. *Widerstand oder Anpassung? Katholizismus im Dritten Reich*. Munich: Piper, 1984.

Dibelius, Otto. *Obrigkeit*. Stuttgart: Kreuz, 1963.

———. "Christ against Tyranny." *Christianity Today* 5 (1963).

Dicey, Albert V. *Introduction to the Study of the Law of the Constitution*. London: Macmillan, 1915.

Dönitz, Karl. *Memoirs: A Documentary of Nazi Twilight*. New York: Elmont, 1961.

Dorpalen, Andreas. *Heinrich von Treitschke*. New Haven, CT: Yale University Press, 1957.

Droysen, Karl-Gustav. *Die Geschichte der preussischen Politik*. Leipzig: Veit, 1968.

Dunn, James. *Romans*. Dallas: Word, 1988.

Ehlert, Hans, ed. *Der Schlieffen Plan: Analysen in Dokumenten im Auftrag des Militärischen Forschungsamtes*. Paderborn: Schöningh, 2006.

Engelberg, Ernst. *Bismarck—Urpreusse und Reichsbegründer*. Berlin: Akademie, 1985.

Erdmann, Karl Dietrich. *Die Zeit der Weltkriege*. Stuttgart: Ernst Klett, 1976.

Evangelisches Staatslexikon. Stuttgart: Kreuz, 1975.

Eyck, Erich. *Bismarck and the German Empire*. London: Allen and Unwin, 1950.

———. *Das persönliche Regiment Wilhelms II: Die politische Geschichte des Kaiserreichs von 1898–1914*. Zürich: E. Rentsch, 1948.

Faber, Karl-Georg. "Realpolitik als Ideologie." *Historische Zeitschrift* 203:1 (1966) 1–45.

Falcke, Heino. " The Place of the Doctrine of the Two Kingdoms in the Life of the Evangelical Churches in the German Democratic Republic" *Lutheran World* 24 (1977) 22–31.

Federn, Karl. *The Materialist Conception of History: A Critical Analysis*. London: Macmillan, 1939.

Ferguson, Niall. *Empire. How Britain Made the Modern World*. London: Penguin, 2003.

Fischer, Fritz. *From Kaiserreich to Third Reich: Elements of Continuity in German History, 1870–1945.*Translation of *Bündnis der Eliten*, by Roger Fletcher. London: Allen and Unwin, 1986. *Griff nach der Weltmacnt: Deutsche Kriegszielplitik im ersten Weltkrieg*. Düsseldorf: Droste, 1961.

———. *Hitler war kein Betriebsunfall*. Munich: C.H. Beck, 1991.

———. *Krieg der Illusionen; Die deutsche Politik von 1911 bis 1914*. Düsseldorf: Droste, 1966.

Foerster, Friedrich Wilhelm. *Erlebte Weltgeschichte 1868-1953*. Nuremberg: Glock and Lutz, 1953.

Foner, Philip S. "Marx's Capital in the United States." *Science and Society* 31.4 (1967) 461–66.

Footman, David. *The Primose Path: A Biography of Ferdinand Lassalle*. London: Crescent, 1946.

Fredriksen, Paula. *Paul: The Pagan's Apostle*. New Haven, Ct: Yale University Press, 2017.

Fritz, Hartmut. *Otto Sibelius: Ein Kirchenmann zwischen Monarche und Demokratie*. Göttingen: Vandenhoeck and Ruprecht, 1998.

Fulbrook, Mary. "The Limits of Totalitarianism: God, State and Society in the GDR." *Transactions of the Royal Historical Society* 7 (1997) 25–52.

Funder, Anna. *Stasiland: True Stories from behind the Berlin Wall*. Melbourne: Text Publications, 2003.

Gascoigne, John, and Hilary M. Carey, eds. *Church and State in Post Reformation Germany*. Leiden: Brill, 2011.

Goeckel, Robert F. *The Lutheran Church and the East German State*. Ithaca, NY: Cornell University Press, 2019.

Goethe, Johann Wolfgang von. *Werke*. Edited by Gustav Loeper et al. Weimar: 1887–1919.

Gorbachev, Mikhail. *What Is at Stake Now: My Appeal for Peace and Freedom*. Cambridge: Polity, 2020.

Grab, Walter. "The German Way of Jewish Emancipation." *Australian Journal of Politics and History* 30.2 (1984) 224–35.

———. *Meine vier Leben: Gedächtniskünstler, Emigrant, Jakobinerforscher, Demokrat*. Cologne: Papy Rossa, 1999.

Gruner, Wolf. *Der Deutsche Bund 1815–1866*. Munich: C. H. Beck, 2012.

Gurian Waldemar. *Hitler and the Christians*. Translated by E. F. Peeler. London: Sheed & Ward, 1936.

Gysi, Klaus. "Meine Begegnung mit Albrecht Schönherr." In *Glauben und Lernen in einer Kirche für Andere*, edited by Hans Feil, 76–85. Gütersloh: Chr. Kaiser, 1992.

Gysi, Klaus, and Friedrich Schorlemmer. *Was bleiben wird: Ein Gespräch über Herkunft und Zukunft*. Berlin: Aufbau, 2005.

Habermas, Jürgen. *The Theory of Communicative Action and the Structural Transformation of the Public Sphere*. Boston: Beacon, 1987.

Hancock, Eleanor. *Ernst Röhm, Hitler's SA Chief of Staff*. New York: Palgrave Macmillan, 2008.

Harnack, Adolf. *Militia Christi: The Christian Religion and Military in the First Three Centuries*. Philadelphia: Fortress, 1981.

Hartmann, Matthias. "Der SED-Staat, die Kirchen und die Gruppen" *Deutschland Archiv* 5 Jg. (May 25, 1992) 538.

———. "Frei geblieben? Rückblicke auf die Kirchen in der DDR." *Deutschland Archiv* (Rezensionen) January–February, 1998, 123–34.

Harvey, David W. *A Companion to Marx's Capital*. London: Verso, 2010.

Heep, Stefan. "Hitler—das Heilige in Erscheinung?—Die religiöse Dimension des Nationalsozialismus neu beurteilt." *Zeitschrift für Religionswissenschaften* 26.2 (2018) 323–78.

———. "The Long Way of Political Theology to Religious Germanism' or How National Socialism Could Be Perceived as the Fulfillment of Christianity." *Politics, Religion and Theology* 21.3 (2020) 311–36.

Hegel, G. W. F. *Philosophy of Right.* Translated by T. M. Knox. Oxford: Oxford University Press, 1968.

———. *Vorlesungen über die Philosophie der Religion.* 2 Vols. Hamburg: Felix Meiner, 1966.

Heil, Uta. "Menschenliebe im Superlative: Zur Rezeption der christlichen Lehre von Feindesliebe bei Athenagora." In *Logos der Vernunft—Logos des Glaubens,* edited by Ferdinand, R. Postmeier and Horacio E. Lona, 229–45. Berlin: De Gruyter, 2010.

Heise, Joachim. "Die Ausbildung des theologischen Nachwuches an staatlichen Universitäten der DDR." *Hochschule Ost: politisch-akademisches Journal aus Ost Deutschland* 1 (1996) 45–54.

Heitkamp, Sven. *Walter Markov—Ein DDR Historiker zwischen Parteidoktrin und Profession.* Leipzig: Rosa Luxemburg-Stiftung, Sachsen, 2003.

Henkys, Reinhard. *Gottes Volk im Sozialismus: Wie Christen in der DDR Leben.* Berlin: Wichern, 1983.

Hermann, Ursula. *Der Kampf von Karl Marx um eine revolutionäre Gewerkschaftspolitik 1864–1868.* Berlin: Tribüne, 1968.

Hertfelder, Thomas. *Franz Schnabel: Die deutsche Gesichichtswissenschaft. Geschichtsschreibung zwischen Historismus und Kulturkritik (1910–1945).* Göttingen: Vandenhoek and Ruprecht, 1999.

Hirschfeld, Gerhard, and Lothar Kettenacker, eds. *Der "Führerstaat": Mythos und Realität—Studien zur Struktur und Politik des Dritten Reiches.* Stuttgart: Klett-Cotta, 1981.

Hoffman, Stephen. "East Germany." In *Three Worlds of Christian-Marxist Encounters,* edited by Nicholas Pidiscalzi and Robert G. Thobaben, 99–105. Philadelphia: Fortress, 1985.

Hook, Sidney. *Dictionary of the History of Ideas.* Vol. 3. New York: Scribner, 1973.

Huber, Wolfgang. *Von der Freiheit: Perspectiven für eine solidarischen Welt.* Munich: C. H. Beck, 2012.

———. "Die deutsche Bonhoeffer-Rezeption in ökumenischer Sicht." *rinnerungen an die Zukunft: Zur Deutsch-Deutsch Bonhoeffer-Rezeption. Jahrestagung der Internationalen Bonhoeffer-Gesellschaft* (2022) 8–24.

Hubner, Ernst Rudolf. *Deutsche Verfassungsgeschichte seit 1789.* Vol. 3, *Bismarck und das Reich.* Stuttgart: Kohlhammer, 1988.

Iggers, Georg G. *The German Conception of History: The National Tradition of Historical Thought from Herder to the Present.* Middletown CT: Wesleyan University Press, 1968.

Iwan, Wilhelm. *Um des Glaubens Willen nach Australien: Eine Episode deutscher Auswanderung.* Breslau: Verlag des Luth Buchvereins, 1931. English translation: *Because of Belief: Emigration from Prussia to Australia.* Translated by David A. Schubert. Highgate, South Australia: H. Schubert, 1995.

Jenks, Gregory, ed. *Interfaith Afterlives of Jesus; Jesus in Global Perspective 2.* Eugene, OR: Cascade, 2023.

Jens, Walter, ed. *Um Nichts als die Wahrheit: Deutsche Bischofskonferenz contra Hans Küng.* Munich: Piper, 1978.

Joppe, Christian. *East German Dissidents and the Revolution of 1989: Social Movement in a Leninist Regime.* London: Macmillan, 1995.

Jung, Carl Gustav. "Wotan." *Neue Schweizer Rundschau*, March 11, 1936, 657–69.

Kandler, Karl-Hermann. *Die Kirchen und das Ende des Sozialismus. Betrachtungen eines Betroffenen.* Asendorf: MUT, 1994.

Kennedy, Paul M. *The Parliament of Man: The Past, the Present and the Future of the United Nations.* New York: Random House, 2006.

———. *Preparing for War in the 21st Century.* London: Harper Collins, 1993.

Käsemann, Ernst. *Commentary on The Epistle to the Romans.* Grand Rapids: Eerdmans, 1980.

———. *Perspectives on Paul.* Translated by Margaret Kohl. London: New Testament Library, 1971.

Kautsky, Karl. *Die Diktatur des Proletariats.* Vienna: Verlag der Wiener Volksbuchhandlung Ignaz Brand, 1918.

Kershaw, Ian. *Hitler.* Vol. 1, *1889–1936: Hubris.* Vol. 2, *1936–1945: Nemesis.* London: Allen Lane/Penguin, 1998.

Kettenacker, Lothar. *Germany, 1989: In the Aftermath of the Cold War.* London: Routledge, 2009.

Kiesewetter, Hubert. *Von Hegel zu Hitler: Eine Analyse der hegelischen Machtstaatsideologie und die politische Wirkung des Rechtshegelianismus.* Hamburg: Hoffmann und Campe, 1974.

Klessmann, Christoph. "Opposition und Dissidenz in der Geschichte der DDR." *Aus Politik und Zeitgeschichte* B 5.91 (January 25, 1991) 52–62.

———, ed. *Kinder der Opposition: Berichte aus Pfaarhäusern in der DDR. Zur Sozialgeschichte der protestantischen Milieu.* Gütersloh: Güthersloher, 1993.

Klötzing-Madest, Ulrike. *Der Marxismus-Leninismus in der DDR—Eine politische Religion. Eine Analyse an Hand der Konsequenzen von Eric Voegelin, Raymond Aarons and Emilio Gentile.* Baden Baden: Nomos, 2017.

Knabe, Hubertus. "'Weiche' Formen der Verfolgung in der DDR: Zum Wandel repressiver Strategien in der Ära Honecker." *Deutschland Archiv* Jg. 30 (September–October 1997) 709–19.

Koehne, Samuel. "Hitler's Faith: The Debate over Nazism and Religion." ABC, "Religion and Ethics." http://www.abc.net/religion/articles/2012/04/18/3480312.htm.

Kolakowski, Lesek. *Main Currents of Marxism.* 3 vols. Oxford: Oxford Universtity Press, 1978.

Kraft, Dieter, ed. *Aus Kirche und Welt: Festschrift zum 80 Geburtstag von Hanfried Müller.* Berlin: Brigitte Tiede, 2006.

Krötke, Wolf. "Adolf von Harnack (1851–1930)—Ein Leben für die historische Wissenschaft und einen zeitgemässen christlichen Glauben." *Jahrbuch für Berlin-Brandenburgische Kirchengeschichte* Jg. 64 (2003) 53–66.

———. "Bonhoeffer als Theologe der DDR. Ein kritischer Rückblick." In *Protestantische Revolution*, edited by Trutz Rendtdorff, 301–5. Göttingen: 1993.

———. "Karl Barth und Dietrich Bonhoeffers Bedeutung für die Theologie in der DDR." *Kirchliche Zeitgeschichte* 7:2 (1994) 279–94.

———. "Karl Barth und Dietrich Bonhoeffer in der DDR: Zur Rezeptionsgeschichte ihres Denkens in Kirche und Theologie." *Hochschule Ost* 1 (1996) 55–62.

————. "Die Kirche im Osten Deutschlands als gesellschaftliche Minderheit—Probleme und Chancen." In *Aufschwung oder Niedergang?*, 97–111. Frankfurt am Main: Peter Lang, 2003.

————. "Die Kirche und die friedliche Revolution in der DDR." In *Zeitschrift für Theologie und Kirche* 87:4 (November 1990) 521–44.

————. "Piety in the Church—*Gottesvergessenheit* in Society: Observation on an Aspect of the Church's Task in East Germany." *Toronto Journal of theology* 17.1 (2001) 133–46.

————. "Das Spektrum der Bonhoeffer-Rezeption in der DDR." *Erinnerungen an die Zukunft: Zur Deutsch-Deutsch Bonhoeffer-Rezeption. Jahrestagung der Internationalen Bonhoeffer-Gesellschaft* (2022) 87–103.

————. "Der Zenzierte Bonhoeffer." *Zeitschrift für Theologie und Kirche* 92.3 (1995) 29–56.

Krüger, Hans-Peter. *Demission der Helden: Kritiken von innen 1983–1992*. Berlin: Aufbau Taschenbuchverlag, 1992.

Kruglanski, Arie W., et al. *Right-Wing Extremism in Germany*. Oxford: Oxford Academic, 2019.

Kümmel. W. G. *Introduction to the New Testament*. London: SCM, 1978.

Küng, Hans. *Christentum und Weltreligionen Islam, Hinduismus Buddhismus*. Munich: Piper, 1984.

————. *Christsein*. Munich: Piper, 1974.

————. *The Church*. London: Search, 1968.

————. *Existiert Gott?* Munich: Piper, 1978.

————. *Die Hoffnung bewahren: Schriften zur Reform der Kirche*. Zürich: Benziger, 1990.

————. *Ist die Kirche noch zu retten?* Munich: Piper, 2011. English: *Can We Save the Catholic Church?* London: William Collins, 2013.

————. *Jesus*. Munich: Piper, 2012.

————. *On Being a Christian*. New York: Image, 1984.

————. *Theology for the Third Millenium: An Ecumenical View*. New York: Doubleday, 1988.

————. *20 Thesen zum Christsein*. Munich: Piper, 1975.

————. *Umstrittene Wahrheit: Erinnerungen*. Munich: Piper, 2007.

Küng, Hans, and Jürgen Moltmann, eds. *Fundamentalism as an Ecumenical Challenge*. London: SCM, 1992.

Lambert, Tony. *Chinese Christian Millions*. Oxford: Monarch, 2006.

Laquer, Water. *Fascism—Past, Present and Future*. New York: Oxford Universtity Press, 1996.

Lehmann, Hartmut. "The Germans as a Chosen People: Old Testament Themes in German Nationalism." In *Religion und Religiosität in der Neuzeit*, by Hartmut Lehmann, Manfred Jakubowski-Tiessen, and Otto Ulbricht, 248–59. Göttingen: Vandenhoek and Ruprecht, 1991.

Lewis, Ben. *Hammer and Tickle: A Cultural History of Communism*. London: Pegasus, 2010.

Linke, Dietmar. *Theologiestudenten der Humboldt Universität: Zwischen Hörsaal und Anklagebank. Darstellungen der parteipolitischen Einflussnahme auf eine Theologische Fakultät in der DDR an Hand von Dokumenten*. Neukirchen-Vluyn: Neukirchner, 1994.

Louis, W. R., ed. *The Origins of the Second World War: A.J.P. Taylor and His Critics*. New York: John Wiley, 1972.

Lupo, Salvatore. *Two Mafias: A Transatlantic History 1888-2008*. London: Palgrave Macmillan, 2015.

Mack, Burton L. *Who Wrote the New Testament?: The Making of the Christian Myth*. San Francisco: Harper Collins, 1995.

Macquarrie, John. *Principles of Christian Theology*. New York: Scribner, 1966.

———. "What Still Separates Us from the Catholic Church?: An Anglican Reply." In *Post-Ecumenical Christianity*, edited by Hans Küng, 45-53. New York: Herder, 1970.

Maier, Charles S. *Dissolution: The Crisis of Communism and the End of East German*. Princeton, NJ: Princeton University Press, 1999.

Mann, Thomas. *Die Betrachtungen eines Unpolitischen*. Frankfurt/Main: Fischer Taschenbuch, 1993. English translation: *Reflections of a Nonpolitical Man*. Translated by Walter D. Morris. New York: Ungar, 1982.

Manthey, Barbara. "On the Pathway to Violence: West German Right Wing Terrorism in the 1970s." *Terrorism and Political Violence* 33.1 (2021) 49-70. https://doi.org/1 0.1080/09546553.2018.1520701.

Marx, Karl. "Instructions for the Delegates of the Provisional General Council. The Different Questions." In *Documents of the First International (1864-1866)*, vol. 1. Madison: University of Wisconsin Press, 1988.

Mascall, Eric L. *Jesus—Who He Is and How We Know Him*. London: Darton, Longman and Todd, 1985.

Mason, Timothy W. "The Primacy of Politics—Politics and Economics in National Socialist Germany." In *Nazism, Fascism and the Working Class*, edited by Jane Caplan, 53-76. Cambridge: Cambridge University Press, 1995.

Maul, Conrad. *Egon Bahr und die Ostpolitik der sozialliberalen Koalition*. Munich: Grin, 2005.

Mazeros, Istvan. *Marx's Theory of Alienation*. London: Merlin, 1970.

McClellan, David. *Karl Marx: His Life and Thought*. London: Macmillan, 1973.

McGrath, Alister E., ed. *The SPCK Handbook of Anglican Theologians*. London: SPCK, 1988.

Mommsen, Theodor, *Die Geschichte Roms*. Berlin: Phaidon, 1954.

Moore, Andrew. *The Secret Army and the Premier: Conservative Paramilitary Organisations in New South Wales 1930-1932*. Sydney: UNSW Press, 1989.

Morris, Benny. *Righteous Victims*. New York: Knopf, 1999.

Moses, John. "Bonhoeffer Reception in East Germany." In *Bonhoeffer for a New Day: Theology in a Time of Transition*, 278-97. Grand Rapids: Eerdmans, 1997.

———. "Church and State in Post-Reformation Germany, 1530-1914." In *Church and State in Old and New Worlds*, edited by Hilary M. Carey and John Gascoigne, 77-98. Boston: Brill, 2011.

———. "The Church Policy of the SED Regime in East Germany, 1940-89: The Fateful Dilemma." *Journal of Religious History* 20.2 (December 1996) 228-45.

———. "The Church's Role in the Collapse of Communism in East Germany 1989-90." *Colloquium* 23.3 (1991)122-34.

———. "The Collapse of the GDR in 1989/90: A Protestant Revolution." In *United Germany and Europe towards 1990 and Beyond*, special issue of *European Studies Journal* 10.1-2 (1993) 147-60.

———. "Count von Luckner's Tour of Queensland and *Deutschtumspolitik*." In *The German Presence in Queensland over the last 150 Years: Proceedings of an international Symposium, 25 and 26 August 1987*, edited by Manfred Jürgensen and Allan Corkhill. St. Lucia Queensland: University of Queensland Press, 1987.

———. *Looking over the Fence: Reflections and Reminiscences of an Historian's Journey from the Australian Bush to a Wider World*. Melbourne: Australian Scholarly (Arcadia), 2023.

———. "The Politicisation of Martin Luther in the German Democratic Republic." *Pacifica Australasian Theological Studies* 24:3 (October 2011) 283–99.

———. *Reluctant Revolutionary: Dietrich Bonhoeffer's Collision with Prusso-German History*. New York: Berghahn, 2009.

———, ed. *A Remarkable Tribe : All Souls St Gabriel's School: Perspectives, Recollections, Reflections*. Charters Towers: All Souls St Gabriel's School, 2019.

———. *Trade Unionism in Germany from Bismarck to Hitler*. New York: Barnes and Noble, 1984.

Moses, John A., and Gregory Munro. "Assessing the Role of the German Churches in the Collapse of the GDR." In *Rewriting the German Past*, edited by Reinhard Alter and Peter Monteath. Adelaide: Australian Humanities, 1997.

Moses, John A., with Peter Overlack. *First Know Your Enemy: Comprehending Imperial German War Aims and Deciphering the Enigma of Kultur*. Melbourne: Australian Scholarly, 2019.

Motschmann, Jens. *Die Pharisäer: die evangelsiche Kirche, der Sozialismus und das SED Regime*. Berlin: Ullstein, 1993.

Müller, Hanfried. "Dietrich Bonhoeffer—Christuszeuge in der Bekennenden Kirche für die mündige Welt." *Beiträge zur Geschichte der Humboldt Universität zu Berlin* 5 (1981).

———. *Von der Kirche zur Welt: Ein Beitrag zu der Beziehung des Wortes Gottes auf societas in Dietrich Bonhoeffers Theologischer Entwicklung*. Hamburg-Bergstedt: Rich, 1961.

Münkler, Herfried. *Der Grosse Krieg: Die Welt 1914–1918*. Berlin: Rowohlt, 2014.

Munro, Gregory. *Hitler's Bavarian Antagonist: Georg Moenius and the Allgemeine Rundschau of Munich 1929–1933*. Lampeter, Wales: Mellen, 2006.

Neitzel, Sönke. *Weltkrieg und Revolution: 1914–1918/19*. Berlin: Be.bra, 2008.

Neubert, Erhart. *Eine protestantische Revolution*. Berlin: Kontext, 1990.

———. *Geschichte der Opposition in der DDR 1949–1989*. Bonn: Chr. Links, 1998.

———. "Müller, Hanfried." In *Wer ist Wer in der DDR*. Berlin: Chr. Links, 2010.

———. "'Obwohl der scheinbar tiefe Frieden . . .' Zur Genese der system-immanenten protestantisch geprägten Opposition in der DDR 1972–1978." No publication data available.

———. "Protestantische Kultur und DDR-Revolution." *Aus Politik und Zeitgeschichte* B 19.91 (May 3, 1991).

———. "Sozialethische und charismatisch-evangelische Gruppen in der Kirche aus soziologischer Sicht." In *Das Recht der Kirche*, vol. 3, *Zur Praxis des Kirchenrechts*, edited by Gerhard Rau et al. Gütersloh: Güterloher, 1987.

Neumann, Peter H. A., ed. *Religionloses Christentum und Nicht-religiöse Interpretation bei Dietrich Bonhoeffer*. Darmstadt: Wissenschaftliche Buchgesellschaft, 1990.

Nipperdey, Thomas. *Deutsche Geschichte, 1866–1918*. Vol. 2, *Machtstaat vor der Demokratie*. Munich: C. H. Beck, 1993.

Noack, Axel. "Die evangelische Studentengemeinde in der DDR im Blickfeld des MfS." *Hochschule* (1/96) 81–94.

Nolte, Ernst. *The Three Faces of Fascism*. London: Weidenfeld and Nicolson, 1965.

Nowlan, Kevin B., ed. *Karl Marx, the Materialist Messiah*. Dublin: Mercier, 1984.

Noyes, P. H. *Organization and Revolution: Working Class Associations in the German Revolution*. Princeton, NJ: Princeton University Press, 1966.

Oestreicher, Paul. "Christian Pluralism in a Monolithic State: The Churches of East Germany 1945–1990." *Religion, State and Society* 21.3–4 (1993) 263–75.

O'Grady, Selina. *And Man Made God: Kings, Cults and Conquests at the Time of Jesus Christ*. New York: St. Martin's, 2012.

Ökumenische Versammlung für Gerechtigkeit, Frieden und Bewahrung der Schöpfung. Dresden: Kirchenamt der evangelischen Kirche Deutschland, 1989.

Oltermann, Philip. *The Stasi Poetry Circle: The Creative Writing Class That Tried to Win the Cold War*. London: Faber, 2022.

Oppen, Asta von. *Der unerhörte Schrei: Dietrich Bonhoeffer und die Judenfrage im Dritten Reich*. Hannover: Lutherisches Verlagsanstalt, 1996.

Orlow, Dietrich. *The History of the Nazi Party*. Pittsburgh: University of Pittsburgh Press, 1973.

Otto, Rudolf. *The Idea of the Holy: An Enquiry into the Non-Rational Factor in the Idea of the Divine and Its Relation to the Rational*. Oxford: Oxford University Press, 1923.

Oxford Dictionary of the Christian Church. Edited by E.A. Livingstone. 3rd ed. Oxford: Oxford University Press, 1997.

Pangritz, Andreas. "Dietrich Bonhoeffers Begründung der Beteiligung am Widerstand." *Evangelische Theologie* 55.6 (1966) 491–519.

Parkes, James. *Judaism and Christianity*. Chicago: Chicago University Press, 1948.

Parkes, John. *The Jew and His Neighbour*. London: SCM, 1930.

Perlman, Moshe. *Die Propheten: Auf den Spuren der Rufer Gottes*. Freiburg im Breisgau: Osten, 1975.

Pickering, Roger. *We Men Who Feel Most German: A Cultural Study of the Pan-German League, 1886–1914*. New York: Routledge, 1984.

Pierard, Richard V. "Religion and the East German Revolution." *Journal of Church and State* (1990) 501–09.

Plessner, Helmut. *Die verspätete Nation: Über die politische Verfügbarkeit bürgerlichen Geistes*. Stuttgart: Kohlhammer, 1959.

Polkinghorne, John. *The Polkinghorne Reader: Science, Faith and the Search for Meaning*. Edited by Thomas Jay Oord. London: SPCK Templeton, 2010.

———. *Science and Technology—An Introduction*. London: SPCK, 1998.

Pollack, Detlef. *Kirche in der Organisationsgesellschaft: Zum Wandel der gesellschaftlichen Lage der evangelischen Kirche in der DDR*. Berlin: De Gruyter, 1994.

———. "Der Umbruch in der DDR—Protestantische Revolution? Der Beitrag der evangelischen Kirchen und der politischen alternativen Gruppen zur Wende 1989." In *Protestantische Revolution?*, edited by Trutz Rendtdorf. Göttingen: Vandenhoeck und Ruprecht, 1993.

Prostmeier, Ferdinand R., and Horacio E. Lona, eds. *Logos der Vernunft–Logos des Glaubens*. Berlin: de Gruyter, 2010.

Prunier, Gerard. *The Rwandan Crisis 1959–1994: History of Genocide*. London: C. Hurst, 1998.

Ramet, Pedro. "Disaffection and Dissent in East Germany." *World Politics* 37 (1984–1985) 85–101.

Rau, Gerhard, et al. *Das Recht der Kirche*. Vol. 3, *Zur Praxis des Kirchenrechts*. Gütersloh: Gütersloher Verlagshaus, 1997.

Reich, Jens. "Warum ist die DDR untergegangen? Legenden und sich selbst erfüllende Prophezeihungen." *Aus Politik und Zeitgeschichte* B 46.96 (November 8, 1996) 3–7.

A Remarkable Tribe: All Souls St Gabriels School 1920–2020: Perspectives, Recollections, Reflections. Charters Towers, Queensland: All Souls St Gabriel's School, 2019.

Richter, Edelbert. *Christentum und Demokratie in Deutschland: Beiträge zur geistigen Vorbereitung der Wende in der DDR*. Munich: Kiepenhauer, 1991.

———. "Die Zweideutigkeit der lutherischen Tradition—Zur Aufarbeitung der Vergangenheit in der evangelischen Kirche der ehemaligen DDR." *Deutschland Archiv* 4 Jg. (April 26, 1999) 407–17.

Ritner, Susan Rennie. "The Dutch Reformed Church and Apartheid." *Journal of Contemporary History* 2.4 (1967) 17–37.

Ritter, Gerhard. *The Schlieffen Plan: Critique of a Myth*. London: Batsford, 1967.

Rodden, John. *Re-Painting the Little Red Schoolhouse: A History of Eastern German Education, 1945–99*. Oxford: Oxford University Press, 2002.

Röhl, John C. G. *Germany without Bismarck: The Crisis of Government in the Second Reich*. London: Batsford, 1965.

———. *Wilhelm II: The Kaiser's Personal Monarchy*. Cambridge: Cambridge University Press, 2004.

Röhl, John C. G., and Guenther Roth. *Aus dem grossen Hauptquartier: Kurt Riezlers Briefe an Käthe Liebermann 1914–15*. Wiesbaden: Harrassowitz, 2016.

Röhr, Werner. *Hundert Jahre deutsche Kriegsschulddebatte: Vom Weissbuch 1914 zum heutigen Geschichtsrevisionismus*. Hamburg: VSA, 2015.

Runciman, Stephen. *History of the Crusades*. Cambridge: Cambridge University Press, 1975.

Schmidt, Hans-Jörg. "Ulbricht klopft and die Himmelspforte . . . Der politische Witz in der DDR als historisches Kondensat." *Kirchliche Zeitgeschichte* 17.2 443–46.

Schmidt, Jürgen. *Martin Niemöller im Kirchenkampf*. Hamburg: Leibniz, 1971.

Schnabel, Franz. *Deutsche Geschichte im Neunzehnten Jahhundert*. 4 vols. Freiburg im Breisgau: Herder, 1949–1959.

Schönherr, Albrecht. "Bedeutung Dietrich Bonhoeffers." In *Glauben und Lernen in einer Kirche für Andere*, edited by Ernst Feil. Gütersloh: Chr. Kaiser, Gütersloher, 1993.

———. *Zum Weg der Evangelischen Kirche in der DDR*. Berlin: Union, 1986.

Schroeder, Richard. *Deutschland schwierig Vaterland*. Freiburg: Herder, 1993.

Schubert, Jarausch, Konrad. "The Failure of East German Anti-Fascism: Some Ironies of History and Politics." *German Studies Review* 14.1 (February 1991) 85–102.

SED und Kirche. *Eine Documentation ihrer Beziehungen*. Vol. 2. Edited by Frédéric Hartweg and Horst Dohle. Neukirchen-Vluyn: Neukirchener, 1995.

Seidenkop, Larry. *Inventing the Individual: The Origins of Western Liberalism*. Cambridge, MA: Belknap, 2017.

Sherratt, Yvonne. *Hitler's Philosophers*. New York: Barnes and Noble, 2014.

Simpson, William W. "Jewish-Christian Relations since the Inception of the Council of Christians and Jews." *Jewish Historical Society of England* 28, 89–101.

Simpson, William W., and Ruth Weyl. *The Story of the International Council of Christians and Jews*. London: International Council for Christians and Jews, 1948.

Siracusa, Joseph. *Reagan, Bush, Gorbachev: Re-Visiting the End of the Cold War.* Westport CT: Praeger Security, 2008.

Siracusa, Joseph, with Aidan Warren. *US Presidents and the Cold War: Nuclear Diplomacy.* New York: Palgrave Macmillan, 2021.

Smith, Woodruff D. *The Ideological Origins of Nazi Imperialism.* Oxford: Oxford University Press, 1986.

Srbik, Heinrich Ritter von. *Deutsche Einheit: Idee und Wirklichkeit vom Heiligen Reich.* Munich: F. Bruckmann, 1942.

———. *Geist und Geschichte Vom deutschen Humanismus bis zur Gegenwart.* 2 vols. Munich: F. Bruckmann, 1950.

Steinbach, Peter, and Angela Borgstedt, eds. *Franz Schnabel: Der Historiker des freiheitlichen Verfassungsstaats.* Berlin: Lukas, 2009.

Steinberg, Jonathan. *Bismarck—A Life.* New York: Oxford University Press, 2011.

Stern, Fritz. *The Failure of Illiberalism: Essays on the Political Culture of Modern Germany.* New York: Knopf, 1972.

Swidler, Leonard, ed. *Küng in Conflict.* New York: Image, 1981.

Taylor, A. J. P. *The Origins of the Second World War.* London: Penguin, 1991.

Todt, Elisabeth. *Die gewerkschaftliche Betätigung in Deutschland von 1850–1859.* Berlin: Die freie Gewerkschaft, 1950.

Todt, Elisabeth, and Hans Radant. *Zur Frühgeschichte der deutschen Gewerkschaftsbewegung 1800–1849.* Berlin: Die freie Gewerkschaft, 1950.

Tyndale, Wendy R. *Protestants in Communist East Germany: In the Storm of the World.* London: Routledge, 2010.

Ulbricht, Walter. "Referat zum Grundriss der Geschichte der deutschen Arbeiterbewegung." *Zeitschrift für Geschictswissenschaft* 6 (1962) 1255–1514.

Victor, Barbara. *A Voice of Reason: Hanan Ashrawi and Peace in the Middle East.* San Diego: Harcourt Brace, 1994.

Voslensky, Michael. *Nomenklatura: The Soviet Ruling Class. An Insider's Report.* New York: Doubleday, 1984.

Wallach, Jehudah. *The Dogma of War of Annihilation: The Theories of Clausewitz and Schlieffen and Their Impact on German Conduct of Two World Wars.* Westport, CT: Greenwood, 1986.

Weber, Max. *Soziologie, Universalgeschichtliche Analysen, Politik.* Edited by Johannes Winckelmann. Stuttgart: Alfred Kröner, 1973.

Weitz, Eric D. *Creating German Communism 1890–1990: From Popular Protest to Socialist State.* Princeton, NJ: Princeton University Press, 1997.

Willms, Johannes. *Bismarck: Dämon der Deutschen.* Munich: Kindler, 1997.

Wilson, A. N. *C. S. Lewis: A Biography.* London: William Collins, 1990.

Wink, Walter. *Naming the Powers.* Vol. 1. Philadelphia: Fortress, 1983.

Winter, Gerhard. "Dietrich Bonhoeffer—Kämpfer gegen Krieg und Faschismus." *Beiträge zur Geschichte der Humboldt Universität zu Berlin* 5 (1981) 9–26.

Wolin, Sheldon S. *Democracy Incorporated: Managed Democracy and the Specter of Inverted Totalitarianism.* Princeton, NJ, Princeton University Press, 2008.

Woolf, Stuart J. *The Nature of Fascism.* New York: Random House, 1968.

Wright, N. T. *Paul for Everyone.* London: SPCK, 2004.

Zimmerling, Paul. "Ja zur Entfaltung der Kraft des Lebens": Hanfried Müllers Interpretation der Theologie Bonhoeffers." *Erinnerungen an die Zukunft:*

Zur Deutsch-Deutsch Bonhoeffer-Rezeption. Jahrestagung der Internationalen Bonhoeffer-Gesellschaft (2022) 71–86.

Zwahr, Hartmut. *Das Ende der Selbstzerstörung. Leipzig und die Revolution in der DDR.* Göttingen: Vandenhoeck and Ruprecht, 1993.

Index